PRAISE FOR
More On Learning Golf

"John Ward and Paul Woods' book, entitled *More On Learning Golf*, is a masterpiece follow-up to Percy Boomer's original book. *More On Learning Golf* captures the simplicity of Percy's book *On Learning Golf*. Golf is a feel game, and John and Paul capture Percy's thoughts on what fundamentals to focus on to create that feel.

"This book is a MUST-read for all golfers wanting to get better."

—Dr. Jim Suttie, PGA Teaching Professional, *Golf Magazine* World Golf Teachers Hall of Fame, *Golf Digest* Top 50 Teachers, Illinois Golf Hall of Fame

"I'd like to buy Percy Boomer a beer. The man wrote a golf instruction book eighty years ago, and believe it or not, his words are still relevant. A classic, balanced golf swing is timeless, just like Boomer's words. We've seen stunning technological advancement in twenty-first-century golf equipment, not to mention in the twenty years before that, too. I've been a golf writer for more than forty years, writing about pro golf for assorted newspapers and magazines (if you remember such antiques), including *Golf World* and *Sports Illustrated*, and watched the transition from persimmon to metal (even titanium) and the pre- and post-Pro V1 worlds.

"I would've bet a large sum of cryptocurrency that eighty-year-old golf instruction would be as obsolete as a stymie. But I tip my hat to Mr. Boomer for keeping things timelessly simple: Treat golf as 'all one shot' (a driver, a 7-iron, a pitch—whatever) and swing as 'all one piece.' (Isn't that what US Open champ Bryson DeChambeau wanted by cutting his irons the same length?) Making an in-to-out swing path is 'an essential feel of good golf' and 'the swing becomes the aim.' These Boomer-isms are nearly self-explanatory, but they come to life thanks to Boomer's real-life anecdotes of helping fellow golfers. Boomer is full of common sense that flows through his book like beer from a tap—a simple golf swing that is easy to swallow.

"Boomer was also ahead of his time regarding the mental side of golf, which he embraced with this counterintuitive thought: 'A golfer can only produce his true quality when he can play without concentrating.' Sign me up for that.

"What this book's authors did was more than just refresh and translate Boomer's original work; they rescued it for golfers of a different century. They added the user manual that modern Boomer readers need—the hands-on, how-to specifics—in order to 'Boom It Like Boomer,' a T-shirt catchphrase waiting to happen. There is still great value in Percy Boomer's words, and now they have been preserved and explained. For that, I owe the authors a beer, too."

—**Gary VanSickle, Award-Winning Golf Writer;** *Sports Illustrated* **(1996–2016); Past President, Golf Writers Association of America**

"John Ward is unlike any other golf coach and is the best swing coach I have ever had, bar none. Like all the best coaches, John uses a system of fundamentals that are connected with one leading to and supporting the next. This simple system provides everything you need to get better and be successful. Golf at my best now is far better than it has ever been. Even my worst play now is better than my best golf was in the past.

"The system of the golf swing presented in *More On Learning Golf* gives much more than swing tips. This system allows me to analyze my swing, find answers to my own questions about the golf swing, and even help others with their swings based upon solid and connected fundamentals.

"After a lot of questioning, thinking, and practice, I have become a firm believer that I can successfully use the same movement to drive, pitch, chip, and putt. By embracing this principle, the golf swing has become simpler and my overall golf game has improved by leaps and bounds.

"Using what I have learned, I look forward to another thirty years of enjoyable golf with my beautiful wife, who is also a lover of golf and committed follower of John and his teachings."

—**Chris Marlowe; Professional Basketball and Olympic Volleyball Sportscaster; 1984 US Olympic Volleyball Team Captain and Gold Medalist**

"As past captain of La Moye Golf Club in Jersey, Channel Islands (childhood home of Percy Boomer), I corresponded with Paul Woods, co-author, then subsequently met him in 2019 when he visited Jersey as part of his research into Percy Boomer. His enthusiasm for Percy was clear from the outset.

"John Ward, professional golf instructor and co-author, and Paul kept the principles of Percy's teaching alive in their previous book, *Feel Simple Golf*. As you read through *More On Learning Golf*, John and Paul continue to clearly explain in simple and understandable language the modern interpretations of Percy's historical methods.

"This is easily summarized by one of Percy's principles: 'It is essential to feel and control the swing as a whole and not to concentrate upon any part of it.' This is reflected in John's intuitive approach. Paul's background in organizational psychology is very much in line with Percy's principles by emphasizing that 'mental visualization with body movement plus actual practice result in greatest learning and improvement.'

"John and Paul have enhanced Percy's timeless teachings. I hope you enjoy this book as much as I have and it leads you to better golf and greater enjoyment of the game."

—George Kean, La Moye Golf Club, Jersey, Channel Islands

"Sometimes you read a book that relates perfectly to your lived experience and think, 'Aha! This could be a game-changer!'

"Learning to correctly set up my swing with bracing and then pivoting my lower body with good balance feels right based on my years of yoga training. Allowing my power to come from the lower body and pivot lets the club do the work for me. I can swing with confidence now, knowing I won't end the round with pain in my low back and hip.

"There are many variables in golf, but implementing the same body mechanics for putting, chipping, and driving the ball has allowed me to play with ease. I'm a perfectionist, which can be paralyzing when it comes to your golf swing. This system showed me how to simplify my swing, build a strong mental game, and play by feel with a quiet brain. I'm able to get creative, read the greens, and enjoy being outside with friends during the round.

"Bottom line, I'm having more fun and playing better than ever!"

—Laurie Marlowe, Feel Simple Golf Student, Centennial, Colorado

"Percy Boomer is a legendary teacher of the game. So many great players and teachers of the game have alluded to his book and teachings.

"John Ward has diligently studied Percy's work and applies it in a simplistic manner to his students. I have witnessed this firsthand for well over a decade of working with John as a teacher. This book lays out a straightforward set of fundamentals that have helped me play better and much more consistent golf."

—Brandon Barron, Feel Simple Golf Student, Aurora, Colorado

"George Boomer, Percy's father, was a local teacher who claimed Harry Vardon, a six-time Open champion and US Open champion, along with Ted Ray, also an Open and US Open champion, amongst his students. George founded La Moye Golf Club in 1902.

"George's youngest son, Aubrey, was a top player in the 1920s and '30s. Aubrey Boomer won many tournaments, including five French Opens, and was runner-up to Bobby Jones in the 1927 Open at St Andrews. Aubrey was also a member of the Great Britain Ryder Cup teams of 1927 and '29.

"George's oldest son, Percy, was also a very good golfer who won the Belgium, Swiss, and Dutch Opens in the 1920s. Percy became far better known as a teacher and authored *On Learning Golf*, a book that remains heralded today.

"On behalf of La Moye Golf Club, we are very grateful to authors John Ward and Paul Woods for continuing to promote the teaching methodology of Percy through this, their latest book, *More On Learning Golf*. We wish you all enjoyable and instructive reading."

—Dennis Lavin, Club Captain (2021/2), La Moye Golf Club, Jersey, Channel Islands

"As a casual golfer, I really appreciate how John Ward and Paul Woods take a seemingly complicated topic like the golf swing and simplify it into easily understandable movements. I have always struggled with trying to implement the dozens of different swing tricks and tips I have heard over the years. Because of this book, I now realize that each time I adjusted my swing using one of the new ideas I picked up from a friend or by watching a video, it would throw something else off. In *More On Learning Golf*, John and Paul break down and expand upon Percy Boomer's concepts into five easy-to-follow steps that make the golf swing one that can be repeated time and time again. I am confident this book will improve anyone's golf game if they are willing to put the lessons into action!"

—Brent Berninger, Littleton, Colorado

"I came across Percy Boomer while writing a history of golf in Belgium. The Boomer brothers, Percy and Aubrey, played an important role in the golf history of my country. When they were both professionals at St. Cloud Golf Club near Paris, they would often come to Belgium to take part in tournaments and challenge matches, which were popular in the 1920s.

"While Percy gave lessons at St. Cloud and subsequently at Sunningdale Golf Club in England, Aubrey came to Belgium to teach at the Waterloo Golf Club and then at the Royal Golf Club of Belgium. Their golfing philosophies were similar, and both followed the same swing principles. Percy was probably the better at explaining the swing and communicating this to pupils. His teaching skills were most likely inherited from his father, George, who was a school teacher.

"Aubrey was the better golfer, though Percy was more than just an average performer. Their shared principles of the golf swing led each to international success. Aubrey won twelve European national titles: the French Open five times; the Dutch Open four times; the Belgian Open twice, and the Italian Open once. Aubrey was runner-up to the great Bobby Jones in the Open and played twice in the Ryder Cup. Percy won the Belgian Open in 1923 and went on to win the Swiss Open the following year and then the Dutch Open in 1927.

"Percy was a prolific writer, not just authoring his book, *On Learning Golf*, but also a regular contributor to golf magazines of the period. Percy Boomer's teaching methods and swing principles remain relevant today. As someone interested in the history of golf, I am happy to see Percy Boomer's legacy live on through this book, *More On Learning Golf*, that explains and extends Percy's teachings."

—Theodius Lennon, Brussels, Belgium

"No one has taught me more about the golf swing than John Ward."

—**Rod Johns, Feel Simple Golf Student and Colleague, Lone Tree, Colorado**

"I have been a Percy Boomer *On Learning Golf* advocate for over ten years. When I first came across Ward and Woods' book, *Feel Simple Golf*, I was amazed how well John was versed in the teachings of Percy Boomer. John's work continues to focus and highlight all the key areas that help bring this swing to life.

"Along with Percy, I would call myself an unnatural golfer—someone to whom the correct motions and feels of the swing do not come naturally. John helped me understand how to implement the correct sequencing. I was then able to build up the feels in my own feel cabinet and build up a reliable system that is built on controls. By implementing these simple series of sequencing put forth in this book, I was able to start building the proper feels and sensations that grew out of consistently following and implementing a correct set of controls in my setup and starting movements. Pivot, body balance, starting positions, swing width, and golf psychology are all areas of your game that will come into a new light after reading this wonderful book."

—**Matt Scaramuzzo, PGA Superstore Manager, Palm Beach Gardens, Florida**

"I have been a golf addict for over 39 years and constantly find myself referring back to Percy's teachings whenever things start to go wrong. *More On Learning Golf* clarifies Percy's ideas to make them more easily understandable. This book keeps his teachings and concepts alive, such as connection, pivot, bracing, intentional actions, and automatic reactions. The authors give an expanded explanation of passive and active swing components and provide a summary that highlights key points for each chapter.

"What I really like about this method is that every shot from putting to driving uses the same basic motion. I have found this to hold true after countless hours on the driving range and putting green. This gives a system that allows you to self-analyze and correct your swing. This book focuses on doing the fundamentals of a good swing, not the end-result, for all shots and building a repeatable swing based on feel."

—**Loui Cuppari, Sale, Victoria, Australia**

"After being approached by the grandchildren of the late Percy Boomer to help dispose of 'a few books' owned by their grandfather, a fascinating course of events took place. Firstly, a few books turned out to be approximately 600—all of which Percy acquired before his passing in 1949. Percy was a great student of the game. Included in the collection are some of the rarest and most-sought-after golf books in history. Percy's personal copy of his 1942 classic, *On Learning Golf*, is part of the collection.

"Secondly, while researching Percy Boomer, it was a sheer pleasure to unexpectedly make contact with two individuals who have made it 'a life's work' to study and develop even further Percy's original principles in *On Learning Golf*. John Ward, golf professional and author, and Dr. Paul Woods deserve every accolade for enhancing and extending (and dare I say, improve) an already fine piece of literature, Eighty-years later, they have pieced together in a simple way ALL of Percy's principles and answer some of Percy's unanswered questions.

"*More On Learning Golf* carries the words and wisdom of Percy Boomer into the 21st century and no doubt beyond. This book will help a high-handicap beginner through to the battle-hardened Tour pro. The authors have simply made a timeless classic even greater. Well done."

—**Peter Grunwell, British PGA Member, Fine Golf Books, St. Andrews, Scotland**

More on Learning Golf:
Modernizing Percy Boomer's 1942 Classic

by John E. Ward and Paul K. Woods, Ph.D.

© Copyright 2022 John E. Ward and Paul K. Woods, Ph.D.

ISBN 978-1-64663-673-0

All rights reserved. No part of this publication may be reproduced, stored in a retrieval system, or transmitted in any form or by any means—electronic, mechanical, photocopy, recording, or any other—except for brief quotations in printed reviews, without the prior written permission of the author.

Published by

Feel Simple Golf
2564 Civic Lane
Grand Junction, Colorado 81505

more ON LEARNING GOLF

Modernizing
Percy Boomer's
1942 Classic

John E. Ward & Paul K. Woods, Ph.D.

A "GOOD OUT"

PERCY

To Percy—may his legacy live on!

Table of Contents

Plan of the Course 1

Part One: The Genesis of this Book 9

1. What Teaching Taught Me 19
2. Fundamentals—Golf and the Senses 29
3. Fundamentals—The Swing 35
4. Golf Bogey No. 1 46
5. The Road to Golfing Health 54
6. The Concentration Fallacy 62

Part Two: On Learning and Teaching 71

7. The Controlled Golf Swing 79
8. Preparatory to the Swing 89
9. Interlude for Instruction—What We Mean When We Say 100
10. Fundamentals—Centered on Wrist Action 111
11. To Keep—or Not to Keep—Your Eye on the Ball 122
12. Interlude for Instruction: It Is the Pupil Who Must Learn 131
13. The Feeling of In-to-Out 144
14. The Force-Center 152

15.	Interlude for Instruction—Monologue. 165
16.	Rhythm. 171
17.	Interlude for Instruction—As a Dancer Sees It. 187
18.	Power 195
19.	Interlude for Instruction—A Mathematician Explains . . .206
20.	Temperament 213
21.	Interlude for Instruction—Largely Concerned with the Waggle 223
22.	Putting 236
23.	Interlude for Reminiscence. 247
24.	Golf Analysis. 251
25.	Inverse Functioning 262

Afterword. 274
Acknowledgments. 277
Appendix: Feels of the Golf Swing 278
Index 286
About the Authors 290

Plan of the Course

DO YOU KNOW Percy Boomer? If you are like most golfers, you may possibly have heard his name. Of course, Percy's last name is a very good one for a golfer. You may also have heard of Percy's swing principle of "turn in a barrel," but never considered when and where it originated.

Photo Courtesy of St. Cloud Golf Club, Paris, France

Percy Boomer was inducted as a member of the inaugural class into the World Golf Teachers Hall of Fame in 1998. Percy Boomer was ranked the number one golf swing guru of all time by *Sports Illustrated* magazine in 2005. Percy's book, *On Learning Golf*, was first published by John Lane, the Bodley Head, in London, England, in 1942 in the World War II era. Imagine that your only book was published in the heat of a world war when resources were scarce and people feared for their lives. Percy's book was then published in the United States in 1946 by Alfred A. Knopf. *On Learning Golf* has been reprinted nearly forty times. Given all this, don't you think he would, rightfully, be well known in his field?

Percy Boomer has undoubtedly left his mark on the game of golf. Yet Percy is relatively unknown to most golfers today. It is our hope that this book will help change that. We want to recognize Percy's legacy and extend and modernize his timeless teachings to help golfers improve their game and have more fun.

This book integrates Percy's classic teachings of the golf swing with John Ward and Paul Woods's books inspired by *On Learning Golf*. Percy's teachings are reviewed, explained, expanded upon, and modernized for today's game. To keep this book at a reasonable length, less substantive portions of Percy's writings have been removed without detracting from the essence of his teachings.

Today's Takeaway

While Percy's teachings from more than eighty years ago remain very relevant to today's golf swing, *On Learning Golf* provides the puzzle pieces of an integrated golf swing but doesn't put all the pieces together for us. Percy's book was published a few short years before he passed away in Sunningdale, England. Percy never had the opportunity to write a more extensive follow-up book on the details of the golf swing. We have respectfully written our golf instructional books in honor of Percy Boomer. We hope that he would be pleased with our efforts.

In addition to using "learn" in the title of his book, Percy repeated this word three times in the opening paragraph. Percy's book is more than about the mechanics of the swing; it is about "learning" golf. Percy knew the importance of swing mechanics, but more importantly, he understood that learning golf had to be done visually (e.g., using words, photos, and illustrations), auditorily (e.g., using spoken words), and kinesthetically (i.e., understanding through the feel of doing).

Percy spoke of the fundamental sensations of the golf swing and emphasized that it was through feel that he played and taught. *Feel*, a sensation experienced in the body in setting up and making a good golf swing, is key to Percy's teachings. It is the feel (or feels) of a good swing that we seek when we play. Experiencing the desired feels means that we have correctly implemented the fundamentals of a good swing. Implementing the correct fundamentals results in the desired outcome. When a particular feel is missing, we gain valuable insight into a fault in our swing. In this book, we highlight and build upon the feels Percy introduces.

We have published two books and a companion seminar and instruction manual based entirely on Percy's teachings. John is arguably the foremost teacher of Percy Boomer's principles of the golf swing in the world today. Our books are a culmination of John's more than a decade of study, experimentation, understanding, and effective golf coaching entirely based on *Feel. Simple. Golf.*, an expansion of Percy's *On Learning Golf.*

- *Experience the Feel of Simple Golf* by John E. Ward and Dr. Paul K. Woods (2016)

  This book is a thorough and detailed technical reference manual to the integrated system of the golf swing based on Percy Boomer's principles.

- *Feel. Simple. Golf.* by Ward and Woods (2017)

  This book is a simplified instruction manual on the integrated system of the golf swing based on *Experience the Feel of Simple Golf.*

- *Feel. Simple. Golf.: Instruction and Seminar Manual* by Ward and Woods (2018)

This concise manual is for students of *Feel. Simple. Golf.* who are learning the integrated system of the golf swing based on the teachings of Percy Boomer. This companion manual supplements hands-on instruction and seminars provided by John Ward and his team.

Percy's Teachings in His Words (p. xi-xii)

This is not a book on the science of golf, but about learning it. Everything on the science of the game has been written, little on how to learn it. So I outline a method of learning and stress certain points about the golf swing. And please remember that long experience has told me what to emphasize when teaching. Some of the points which you will find me making a fuss about are considered minor details in the science of the game, but they are important to me because they relate to feel rather than to mechanics—and it is through feel that I play and teach.

I believe that the mechanical details, like the ball, should become incidental. They are of course of extraordinary interest and if this book arouses interest in the fundamental sensations of the golf swing I shall be tempted to write another (and much more extensive one) on its detail. But that is another matter.

In brief, the plan of this book is that in the six chapters of Part One I outline my theory of golf, and explain how I came by it and why I hold it; while Part Two consists of chapters which elaborate the various technical points, interspersed with Interludes for Instruction and Reminiscence which enable certain very essential points to be emphasized as well as providing a little light relief from the more solid matter.

—**PERCY BOOMER**

Beyond Percy—Feel Simple Golf

We were fortunate to have personally met Rick Bradshaw several months before his way-too-early passing. Rick was PGA Teacher of the Year, North Florida Section (2004 & 2006); director of instruction at the Jim Dent/Rick Bradshaw School of Golf, Tampa, Florida; and a fellow follower of Percy Boomer and renowned teacher of Percy's principles. Without us knowing he was in the last few months of his life, Rick accepted our invitation to write the foreword to *Feel. Simple. Golf.* (2017). We wish to memorialize Rick's love of golf, passion for golf instruction, and admiration for Percy Boomer by including his words in this book.

In John E. Ward's and Paul K. Woods' book, *Feel. Simple. Golf.*, they have written the secret, like no other golf instruction book to date, a once and for all way for golfers to learn and understand the true answers to swinging the golf club with effortless power, a consistent repetitive swing arc, and with virtually one thought and sensation for all shots. Could the golf swing be that simple? You better believe it is!

Over the more than 35 years that I have been teaching and studying the theories and history of teaching the golf swing, I seldom find an instructor who has discovered the secret to how simple the golf swing is and be able to relate those concepts to their students. John Ward is one of those golf instructors! I often refer to learning the secret to the golf swing as like finding a needle in a haystack. It's not that the needle is complicated in its design; it's just difficult to find the needle. The ability of a golf instructor to make things simple to achieve, rather than technically difficult, is an art in itself. I often say to my golf students that I want them to discover one or two thoughts that make thirty things happen versus thinking about thirty thoughts to make one thing happen. John Ward is an accomplished golf professional both as a player and golf instructor, and has found that needle in the haystack!

John Ward and Paul Woods have tapped into the techniques that were taught by Percy Boomer. Percy Boomer's book, *On Learning Golf*, was written in 1942 and published in the U.S. in 1946. His book is considered the number one most influential read in the history of golf instruction. Yet few golfers have ever heard of Percy Boomer. Boomer taught as does John Ward that the golf swing is centrifugal in nature, powered from the ground up. Percy wrote; why else would they put nails in your shoes if the power did not emanate from the ground. Picture a tornado swinging a golf club with a controlled swing arc and you'll be close to what John is teaching.

This book has been written to teach the feel of how the golf swing works. It is a book of true answers to effortless power. It is a book that presents a "mindful, not thoughtful" approach to swinging the golf club the same way for all shots. John's explanation and repetitiveness of concepts and thoughts are to make sure that you the reader ingrain the essential factors that will ensure your success and understanding of the swing. This book is a true treasure and one of a kind, and has been written with a lot of heart and soul. I do not write this foreword unless I truly believe in this book's content. Read carefully and study the concepts and you will find the secret to successful golf.

—Rick Bradshaw (1949-2016)
Tampa, Florida

more ON LEARNING GOLF

Part One

The Genesis of This Book

Today's Takeaway

JOHN LOVES PLAYING and coaching golf. He has been playing golf for over fifty years, since he was nine years old, and teaching for over thirty. John has played at all levels of competition, from one-day tournaments to the US Senior Open Championship. Thirty years ago, his passion for playing golf led him down the path of becoming a professional golf instructor. Despite his love of the game, in 2009 he told the love of his life, Suzy, that he was getting ready to quit instructing and coaching golf.

Over the years, John had become more and more frustrated seeing golfers walk away from the game. While golf clubs are made to hit balls farther than ever and golf balls are made to fly longer and straighter, the number of golfers is declining. John believes this is partially due to the complexity of learning the golf swing; the large amount of time needed to play, learn, and improve one's swing; and the frustration of inconsistent results.

John saw and felt the frustration in his students earlier in his teaching career. Years ago, he became frustrated with being part of making the golf swing so complex and difficult to learn. Unless he was able to find a simple way to teach the golf swing that consistently led to rapid improvement and fun, John wasn't interested in continuing to be a professional golf instructor. His conviction peaked as he walked off the course, having played in the 2009 US Senior Open Championship. John knew then that he could play better and needed to be a better instructor. He wanted to develop a simple, powerful, accurate, and consistent golf swing for himself, and he wanted his students to experience similar success and fun. John wanted to be a better professional golf instructor.

In his journey to find a better way, John read everything he could get his hands on, thought about what he had learned over the years as a player and instructor, and analyzed tons of golf swings. As a result of his efforts, John now knows without a doubt that the teaching and learning of the golf swing can be simple. The breakthrough was when Suzy insisted that he reread Percy Boomer's book. Over the past decade, *On Learning Golf* has been a guiding, although sometimes challenging, light that has led him to a simple and integrated approach to the golf swing. Our hope in writing this book that integrates *On Learning Golf* and *Feel. Simple. Golf.* is that it honors and does justice to Percy's major contribution to helping us learn, play, and love golf.

Returning to Percy's book—after years of searching, Percy discovered the power of grasping the relationship between the mental and physical in his effectiveness as a teacher of the golf swing. This blending of the mental and physical is also key to developing and maintaining an effective, consistent, and results-producing golf swing. Understanding and effectively using an active brain and a quiet brain at the appropriate times is the foundation of the mental part of the golf swing. Following Percy's lead, John has built these principles into Feel Simple Golf.

Percy's Teachings in His Words (p. 3-9)

Golf is in the Boomer blood. My father was a village schoolmaster in Jersey. As an educationist he was generations ahead of his time. He saw no use in forcing a boy to try to learn subjects which he was obviously incapable of absorbing—and of which he could make no use anyway, but he did help his pupils to develop such talents and natural aptitudes as they possessed.

In consequence, though so far as I know his school never produced a Senior Wrangler and maybe did not show up too well when the Inspector came round, it did have the very remarkable record of producing five golfers of international rank in one generation.

I imagine that it is a world's record for a village school and one never likely to be beaten and if any memorial were needed to my father's devotion to the game the records of the great Channel Island golfers who were his pupils—incomparable Harry Vardon and his brother Tom Alfred, the three Gaudins, Renouf, and Ted Ray—would provide it.

. . . .

About myself. It was intended that I should follow my father as a schoolmaster, but as it fell out I preceded him as a golf Pro! After very few years of school-teaching I decided that any talents I had lay elsewhere and being by then a pretty good amateur golfer I obtained the job of 8th Assistant at Queen's Park, Bournemouth. I was then twenty-two. After a short period at Bournemouth I moved to Barton-on-Sea, and from Barton to St. Cloud in 1913. My long period at St. Cloud was interrupted by the first Great War (when I served in the Royal Naval Air Service) and at least broken again by the second. It was at St. Cloud that I developed my ideas about the game and built up my experience as a teacher of it.

Though I have never had the physique required for the hard mill of championship golf I have won three International Open Championships, the Belgian in 1923, the Swiss in 1924, and the Dutch in 1927.

My brother Aubrey is thirteen years my junior. He joined me at St. Cloud when he was seventeen, with a fine athletic record at Victoria College behind him. Shortly after he also joined the R.N.A.S. and we both returned to St. Cloud early in 1919. In our first fourball match together there we played the two top Americans in the Inter-Allied games. The Yanks won the tournament, but Aubrey and I halved our match.

The best Aubrey has done in the British Open was second to Bobby Jones at St. Andrews. He holds the record for the French Open having won it five times; he has also won the Belgian and Dutch titles several times and the Italian once. By winning the *Daily Mail* tournament, the *Glasgow Evening Herald* meeting at Gleneagles and the Roehampton show, he played himself into the British team in three matches against the Americans—two of them for the Ryder Cup.

It is also not to be forgotten that Aubrey holds the world's record for a single round. His 61 was done at St. Cloud in a French P.G.A. tournament against the American Ryder Cup team. The tournament was won by Horton Smith, Aubrey following him in second place.

. . . .

Aubrey and I toured the Argentine together. We were in fact the first visiting Pros to do so—and the first to play that dynamic golfer Jose Jurado. I have always considered that the tournament that Aubrey won there against the best of their Pros and in most difficult and unfamiliar conditions, one of his finest feats.

Some years ago I was playing in a four-ball match with George (Theory) Duncan, my brother Aubrey, and Mr. E. Esmond. We were discussing a shot that Aubrey had just played and Mr. Esmond said to George, "You know Percy was a schoolmaster at one time." George looked at me with his quaint grin and said, "I thought so—he plays like one!"

He was quite right, though it is not because of my early schoolteaching that my game looks as studied and considered as it does. The truth is that though I learned the game in Jersey as soon as I could walk and Harry Vardon was my boyhood idol, I was not what is known as a natural golfer. There is nothing instinctive about my game. Everything I have ever done in golf I had to *learn to do*. Maybe having to teach myself was not a bad preparation for my future work of teaching others.

As a boy I was just a plodder, but I stuck to it and before I took my first professional job I was a good three handicap amateur and held the amateur record of La Moye with 78. I went back there a few years ago and did an approximate 64 in a four-ball match—nearly a stroke a hole better as a result of twenty-five years' hard work and study. But probably the more valuable gain was in the matter of *consistency* and in being able to play my best when I *needed* to play my best.

Do not think that this consistency and control "come naturally" to a professional. Far from it. My first shot as a Pro was at Meyrick Park, Bournemouth—and I topped it! Indeed the whole time I was with the Bournemouth Club I hardly hit a single really clean shot from that tee. *The very fact that my living depended upon my golf made a shot which as an amateur I should have found easy enough, one of almost insuperable difficulty.* Keep that in mind please, and so remember that when I talk of golfing "nerves" I have had practical experience.

It was probably due to my father's influence that when I set out seriously to teach myself golf, I decided I must teach myself a *simple* style. For my father was always insisting that *simplicity* was the greatest of all gifts and the most laudable of all attainments. To illustrate this, he took me to London to see Gerald du Maurier act. How utterly easy he made acting look! You were not conscious of the years of toil that must have gone to the building of that superb technique. Remember that when next you envy the effortless ease with which a crack Pro drives!

So it came about that I set out at first to find a simple swing and then, at a later date to find a simple method of imparting this to others. The discovery, or rather the development of the swing itself was not so difficult, but it is only comparatively recently that I have learned how to teach it. And I freely admit that the teaching is still less simple than I would like it to be.

I have started to write this book twenty times in the last twenty years and I might still hesitate to write it had I nothing more than the theory of a satisfactory swing to impart. But now, teed up for my twenty-first start, I know I am going on until the book is finished. And why? Because this time I feel I have a solid contribution to offer to the teaching and learning of golf. It is upon an aspect of the matter which has been practically ignored by writers, teachers and players alike—but one which I have proved beyond doubt to be of fundamental importance.

So in this book, superimposed upon the fruits of my knowledge, experience, and theories of the game, you will find my account of the relation between the physical and the psychological in golf—a relationship which lies at the root of every form of *control*—of both individual shots and of one's game as a whole. Until I realized the importance of this relationship and discovered how to use it everything that I wrote seemed *inconclusive*. At so many points there seemed nothing further to be done but to shrug one's shoulders and repeat "Golf is a funny game!" But once the relationship between mental and physical was rightly realized these blanks filled in—and the practical results in teaching were astounding.

Beyond Percy—Feel Simple Golf

Keeping with Percy's insistence that simplicity is the greatest of all gifts and the most laudable of all attainments, the following is a simple one-hundred-word description of our Feel Simple Golf integrated system for a simple golf swing. Highlighted in bold are the five fundamentals of the swing upon which the integrated system is built.

- **Pivot** creates power and direction.
- **Body balance** allows a full and unrestricted pivot.
- Balance is lost when weight moves closer to or further from the (1) ball, (2) target, or (3) ground during the swing.

- Body balance is maintained using (1) upward, (2) inward, and (3) behind bracing built into the **starting position**.
- **Swing width** increases power and is built into the starting position with bracing.
- **Psychology of the swing** involves (1) an actively thinking brain to establish the starting position and initiate the starting movement and (2) a quiet brain to repeat a practiced swing movement based on feel.
- This applies from putting to driving.

Unless you are Percy or John, reading this description for the first time may not seem that simple. Although Percy didn't talk about five fundamentals of a controlled, powerful, and consistent golf swing, these fundamentals are deeply rooted in Percy's teachings. We hope that Percy would feel delighted in such simplicity of words that mean so much.

CHAPTER 1

What Teaching Taught Me

"The self-taught golfer is usually a badly taught one."

"The soundest and most permanently profitable motions in golf feel unnatural and 'all wrong' to most people when first tried."

"It is just impossible to build up a sound game by accepting tips and instructions and advice from all those who are willing to offer them."

"The mechanical muscular movements employed in golf are not the whole secret of it."

"Teaching golf as all one shot simplified her game."

Chapter Summary

GOLF CANNOT BE self-taught since a good golf swing initially feels unnatural and all wrong. Learning golf requires a whole and comprehensive system, not a selection of stand-alone swing tips from others. Using the same basic shot to drive, pitch, chip, and putt simplifies the game.

Today's Takeaway

A good swing uses a fifty/fifty blend of the mental and physical. This blend is the glue that holds the swing together and leads to power, control, and consistency. Percy said the muscular movements (mechanics) of the swing need to be simple. The simpler the movement, the more repeatable and, therefore, more consistent the swing becomes and the better the golfer becomes.

System Versus Swing Tips

If we are honest with ourselves, Percy's words likely make most of us lower our heads with a sense of guilt. We have searched and searched for the right swing tip at the right time that would lead us to golf glory. We all wish mastering a golf swing were only that simple. But there are just too many individual tips to learn and master.

Percy briefly mentions a consistent "system" that underlies his teaching of the golf swing. A *system* is a set of things working together as interconnected parts of a mechanism. Change one part of the system and the other parts are affected. Accepting a standalone "swing tip" from a friend to fix a fault in your swing when that tip does not fit into your system will only lead to other faults. Percy doesn't offer a buffet where you get to pick and choose which pieces you adopt, follow, and consume. Following Percy's systems-based teachings means you partake of all that is offered. As Percy emphasizes, he is not a merchant of swing tips.

Consider the book that presents golf's "500 Best Tips Ever!" If there are 500 "best" swing tips, how many more "pretty good" tips to a golf swing are out there? We don't mean to entirely dismiss the value of the book or the swing tips. Our concern is that these tips are stand-alone and not tied together into an integrated understanding (i.e., system) of the golf swing. Another of our concerns is with trying to tweak a swing by applying a Band-Aid when the proper foundation of a swing is not in place and needs work. It is like trying to install a hardwood floor and hang curtains in a house under construction when the foundation and framing are not complete. The effort is doomed to fail.

Unfortunately, most golfers need work on the foundation of their swings, not Band-Aids. The position of the right elbow at the top of the backswing makes little difference if the golfer nearly falls over from being out of balance. Quick fixes for a troubled swing don't work.

A perfectly horrible example of a swing tips-based approach to learning, improving, and troubleshooting a golf swing is an experience John had at the driving range. While hitting balls next to a man helping a woman with her swing, John counted twenty-eight swing tips given to the pale-faced and glassy-eyed woman during a thirty-minute lesson. When one swing tip didn't perfect her swing, there were many more in the friend's bag of swing tips to give. John wondered how likely it was that this woman would continue to subject herself to such instructional abuse and eventually make it to the course to enjoy the game. The incident screamed for the simplicity of the integrated system of the golf swing!

Percy emphasizes the critical importance of having an integrated approach to the golf swing such that you putt as you drive and drive as you putt. An integrated system eliminates the need to have a cabinet with tens, if not hundreds, of stand-alone golf swings. This simplifies the golf swing, reduces the time investment to refine each swing movement, increases your ability to repeat good swings, simplifies the troubleshooting of a faulty swing, and increases the fun of the game.

Since *On Learning Golf* was first published in 1942, many gurus of the golf swing have taken bits and pieces of Percy's teaching and built coaching careers—some very famous and successful. But to our knowledge, Feel Simple Golf is the only golf instruction that has been completely built on Percy's full integrated system of the golf swing. Nothing has been altered, only value-added elements have been built into Feel Simple Golf to extend and modernize Percy's teachings.

Controls and Bracing

Consider Percy's "line of controls," which is central to his teaching. ***Line of controls*** refers to taking a series of steps to set up a good swing before the club is moved on the backswing. This simple process includes building a number of braces into the starting position. A ***brace*** is the positioning a part of your body (e.g., knees, elbows, wrists, head) to allow your body to move in desirable ways and keep destructive movements out of your swing. What's also important is to build these braces into your starting position in the same order from swing to swing, from putting to driving. This is key for the mental part of the game, which is considered later.

Alignment

Before moving to the next chapter, we want to point out Percy's single paragraph about the relationship between the length of the club and positioning of the feet to the ball. This is one of the very few times in his book when Percy talks about alignment, an important piece of the fundamental starting position.

Proper alignment in the starting position for the driver is square (graphic 1). The feet are an equal distance away from the target line. The club head points directly down the target line. The right foot points perpendicular (ninety degrees) to the target line. The left foot points slightly toward the target, allowing the hips to rotate more easily into the follow-through.

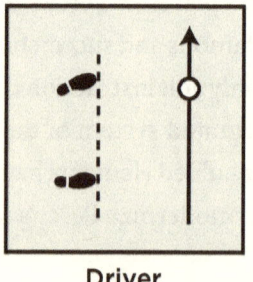

Driver

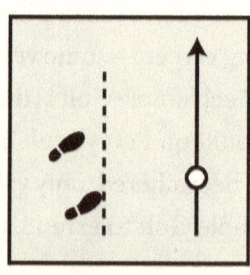

Short Iron

> **As club shortens:**
>
> Feet get closer
>
> Ball moves back in stance
>
> Position becomes more open

Alignment changes as the club becomes shorter (graphic 2). As club selection goes from driver to fairway metals, irons, wedges, then putter, the alignment of the feet becomes more and more open. The left foot gets further from the target line and points more and more toward the target. The right foot stays parallel to the target line but opens and points more toward the target. The belt buckle turns slightly toward the target. The position of the ball on the target line moves gradually back in the stance.

A slight opening of the stance and moving the ball back as the clubs become shorter allow the body to rotate properly throughout the swing. It is easier for the upper body to react to (i.e., follow) the lower body rotation/pivot, which powers the swing. These changes help keep the arms and hands from getting actively involved (by rotating) to bring the club head back squarely to the ball through impact.

Slight changes to alignment in the starting position keep the swing simple while producing a powerful straight shot. The following table from *Feel. Simple. Golf.* shows proper alignment changes for clubs.

Club	Ball Position	Feet Position
Driver	Three inches forward of center (closer to left foot)	Square
Through	Half inch increments back per club	Open two degrees per club
Putter	Three inches back of center (closer to right foot)	Open twenty-six degrees

While alignment for the driver is square, alignment for putting is fairly open (approximately twenty-six degrees).

Percy's Teachings in His Words (p. 11-15)

Anyone who has taught golf or who has even watched closely a number of beginners at the game knows that there are two great classes—those who are *natural* golfers and those who are not. My brother Aubrey was born a golfer; I had to make myself one and a hard time I had doing it. Indeed we were both extreme members of our respective classes.

A study of the difference in mental and physical make-up between the *natural* golfer and the *made* one is intensely interesting. So is a study of their ultimate capacity for the game. Not all the advantages are on the side of the natural player. Of course, if his early game is guided by a far-seeing nature, as Aubrey's was, he is fortunate. But too often the natural golfer is so successful at first that he is content to be self-taught—and the self-taught golfer is usually a *badly* taught one. Why? Well for a number of reasons which this book will make clear, not the least important being the fact that the soundest and most permanently profitable motions in golf feel unnatural and "all wrong" to most people when first tried.

Further we are all imitative to some degree and unless we learn a whole and comprehensive technique of the game from a teacher who has a coherent idea of the relationship of the various shots, we are apt to pick up a bit here and a bit there by watching others. The result is a patchwork game, full of pretty shots maybe when it is running well, but so loosely hung together and so self-contradictory in some of its component parts that it is *unreliable* and may be expected to break down or blow up when the strain comes.

A well-taught golfer rarely breaks down and rarely goes off his game completely and if he does strike a bad patch one or at the most two lessons will pull him back again. But patching up a badly taught player is one of the most difficult and thankless tasks a teacher can undertake. I have refused to take on hundreds of such cases, because I do not believe that any instruction that is not part of a *consistent* system can be of any permanent benefit.

"Tips" which are guaranteed to improve your game are easy enough to come by. Every club-house is full of them, and you have only to go a few holes with a friend to know what his own particular disease is by the "cures" he hands out to you! It is human nature to feel sure that everyone else is afflicted by the same troubles as those which torment ourselves. But all this advice is dangerous for it is just *impossible* to build up a sound game by accepting tips and instructions and advice from all those who are willing to offer them.

Does this apply only if we copy or take advice from bad examples? Oh no!—anyone from a beginner to an experienced golfer who has tried to take too much expert advice from too many sources will have been baffled and confused both in his mind and in his style by the opposite theories and contradictory practices of acknowledged masters. This fact alone is sufficient to prove one of the main contentions of this book, that the mechanical muscular movements employed in golf are not the whole secret of it.

The truth about the conflicting theories of experts is quite simple. The masters play as it suits them to play and then evolve theories to explain why the particular movements which they discover themselves employing are *right*! Unfortunately, a shot that may be effective enough in the hands of a master may have disastrous results if "copied" by some less expert player.

Of course, the muscular-mechanical movements in golf are extremely important but they are not everything. After teaching myself first and then for thirty-five years teaching others, I have arrived at concrete conclusions as to what the important factors are and I would summarize them roughly as follows:

1. Every good golf shot is the outcome of a satisfactory psychological-physical relationship.
2. It is this relationship which gives *control* and *consistency*.
3. These good relationships (and consequent controls) are built up most easily and firmly when the muscular-

mechanical requirements of the game have been simplified. And so—

4. It is desirable to learn to play as many of the shots as possible *with the same movements*.

Let me illustrate this last point which is fundamental in my theory of teaching, by describing the case of a pupil of mine, a lady no longer young who came to me more or less in despair. She had tried hard to play golf but had been defeated because she had never succeeded in driving even one hundred yards!

I taught her golf *with one club only*, her driver, and only off the tee. All I taught her was *how to drive*. When she came to me later and said, "How do I play pitch shots?" I replied, "As you drive." When she asked, "How do I putt?" I replied again, "As you drive."

I continued, "As the shot, and consequently the club, becomes shorter, we stand a little more open to the hole and draw the feet closer together and bring the ball back nearer to the right foot. When playing with the driver the ball will be placed just inside the line of the left heel—with a No. 8 iron it will be just inside the right heel."

I did not need to explain to her that the more we face the hole the nearer to the line of flight will the club head go back—or that the nearer we stand to the ball the more vertical will be our swing (because we are looking more directly down, our shoulders *dip* more on the way back and in consequence our club head comes up more steeply "naturally"). I did not need to explain these points because the correct action is the natural outcome of the position taken up—provided that the fundamentals of the swing are not interfered with.

Teaching golf as *all one shot* simplified her game. It prevented her other shots from interfering with her drive or her drive confusing her other shots, because all the shots were fundamentally the same. And though this pupil was taught with a driver only she now plays the most delicate run-up shots, and pitches excellently, in fact, she runs up better than do many players with handicaps lower than her own 15. Incidentally I look on that 15 as one of the outstanding proofs of the soundness of the theories propounded in this book.

The fault with much of the golf teaching of today, professional as well as amateur, is that the teacher tries to eradicate specific faults by issuing specific instructions. In short, the "good tip" system again. This is fatal, mainly because it is no system at all but just a conglomeration of golf patent medicines. The true aim of the teacher who desires to build up a sound and dependable game in a pupil, must be to link up in the pupil a *line of controls*. And for reasons which will become obvious as this book is read, the aim of the pupil must be to carry out the teacher's instructions *irrespective of immediate results*.

Beyond Percy—Feel Simple Golf

In 1993, John underwent back surgery. John's doctor told him to rest and not do anything strenuous for six months, including golf. After a few weeks, the doctor gave John the okay to begin putting and chipping—but nothing that involved major turning or twisting of his body. John practiced putting and chipping a lot and improved those parts of his game quite a bit. Before his six-month recovery period ended, a friend invited John to play golf. John initially declined but was convinced to at least walk the course and do some chipping and putting. John went and took his clubs.

After the three players teed off on the first hole, they looked at John, waiting for his tee shot. Up to that time, even though John felt totally healed and ready to play golf, he had not taken a full swing. John wasn't able to resist. He gripped his driver, paused, and then screamed "Fore!" to those in front and to the sides of the tee box. His playing partners were stunned and asked what he was doing since he hadn't even hit the ball. John told them that he had no idea where his shot was going and felt he needed to warn everybody around him. John's full swing shots that round were spread in every direction from far left to far right. But his chipping and putting were spot on, like he had never stopped playing.

The lesson learned is that all John's chipping and putting practice didn't help his full swing. At that time in his golf career, his full swing movement was different than his chipping and putting movements. Unlike today, when putting practice helps his full swing, John didn't have an integrated system that uses the same basic movement from putting to driving. Back then, John needed to practice one movement for the full swing and two completely different movements for chipping and putting.

Feel Simple Golf's integrated system of the golf swing simplifies things because the same swing movement is used from putting to driving. Practicing putting directly helps the full swing. Had John been using this system in 1993, he believes the results of his full swing that day would have been better because of all his chipping and putting practice.

CHAPTER II

Fundamentals: 1. Golf and the Senses

"Here was an intelligent fellow who knew that he *should* look right before stepping off the curb, but who could not do it merely by knowing that he should do it, because he had been brought up to look left. Looking left had become a muscular memory with him, and in the control of actions, knowledge and thought can never equal muscular memory. Finding this so, this very intelligent young man decided to build up a *new muscular memory* with the sequence: edge of curb—raise right arm, clench fist—*look right*. And it worked.

"Now here was a clear case of an effective psychological-physical control being developed out of the necessities of the moment with no formal knowledge of the concept whatever.

"*Exactly the same development has taken place in the game of every successful golfer.*"

Chapter Summary

PLAYING GOOD GOLF requires blending the physical and mental parts of the game. The physical (mechanical) part of the game is hurt by poor thinking and strong emotions. Building a golf swing on a set of controls, based on feels, and muscle memory helps keep the destructive effects of thinking and emotions from damaging your swing.

Today's Takeaway

Although neuroscience was not very advanced at the time and Percy was not a medical doctor or researcher, he knew of the impact of the brain on the golf swing. Percy saw the destructive effect of emotions and the useful role of muscle memory in the golf swing. Emotions, such as fear, excitement, anxiety, and joy, come from the amygdala. Developing mental concepts and problem-solving, such as learning a swing fundamental or fixing a troubled swing, take place in the brain's prefrontal cortex. Muscle memory is rooted in the basal ganglia.

An active brain is not helpful for playing your best golf when on the course. An active brain is certainly not involved when you are "in the flow" or "in the zone" and muscle memory has fully kicked in. Emotions and problem-solving get the brain to become active. Once the brain becomes active, muscle memory is dismissed. This is like using cruise control to assist you in driving your car. Once you step on the gas pedal or brake, cruise control is immediately stopped, and you are left to control the speed of your car through intentional actions.

Percy identified muscle memory, playing by feel, and following a sequence as important and useful elements of the mental part of the golf swing.

Once in place, muscle memory resists being changed. That is good for positive muscle memory that leads to good results but is not good for ineffective muscle memory that pulls you toward poor results.

There are times when an active brain is useful in golf. An active brain helps learn, improve, and fix your swing. Conscious control, by activating your brain, is needed to change ineffective muscle memory into positive muscle memory. Using an active brain to think through a needed change and develop steps to make it, then repeatedly practicing the new steps, is necessary to build new muscle memory. Developing and consistently following a ***sequence***, a series of steps, swing after swing helps create new positive muscle memory that leads to desired results.

Percy's Teachings in His Words (p. 16-22)

Every intelligent person who has played golf must have speculated on the relation between the mental and the physical aspects of the game. This is one of the fundamental problems of golf and I had every reason to think about it.

....

When we consider the make-up of a good games player we usually start with a catalogue of *physical* qualities, such as a good eye, steely wrists, good reach, etc. To these we may add—if we are advanced enough to be conscious of psychology—two or three purely mental qualities, such as "good nerves" and intelligence. For years and years I tried to strike a fair balance between the qualities in the two groups, and decided at various times that golf was 50 per cent physical and 50 per cent mental, then 40 per cent/60 per cent and 80 per cent/20 per cent, and all sorts of other proportions. But I admit that however I considered the matter I never felt convinced that I had found a correct answer. I already knew that we play reflex golf, and that a reflex was muscular memory, and this should have told me that any clear-cut division between mental and physical was impossible. I now know why!

Of course, this division of golf into separate physical and mental departments was not an idea of my own. It was the way we all thought about the game. I remember spending one of the most stimulating evenings of my life listening to—and occasionally chipping in on—a debate on the light-ball, between some Americans and members of the Committee of the R. & A.

....

I had in fact reached the conclusion that any separation of the mental and physical functions in the playing or teaching of golf must be artificial—because in the practical job of playing or teaching no such separation is possible.

. . . .

I realized at once that this *conscious control* was exactly what I was already trying to teach because I recognized it as a form of control that would *replace thinking*. And thinking had to be replaced because I knew by experience that if your golf was dependent upon *thinking* it was at the mercy of your mental state. Excitement, depression, elation—any emotion could destroy you.

I had always been considered a good teacher, but I had never been satisfied because I could not teach a pupil to play exactly and consistently—independent of his mental and physical feelings and of the state of the game. And I felt that I ought to be able to teach this. And now I am able to do so, provided that the pupil is willing to work at the game on a "long term" policy.

With my broadening view of the relation between physical and mental, and the possibilities of conscious control I have definitely gained a new capacity in teaching, enabling me to build up in my pupils one control upon another, by building up *feel*. I build up a *feel* of what is right in his golf. So when he gets to the first tee in front of a gallery or is faced by a tricky shot at a critical moment in the game, *mental excitement* can no longer tie his swing up and he can make his shots normally even if his brain is befogged.

. . . .

Now here, for those who collect coincidences, is a true story which shows an independent and extremely practical application of the ideas on which my teaching is based.

I was giving a lesson to a young American, a thoughtful, analytical fellow who up to that time had taught himself all the games he had played. He came to me because he could not connect what he knew he *should* do at golf with the physical action of doing it. So as briefly as possible I explained to him the idea of control by remembered feel. He was deeply interested, for though he had taken a course in psychology at college he had not thought of golf as one of the interests in which a knowledge of the subject might help him. He saw the point, and when he had reflected on it told me this very curious story.

"When I first came to England, the traffic keeping to the left instead of to the right as it does back home nearly got me time after time. Whenever I was going to step off the sidewalk I looked to the left instead of to the right as I should have done.

"This got so dangerous that I had to take a dip into my brain-box to find a way of checking it. It wasn't any good just *telling* myself to look right; I had done that and promptly looked left again! So I decided that every time before stepping off a curb I would raise my right forearm and clench my fist. I reckoned it would draw my attention to the right as desired, *and it did*. In a few days I was cured."

Do you see the full significance of that story? Here was an intelligent fellow who knew that he *should* look right before stepping off the curb, but who could not do it merely by knowing that he should do it, because he had been brought up to look left. Looking left had become a muscular memory with him, and in the control of actions, knowledge and thought can never equal muscular memory. Finding this so, this very intelligent young man decided to build up a *new muscular memory* with the sequence: edge of curb —raise right arm, clench fist—*look right*. And it worked.

Now here was a clear case of an effective psychological-physical control being developed out of the necessities of the moment with no formal knowledge of the concept whatever.

Exactly the same development has taken place in the game of every successful golfer.

Beyond Percy—Feel Simple Golf

Percy's focus on the mental part of the golf swing is more completely addressed in *Feel. Simple. Golf.* Psychology of the swing is fundamental five in Feel Simple Golf.

Each of us loves our brain when it helps us. Much less love is present when it gets in our way. No matter where we go or what we do, including playing golf, our brains are always our companions. When it comes to playing golf, we need to take full advantage of an actively thinking brain when it is our friend and learn how to quiet our brain when it can become our foe.

Muscle Memory

Muscle memory allows us to swing our golf clubs with a quiet brain. Remember climbing on a bicycle after a long time away from riding. You pedaled, steered, and balanced with very little active thinking or conscious control. You relied on muscle memory, which is a well-developed mental procedure created through prior repetition. After repeatedly practicing your swing fundamentals (i.e., pivot, body balance, swing width, and starting position), you develop and use muscle memory to repeat them with less and less active thinking and intentional conscious control.

A word of caution about muscle memory: continuing to use a bad swing movement strengthens the muscle memory of doing that bad movement. Once in muscle memory, the swing problem is harder to fix. Replacing bad muscle memory with good muscle memory requires an active brain.

CHAPTER III

Fundamentals: 2. The Swing

"As I have said, this controlling *feel* is built up through the constant repetition of the correct movements. We do not know just where in the system it resides, but whether it is muscular memory, or the wearing of certain grooves or channels in the mind, or—as is probable—a combination of the two, it is obvious that the more often the same succession of movements can be repeated the clearer the memory will be."

Chapter Summary

THIS SHORT CHAPTER is loaded with concepts on both the mental and physical parts of the swing. The overall fundamentals of the golf swing are outlined. Wrapped within these fundamentals and introduced in this chapter are the concepts of muscular memory, focusing on the feel of the swing, the feel of the club head swinging in-to-out, using one swing movement from putting to driving, the six essentials of a good swing, the swing as an indivisible whole, the breaking apart of the swing on the forward swing into a one-after-another movement, and the waggle.

Today's Takeaway

This short five-page chapter is deceptively full of gems—many of which may easily escape notice.

Simplicity

Percy talks about three ways to simplify the learning and playing of golf: (1) use the same swing movement from putting to driving, (2) play by feel, and (3) build and rely upon muscle memory.

Psychological Simplicity

One of Percy's many contributions to learning golf was recognizing that the golf swing involves both physical and psychological parts. His concept of muscular memory, although not grooves or channels in the brain as he thought, has proven to be fairly accurate.

Simplicity in the psychological part of the swing involves developing **automaticity** to repeat a good swing. Through repeated practice, automaticity is created, and the brain becomes more and more quiet during a swing. Playing your best golf happens when automaticity is fully engaged and things happen naturally without much thinking. When this occurs, you are in the zone or flow.

Using an active brain to try to intentionally control your swing mechanics (e.g., bending and unbending your wrists) or being emotionally aroused (e.g., excited, angry, afraid, uncertain) dismisses automaticity and your swing will crumble. Following a well-practiced sequence to set up every desired swing keeps your brain appropriately involved and allows automaticity to make the swing. The physical part of golf, including good swing mechanics, works best when the psychological part of the game is solid.

<u>Playing by Feel</u>

Playing by feel (versus intentional control) is another way to simplify the swing. When the fundamentals of pivot, body balance, swing width, and starting position are done correctly in a swing, you experience various feels. When you experience these sensations in your body, you know you have done the swing fundamentals correctly. Percy identifies throughout his book more than seventy feels of a good golf swing. Throughout Chapter III, he talks about the following feels associated with the swing fundamentals.

Feel	Swing Fundamental
Weight between both feet, perfectly free and active yet firmly planted	Starting position and body balance
Back and along, then along and through	Pivot
Full stretch	Swing width
Lag	Pivot (forward swing)
Nonstop movement from backswing to forward swing pivots (no "checks")	Pivot
In-to-out	Combined pivot, body balance, and swing width

You don't make these feels happen. These feels happen automatically when you do the swing fundamentals correctly.

Percy felt strongly that golf instruction based on bits and pieces of the swing does not help the student. As your golf skills increase, so too does your ability to sense the linked feels of the desired shot in the preparatory waggle. When you don't experience a specific feel in the waggle or in your swing, it means that the related swing fundamental needs some work.

Physical Simplicity

The golf swing is simpler when one swing movement is used from putting to driving. There is no need to learn, practice, and develop separate automaticity for the full swing, chipping, and putting. When you drive as you putt and putt as you drive, you can work on and develop automaticity for a good full swing while practicing on the putting green.

All the desired feels of a good full swing can be experienced when chipping and putting. In fact, these feels can be more easily felt in the smaller, less extensive, and less bold swing movements. You can also troubleshoot your full swing on the putting green. Putting as you drive and driving as you putt is one of Percy's most powerful and significant contributions to learning and playing golf. Because it goes against what we think is the right way to swing a golf club, this concept is also one of the most challenging to accept and build into one's game.

Power

Without calling it to our attention, Percy gives insight into how power in the swing is created. Since golf is a game in which you strike the ball from the side (e.g., not from behind as in soccer), power is generated through the rotation of your body. This power comes from **centrifugal force**. Think of this as the rotational power of a tornado.

Body rotation can occur in two ways. Rotation can start with the lower body, in which the hips and legs pull the upper body around. Or rotation can start with the upper body where the shoulders and arms pull the lower body around. Percy builds the golf swing around the rotation of the lower body, which has stronger muscles. To keep the swing simple, the upper body reacts to the rotation of the lower body. The upper body does not get actively involved in creating power. Related to this, one of Percy's six essentials of a good swing is "not to tighten any muscle concerned in the reactive part of the swing (movement above the waist)." An added benefit of a lower body-powered swing is that less stress is placed on the spine, which helps protect the lower back from injury.

1. Power from Pivot

Rotation in the golf swing is called ***pivot***. A useful mental image of pivot is the nonstop back-and-forth motion of the agitator in a washing machine. Increasing the size and speed of the pivot increases power in the swing.

2. Power from Swing Width

One of Percy's six essentials of a good swing is keeping the arms extended from the beginning to the end of the swing. This feel of a "full stretch" results from increased ***swing width***. Swing width is the distance from the center of your chest to the tip of your right thumb. Swing width increases the speed of the club head as it accelerates through impact. Think of the power from swing width as what a child experiences when she is on the outside of a line of children playing the playground game of crack the whip. The further she gets from the fixed center of the rotating line of linked children, the faster the child is whipped around through centrifugal force.

3. Power from Lag

Lag is the third source of power in a golf swing. To understand lag, think of a resting train starting to move forward. The engine moves forward first. With a slight lag, the second car moves forward. Then, following more lag, the third car moves forward, etc. Percy instructs that on the forward swing pivot,

the lower body rotates forward first. With a slight lag, the shoulders are pulled forward. Then, with more lag, the arms are pulled forward. Finally, the hands are pulled forward, as the hips have rotated forward quite a bit. The lagging hands are automatically whipped forward and accelerate through impact with the ball.

Percy's Teachings in His Words (p. 23-27)

I have already explained briefly why, both in my own game and in my teaching, I have adopted the simplest possible swing and have insisted that as many shots as possible should be played with fundamentally the same movements. Now that I have outlined the idea of teaching by feel you will better understand why I attach such importance to this point.

To put the lesson of the concept of control by feel as briefly as possible, we must give up *thinking* about our shots. In place of thinking there must be *conscious control*, obtained by building up (by constant repetition of the correct action) a comfortable and reliable *feel*, a feel that will tell you infallibly through appeal to your muscular memory, what is the right movement—and which will remain with you and control your shots whatever your mental state may be. Not being a matter of *thought*, this control stands outside the mental state.

As I have said, this controlling *feel* is built up through the constant repetition of the correct movements. We do not know just where in the system it resides, but whether it is muscular memory, or the wearing of certain grooves or channels in the mind, or—as is probable—a combination of the two, it is obvious that the more often the same succession of movements can be repeated the clearer the memory will be. Also, and this is most important, it is highly desirable that the memory should not be confused by the frequent or even occasional introduction of other and different movements—as happens when the swing is fundamentally changed for certain shots.

It is mainly for this reason that I teach and preach and practice that every shot from the full drive to the putt should be played with the same movement. Of course in the drive the movement is both more extensive and bolder than for the shorter shots, but fundamentally it is the same. The result must be a feeling of **"*in-to-out*"** stroking across the face of the ball—played not at the ball, but through it. The "in-to-out" refers to the relation of the feel of the path of the club head to the desired line of flight of the ball.

The only shots in golf which I have been unable to play or to teach as sections of the fundamental "in-to-out" swing are certain shots which call for cut pulled under and across the ball.

But for ninety-nine out of every hundred shots a golfer must play, *the swing* is the movement necessary. So to clear the ground I will list what I consider to be the essentials of the swing:

1. It is essential to turn the body round to the right and then back and round to the left, without moving either way. In other words this turning movement must be from a fixed pivot.
2. It is essential to keep the arms at full stretch throughout the swing—through the back swing, the down swing, and the follow through.
3. It is essential to allow the wrists to break fully back at the top of the swing.
4. It is essential to delay the actual hitting of the ball until as late in the swing as possible.

5. It is essential not to tighten any muscle concerned in the reactive part of the swing (movement above the waist).
6. It is essential to feel and control the swing as a *whole* and not to concentrate upon any part of it.

In a sense this last point is the most vital. The swing must be considered and felt as a single unity, not as a succession of positions or even a succession of movements. *The swing is one and indivisible.*

Now I consider that our golf is liable to go wrong if we lose sight of any of these essentials. There are of course innumerable incidentals that could be added that are important enough to have a considerable influence on one's game, but I will go so far as to say that if you have these six essentials well embedded in your system and if you have developed some conscious control of your swing by getting the *feel* of the right movements—your game will rarely or never desert you.

Of course the comfortable, reliable, *right* feel is not a thing that comes all at once. For instance, it takes years—though not if your teacher teaches by feel—to feel nicely set and comfortable before the ball; weight between the feet, perfectly free and active and yet firmly *planted*.

Then the waggle. About the waggle a whole book could be written. Every movement we make when we waggle is a miniature of the swing we intend to make. The club head moves in response to the body and the body opposes the club head. It is a flow and counter flow of forces with no static period, no check.

There is no check anywhere in a good swing. There is no such thing as the "dead top" of a swing—there are four points each one of which might be so considered if it were not for the other three! They are: (1) When the pivot (feet to shoulders) has reached *its* top, the arms are still going up. (2) When the arms have reached *their* top, the body is on its way down. (3) When the arms begin to come down, the wrists have still to break back, and (4) When the wrists break.

Now these four points together make up the top of the swing, and I was talking about the waggle—which is the bottom of an imaginary swing! But do not think I was digressing. I was not, the two are linked together. And why? Because unless you feel the whole of the swing in your waggle, your waggle is failing in its purpose.

The whole meaning and purpose of the waggle is that you shall first feel your swing rightly so that you may then make it rightly. I remember watching Sandy Herd make his first Ciné pictures. In order not to waste film he tried to do without his customary fourteen waggles and in consequence he could not hit the ball. He could not make his shot because he had not *felt* it. They got over the difficulty eventually by letting him have his full fourteen waggles but only starting the camera at about number ten!

There is of course a great deal more to be said about the swing than I have said in this chapter, which is intended simply as an outline of the fundamentals as I see them. Much of the detail will be dealt with in later chapters.

Beyond Percy—Feel Simple Golf

Feel Simple Golf presents an integrated system of the golf swing that is based on five swing fundamentals. These fundamentals build upon and support one another. The fundamentals are pivot, body balance, swing width, starting position, and psychology of the swing. These five fundamentals, built from Percy's teachings, are covered in more detail in later chapters.

In this chapter, Percy's teachings touched upon all five fundamentals of Feel Simple Golf:

- Pivot—"a fixed pivot"
- Body balance—"weight between the feet ... firmly planted"
- Swing width—"keep the arms at full stretch"
- Starting position—"feel nicely set and comfortable before the ball"
- Psychology of the swing—"this control stands outside the mental state"

The power of five fundamentals versus five hundred best swing tips is the ease of learning, improving, and troubleshooting a swing. Using these fundamentals, Feel Simple Golf's integrated system of the golf swing gives a simple, self-directed, seven-step process to spot and fix a troubled swing.

NEARING THE TOP OF THE SWING

POINTS TO STUDY

The impression here is that the weight is being pushed against the left foot. It looks inside.

BELOW THE WAIST

The left knee has moved horizontally forward and around in a semicircle. Because this movement has been horizontal the left heel has been lifted.

The right leg is taut and nearly straight . . . not quite straight. The weight has remained central as at the address so the right leg is not vertical.

The hips are horizontal (like the knees). The right hip has not sagged or moved laterally; it has turned straight back.

ABOVE THE WAIST

The shoulders have turned horizontally to the spine. Became of the upright stance—the spine being very little inclined forward—the shoulders have not dipped appreciably.

The left shoulder has not dipped, but it has come under and along to the chin.

The left arm is not stiff but it is straight, and the hands are held out as wide as possible.

This is the region of the reverse. The arms are near their top, but the wrists have still to break back fully as the left heel returns back to the ground.

NEARING THE TOP OF THE SWING

PERCY

CHAPTER IV

Golf Bogey No. 1

"Golf Bogey No. 1 is the natural urge to act in the obvious way to achieve the desired result. The seductiveness of the idea is clear; its destructiveness lies in the fact that in golf (as in many other affairs in life) the obvious way is not always the right way. Frequently the obvious way is the wrong way and unless the urge to follow it can be inhibited the right way cannot be taken."

Chapter Summary

THE FOCUS SHOULD be on making a swing based on swing fundamentals and letting the desired results come naturally. Many things in the golf swing that seem correct are not. To most golfers, the way a good golf swing feels probably seems wrong.

Today's Takeaway

Percy's story shows how what we think is the obvious and correct way to swing a golf club may not be correct. This lesson applies to other parts of the golf swing besides the in-to-out feel of a good swing.

The feel of the correct in-to-out swing path is not something you make happen through actions you intentionally take. It is something that naturally happens when you swing the club with a balanced pivot, swing width, and bracing to keep your rotating body in the correct position. The feel of an in-to-out swing path is not "caused," it is a "result" of using good fundamentals.

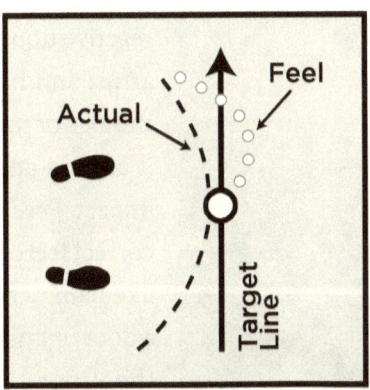

The in-to-out swing is how the club "feels" it is moving, not how it actually moves. As the club head approaches the ball, it swings on an arc from inside the target line. The club head squares through impact with the ball and only briefly travels down the target line. Following impact, the club head continues swinging on an arc inside the target line into the follow-through. At no time does the club head swing to the right of the target line—it only feels like it does. In-to-out is the feel that we seek in making a good swing.

With a good starting position, when the desired in-to-out feel happens, the ball automatically goes where you want it to go—straight down the desired target line.

More Obvious but Wrong

There are other examples of how what we think is the obvious and correct way to swing a golf club is not correct.

It seems obvious that to hit the golf ball, the club must go "back and up, then down and forward." To make this happen, the arms and hands lift the club up from the ground, then pull the club down to the ball. Contrary to this, the correct feel of a pivot-powered swing is "back and along, then along and through."

The lower body pivot automatically rotates the reactive upper body (shoulders, arms, and hands) back around the axis of the spine, then twists it around and forward through impact. Percy later describes the correct feel of a good swing to be like hammering a wedge under a door but not driving a nail into the floor. Percy also warns against trying to hit the ball with the club. Rather, allow the twisting forward swing pivot to accelerate the club through the ball. Contact of the club head with the ball is incidental.

Another example of what seems obvious and correct, but is not, is the loading of weight onto the right foot to make a powerful swing. In baseball, in preparation to hit the pitch, the batter shifts weight onto the right foot. But the golf swing is not a baseball swing carried onto the golf course. Loading weight onto the right foot on the backswing places the golfer in an unbalanced position. The golfer must then shift weight forward in order to hit the ball. This extra movement complicates the swing and makes it harder to repeat consistently.

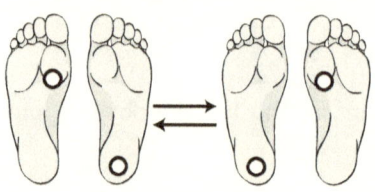

The correct feel for the pivot-powered golf swing is to have weight equally distributed (fifty/fifty) between the two feet on the backswing and forward swing pivots. The weight moves to the ball of the left foot and heel of the right foot on the backswing pivot. The weight moves to the heel of the left foot and ball of the right foot on the forward swing pivot. Only on the follow-through after impact does weight shift more onto the left foot.

As Percy said, "The most effective swing is artificial rather than natural" and "the obvious way is not always the right way."

Percy's Teachings in His Words (p. 29-34)

I have christened it Golf Bogey No.1 because it is the most seductive and destructive medium in the game. It took me most of the years of my golfing life to discover it and even then I could not formulate my ideas about it or counteract it effectively in my teaching until I had come to a proper understanding of the relation between the physical and mental in golf.

Now I can present it to you properly. Golf Bogey No. 1 *is the natural urge to act in the obvious way to achieve the desired result.*

The seductiveness of the idea is clear; its destructiveness lies in the fact that in golf (as in many other affairs in life) the obvious way is not always the right way. Frequently the obvious way is the wrong way and unless the urge to follow it can be *inhibited* the right way cannot be taken.

To use Professor Alexander's excellent phrase, the man who follows the obvious way is an *end gainer*. He is so keen and intent upon gaining his end (getting his ball onto the green and into the hole) that he concentrates upon *that* rather than upon the employment of what he knows to be the correct technique or the *means whereby* the end can best be gained. He is so intent upon his end that he tries to take short cuts to it—or, to put it more accurately, he no longer remembers that it is necessary to go round by a certain road to get there.

That the obvious way is often in conflict with the *right* way in golf is clear on the slightest thought. The most effective swing is artificial rather than natural, and even more closely relative to our point—any experienced golfer knows that it is impossible to make a good drive when thinking of hitting the ball a certain distance in a certain direction on to the green.

But that is where it has to be hit, you say? Agreed. But the point is that it cannot be hit there with any certainty unless the end in view is inhibited—or at least made secondary—and the whole system is concentrated upon performing a proper *swing*, i.e. upon the reasoned means whereby the desired aim may be achieved. In short you must not think about and calculate distance and direction; you must *feel* the swing that will give you the desired distance and direction.

This may seem a simple point, but it is so basically important that I will illustrate it by relating the experience of one of my pupils.

. . . .

Like all good mothers, my pupil took her children to the mountains for the Winter Sports and being an all-round sportswoman—she is a good yachtswoman too—she tried a few easy slopes herself. I have never been on skis, and probably never shall, as I can't afford to risk my limbs, so I cannot say from personal experience how skiing *should* mix with golf—but I know how it did in this case! My pupil came back physically undamaged, fit as ever, mentally happy and untroubled, yet her swing—*What* a mess! Completely slowed up, I told her.

As is my habit when things go seriously wrong, I began all over again: pivot, width, etc. Yet nothing happened except a further crop of half-tops, scoops, and all the lifeless, hopeless shots that a poor swing produces. In a sense, we both knew what was wrong without being able to cure it—we knew her club was coming down "outside" the ball every time. Yet to save her life my pupil could not prevent it!

So it went on until one day in what proved to be a moment of inspiration I said, "You seem to be trying to *guide* the ball down the middle."

"Well," she replied, "that is where you want me to hit it—isn't it?"

"If you insist on putting it that way—yes," I said. "But I would rather you felt that that is *where we want the ball to go*, not where we want you *to hit it*. Certainly you must not try directly to hit it down the middle, by making your club head take the line down the middle."

"But surely," she complained, "the ball goes where you feel the club head goes."

"By no means," said I. "From experience I know that unless I feel my club head goes out to the right my ball will not go down the middle—it will be pulled or horribly sliced. I know—by experience again—that if I want the ball to fly straight down the middle I must feel that I swing my club not in the direction of the hole, but at an angle to what I want to be the line of flight."

"Then you feel you swing your club in one direction to make the ball go in another?" she said.

"I do. And why? Because I could not be a good golfer if I did not!"

So much for the immediate cause of the trouble, but I wanted to dig deeper. Why had the trouble arisen? Before she went to the mountains my pupil was playing beautiful in-to-out shots—sweeping the ball away gloriously with every club. Why, oh why the breakdown?

We puzzled over it a great deal, but she could suggest no reason for it. But one day she said: "I do remember faintly that when you took me in hand first you *did* tell me to swing from in-to-out. You even sketched a line on the ground for me to follow.[1] But I did not realize that was fundamental—I thought it was a stunt of yours to cure some personal fault of mine."

I was angry! All that trouble because my pupil had taken me for a stunt merchant! Whatever I tell a pupil is *considered*, as are the phrases I tell it in. I told that pupil to swing the club head from in-to-out because that is an essential feel of good golf—and for no other reason. At least, all's well that ends well—and I am happy to say that since that day my pupil has never looked back.

What has that to do with Golf Bogey No. 1? Everything. We see the stimulus to put the ball near the flag ruining the lady's game—

---

[1] See diagram on page 147

because she became so intent upon reaching that *end* that she overlooked the means whereby it might be achieved, the correct in-to-out swing that sends the ball down the desired line of flight.

Beyond Percy—Feel Simple Golf

Woven intricately throughout Percy's instruction is the important concept that some golf swing movements result from "intentional actions," while other movements are "reactions," resulting automatically from previous actions.

Actions and Reactions

Keeping the golf swing simple means that the number of intentional actions taken in a swing that lasts from 0.5 to 1.5 seconds must be very small. The key to simplicity is to build a golf swing where (1) most of the intentional actions are taken in setting up the desired shot before the club is moved on the backswing and (2) much of the in-motion swing movements are automatic reactions.

Think of this like the setting up and then the toppling of a series of dominoes. The intentional actions are setting up the dominoes in a series and then tipping over the first domino. The toppling of the remaining dominos in order is an automatic reaction.

Intentional Actions in the Starting Position

The swing fundamental of starting position is where most of the intentional actions in the golf swing take place. Because the club has not yet started its movement on the backswing, you have total control to take as much time as you need to set up the correct starting position to make your desired swing.

The starting position is the foundation of power, direction, and consistency. Recall that building bracing into your starting position involves running a sequence, an important part of the psychology of the golf swing.

Once the starting position has been set up through intentional actions, the final intentional action is to make the starting movement. With bracing in place to keep the body in the correct position, the remainder of the swing is driven by the pivot with the upper body reacting to the pivot.

CHAPTER V

The Road to Golfing Health

"But note that we only arrived at this happy state when reason had dominated instinct..."

"With a properly felt swing, the swing becomes the aim and the matter of where the ball will fly is left (as it should be) to take care of itself."

Chapter Summary

HAVING THE RIGHT concept of what produces a good result (i.e., focusing on doing the fundamentals of a good swing, not the end result), playing by feel, developing automaticity, and not confusing the brain by having different swings for different shots (i.e., using the same swing for all shots) consistently leads to the best results.

Today's Takeaway

Yogi Berra, a famous and witty old-time catcher for and manager of the New York Yankees, once said, "Baseball is ninety percent mental.

The other half is physical."[2] In this chapter, Percy focuses on the 50 percent of the golf swing that is mental—which might actually be 90 percent of the battle. Percy's teachings on the psychology of the swing make the following points:

1. Keep the mechanics of the swing simple. Use the same swing for all shots—from driving to putting. One swing movement—versus separate ones for driving, chipping, and putting—is less demanding on the brain and leads to less mental confusion on what to do for different situations.
2. Use your brain appropriately. Use an active brain to learn, improve, and troubleshoot your swing. Use a quiet brain to play.
3. Make the single objective of every golf shot to experience the feels of a good swing. A good swing automatically produces good results. Focus on the process of the swing, not the desired end result.
4. Rely on automaticity to swing the club.

Use an *active brain* to learn and improve swing fundamentals and troubleshoot a faulty swing. This takes place in the prefrontal cortex of the brain's cerebral cortex. When this part of the brain is active (such as when trying to intentionally control your movements), the neurons in the body's nervous system (e.g., brain, spinal cord) are actively firing. Electrical impulses leading from the brain to the muscles throughout the body light up the brain. The brain is actively churning!

An active brain is useful to learn to use swing fundamentals correctly, experience the related feels that naturally happen, link feels through repeated practice, develop a single feel for the swing as a whole, and create automaticity through repetition of the swing.

---

2   The quote is cited multiple places. One source is: Yogi Berra Quotes; Baseball Almanac, Inc.; baseball-almanac.com; accessed 2/28/22

Once automaticity has been created, the mind quiets, as neuronal pathways have been created that allow you to quickly, efficiently, and automatically make a well-practiced movement (e.g., swinging the golf club, riding a bicycle).

Use a **quiet brain** to play golf. Play by feel, not intentional control. Allow automaticity to repeat a good swing rather than trying to use a series of intentional actions to control your swing mechanics. Automaticity is situated in the basal ganglia located in the base of the brain. The basal ganglia manage repeated physical movements and reduce the activity in the prefrontal cortex.

Automaticity is turned off whenever the brain becomes active by trying to intentionally control swing mechanics or when emotions kick in. Emotions, such as excitement, fear, joy, frustration, or anger, come from the amygdala, which is part of the body's limbic system. When this *fight or flight* part of the brain gets involved, all rational thinking and automaticity are set aside. Think of this as if you were being attacked by a huge, wild and hungry lion. The golf swing crumbles as the excited golfer chokes under the emotional stress.

Your best golf is played when automaticity performs a good swing with good fundamentals, producing the desired feels. When this happens, the prefrontal cortex and amygdala are quiet. The results are good!

Percy's Teachings in His Words (p. 35-39)

Now I could write a whole book on the experience of my pupil briefly outlined in the preceding chapter. It might be made a very interesting book too, for the case contained all the elements of a perfect illustration of the desirability of some sort of *conscious control* that could be used to check the often fatal tendency to do the obvious thing. For do not forget it was Golf Bogey No. 1—the natural tendency to do the obvious thing—that upset my pupil's game.

As soon as she willfully tried to drive down the middle of the fairway she was a mess. When she reverted to the proper method of *considering the stroke*, not the ball and *not* the distant green and tried to sling her club head out into the rough on her right—she became a beautiful, sweeping machine again. But note that we only arrived at this happy state when reason had dominated instinct—when her golf had evolved from instinctive end-gaining to *conscious control* of the stroke.

This conscious control, as I see it, can only be *built up* in some such manner as I have used in my teaching. Conscious control by *feel* certainly cannot be made use of simply by accepting its theoretical basis! Nor can it be made use of by copying the style and swing of someone who possesses it! It has to be *built up* in the individual golfer. And how? My own method will be described in later chapters.

It may be timely to suggest here that the "conscious" in *conscious control* is a warning that a fine and experienced golfer is not *necessarily* a good teacher of the game. Why? Because many cracks do not know how they play themselves—when it comes to anything like a close analysis of their shots—and they have no idea at all of how a beginner must feel in order to make the shots that they make.

Let me illustrate that last point, because it is fundamental to teaching and to learning. All crack players feel that they swing from in-to-out when driving. I have been doing this so long that it no longer feels a "guided" or unnatural swing to me. Indeed if I feel myself making any other sort of swing I know it will result in a bad shot. Yet with the beginner this in-to-out swing *does* feel unnatural and gives an impression that the ball will be pushed into the rough to the right. This feeling will of course be corrected by experience. This disparity in *feeling* about shots as between the crack and the beginner must never be lost sight of in teaching.

Every teacher has to keep continually in mind the fact that the natural thing for any golfer to do if he thinks first of hitting the ball to the hole rather than of making the shot correctly—is to swing the club head down the desired line of flight. The urge to do this is so strong that a merely academic knowledge of where the club head ought to be felt to go cannot stand against it.

William James said that where there is a conflict between the Will and the Imagination, the Imagination *always* wins. So no Will to make a correct swing—unless reinforced by our conscious control—can resist, when imagination of the ball flying straight for the hole supervenes. What usually happens is that before the back swing is completed, the player *transfers his attention from the matter of making the correct swing to the matter of where he wants to hit the ball*, i.e., somewhere at the top of his swing he switches from a correct in-to-out swing to one along the desired line of flight. Consequently he comes down *outside the ball*.

Anyone who is not a pupil of mine will admit that "you came down outside" is their tutor's most frequent admonition. And why do I say, "who is not a pupil of mine?" Well because I never just tell them that! It is quite useless to tell a pupil he has done wrong when acting instinctively *unless you tell him why he did wrong* and so enable him to avoid the fault in future. That I always do.

The player who comes down outside is almost invariably thinking of where he wants to put the ball, and the only effective way of overcoming his trouble is by getting him to concentrate on the swing that experience tells him will place it there. If this is done his conscious control—his feeling for the right movements, plus a steady intention to follow will inhibit his natural desire to take disastrous short cuts.

So Golf Bogey No. 1 can only be defeated by building up a swing which can be accepted by the mind as well as the muscles as a satisfactory means to the end desired, and then concentrating on the production of that swing. With a properly felt swing, *the swing becomes the aim* and the matter of where the ball will fly is left (as it should be) to take care of itself.

And finally, the good golfer feels his swing as *all one piece*. It is produced by a psycho-physical unison and its control is outside the mind of the player. Any control that is *within* the mind is subject to the state of the mind and is therefore unreliable.

Here we come back again to my reason for standardizing as many shots as possible so that they can all be played with the same set of "controls." Only so I believe can you learn to play entirely by sense of feel. Today, if I play a bad shot I do not start asking myself why I played it badly, what I did wrong, etc.—questions which are liable to lead to more bad shots as we all know! I just take an *easy* club and try it until I get the right feel again. Then because my shots are *felt* I know that the right feeling must lead to the right shot—and further, that as all my shots are made fundamentally the same, I know that if I get the right feel with say a No. 5 iron, a very easy club, I shall be making my shots with even the difficult clubs correctly and with confidence.

As I said before, these *controls* to which feeling a club gives the key, are probably in muscular memory *plus* tracks worn in the mind. But wherever they reside it is clear that the fewer there are of them the more reliable they are likely to be. If I play a pitch one way, a drive another, an iron shot in yet another, and a putt quite differently again, it is obvious that no single and consistent line of controls will be set up. Confusion as between one set of controls and another is very likely, and if I go off my game I may go off it very badly!

On the other hand if my system is used, a single sound line of controls is set up—by consistently practicing the same fundamental swing for every shot. Working on these lines and refusing to be side-tracked by extraneous ideas such as "hitting a long ball" or "driving straight down the middle," you can begin to feel a complete assurance that you can at least rely upon producing your best shots every time. They will become a *habit* with you.

Beyond Percy—Feel Simple Golf

The fundamental of the psychology of the golf swing gives ways to keep a quiet brain while playing golf. A quiet brain allows automaticity to drive your swing.

1. Get to the course early enough to warm up and prepare all your equipment so you begin the round loose and calm.

2. Use the same well-practiced pre-shot routine for every shot. This routine, familiar, and comfortable ritual gives a sense of control that quiets the brain. A pre-shot routine may include the following steps:

    a. Visualize the desired shot, select the club that makes that shot, and recall the feels of the intended swing.
    b. Have belief in and fully commit to your intended swing.
    c. Determine the target line for your desired shot.
    d. Set up the intended swing in your starting position, including alignment and grip.
    e. Run your sequence to apply bracing to your swing. Your sequence must follow the same steps, in the same order and in the same amount of time, swing after swing.
    f. Do a preparatory waggle to feel your desired swing.

3. Immediately make the starting movement. Starting the swing immediately after running your sequence keeps your brain from becoming active. Your brain becomes active when you second-guess your intended swing, try to intentionally control the swing mechanics, or let destructive emotions creep in.

4. Think of a positive single thought throughout your swing. This thought might be a desired feel that is key to a good swing, such as "pivot moves shoulders."

5. Once you know the results of your swing, quickly debrief in your mind—but for no longer than thirty seconds. Let your active problem-solving brain engage, quickly manage any emotions, and then move on and return to a quiet brain.

6. Breathe! Take a mental vacation until it is time to prepare for your next shot. Think about or talk with your playing partners about anything other than your round of golf. You might talk about sports teams, dinner plans, past/upcoming vacations, family updates, or other things that don't get you

too excited. The more neutral or slightly positive the topics, the better to keep the brain quiet.
7. Return to step two and repeat until your round is complete.

Just like the physical part of your swing, the psychological part of your swing can be built piece by piece and then improved through repeated practice.

CHAPTER VI

The Concentration Fallacy

"I say that a golfer can only produce his true quality when he can play without concentrating..."

Chapter Summary

CONCENTRATION INVOLVES AN active brain and is an enemy of playing good golf. An active brain dismisses automaticity. An active brain also keeps us from relying on the feels of a good swing to get the desired results. Good results come from consistently experiencing the desired feels (controls) of a good swing. This is based on using the swing fundamentals correctly through automaticity, which requires a quiet brain.

Today's Takeaway

This chapter applies Golf Bogey No. 1 to the psychology of the swing. The mental version of Golf Bogey No. 1 is the natural urge to THINK in the obvious way to achieve the desired results—with the obvious way being the wrong way. For example, it seems obvious that good golf demands good concentration, and great golf demands great concentration. Percy says, not true!

Much of this chapter builds upon Percy's teachings from the last chapter on the psychology of the swing. Specifically, concentration activates the prefrontal cortex, which opens the door to an unwelcome active brain. The feelings of concern or fear of walking across a narrow footbridge or teeing off to a narrow fairway invite the amygdala to join the scene, which also gets the brain churning. Both scenarios work against playing our best golf.

The remedy for such illnesses of the golf swing is *automaticity*. Automaticity that was not interfered with by an active brain (e.g., thinking, problem-solving, emotions), confidence, unwavering commitment and conviction, and a strong physical game likely led Mademoiselle Aline de Gunsbourg (one of Percy's students) to a higher level of success than she thought possible.

Let's look at what Percy means when he calls for "controls-controls-controls" as a key to good golf, rather than concentration. Controls are the series of linked feels of a good swing (e.g., pivot, moving shoulders, full stretch, in-to-out) that are *naturally* sensed in the body when the swing fundamentals are done correctly. Linked feels require the connecting of the swing fundamentals (e.g., pivot, body balance, swing width). When the swing fundamentals are repeatedly done correctly, the resulting feels become linked. The golf swing becomes experienced as a single, indivisible swing movement that produces a single overall feel. When this feel is repeatedly experienced, the linked swing fundamentals have become ingrained in muscle memory and automaticity has been created.

Once automaticity has been created, your only objective is to recall the feel of the swing that gets the desired shot result, set up the desired swing in your starting position, and then do the swing fundamentals correctly through automaticity to experience that feel. Your brain must remain quiet for this to occur. When this objective is met, the desired results of the golf shot will be there. No end-gaining or intentional control of the swing mechanics is involved.

Percy's Teachings in His Words (p. 40-46)

In whatever class of golf you play you will agree that the quality which enables the fellow just above you to give you strokes is not so much his ability to make shots which you cannot, as his knack of keeping his average shot nearer his best than you can. And this prime virtue of consistency is commonly credited to concentration.

And concentration is taken to mean such a pulling of oneself together, such a fixing of the mind on the task in hand, such a tight-lipped determination to do one's best, that golf becomes a trial of nervous strength rather than a game.

Now my own observation of many thousands of golfers from neophytes to tigers is that this form of concentration does *not* assist the production of one's best game. In fact I think the whole "concentration" doctrine a perversion of the truth, almost a reversal of it. I say that a golfer can only produce his true quality when he can play *without* concentrating (in this sense), when he can make his shots without clenching his teeth.

Nothing makes a simple physical action so difficult as does "concentration." Consider this odd fact about walking. We pay less attention to walking down a street than to walking over a plank across a stream—and *because* we pay less attention to it we walk at least as straight and with much better balance, greater firmness, and greater ease.

Simply because the penalties of deviating from the straight are so much greater when crossing the plank, we feel we have to concentrate our attention on the job. And it is this attitude of over-tense attention that makes the simple and familiar act of walking straight so suddenly and curiously difficult.

Now we can translate that directly into a common golfing experience. Put the average good golfer on a tee with a fairway fifty yards wide before him, and time after time he will drive slap down the middle of it. Yet reduce the width of that fairway to fifteen yards and he will become so conscious of its narrowness—

so concentrated on the importance of keeping dead straight—that time after time he will put himself well out in the rough. That is why a course with wide fairways is commonly more popular than a narrow one; the average golfer feels more comfortable about it and *because* he feels more comfortable, plays better.

Hitting a golf ball is not difficult, nor is walking straight, *so long as the penalties of failure are not great*. But introduce the plank bridge or the narrow fairway and the difficulties follow.

The desire to *guide the ball* dead straight increases with the need for a dead straight drive and the greater the desire the greater the difficulty! So when we stand on a tee with a narrow fairway before us, we must use our will power to inhibit the desire to *guide* the ball and simply perform the swing which our golfing sense tells us will send the ball straight. In fact we must forget that the plank is a bridge and simply walk across it!

This is true about the longest shot in golf, the drive; it is equally true and even more obvious about the shortest, the putt. What a simple operation is the five-foot putt on a good green *when there is nothing hanging to it*—and how exasperatingly difficult when it will decide the hole, the match and the half-crown!

So I repeat that if concentration means focusing all our mental attention and capacity on the problems and penalties of the shot in hand, then concentration is destructive of good golf. Good golf, consistent golf, depends upon being able to shut out our mental machinery (with its knowledge of the difficulties of the shot, the state of the game, etc.) *from those parts of us which play golf shots.*

Our conscious mental machinery is obsessed by the problems of getting the ball up to the hole and into the hole. Our golfing self should be concerned with something quite different, with the movements necessary to produce a good shot. These movements are controlled by remembered feel and the only concentrating we must do is in guarding this "remembered feel" from interference.

That is why when a match grows to a climax the great player is apt to become slower and slower. It is not that the putt on the last green is more difficult than that on the first; probably his experienced eye tells him all he needs to know about it at first glance. But he potters about, sometimes to the annoyance of uninitiated spectators, *until he has pushed all that the putt means out of his mind*, until all he is conscious of is the feel of the stroke that will hole the ball. Then, and not until then, he can hole it.

If you want my idea of the ideal mental attitude to the game I will give it you in two words—Walter Hagen's! Walter Hagen was not only one of the greatest golfers, he was one of the most buoyant. Wherever he played he simply oozed with the joy of life. The more he was up against it the better he played. He really enjoyed a fight and the harder it was the more superb his confidence.

The general verdict is that the Hage had a "marvelous temperament for the game." And what do we mean by that? My own interpretation is that the Hage had perfect psycho-physical equilibrium, that his mind and body were perfectly balanced and perfectly correlated for the purpose of the game of golf.

Walter Hagen had found by trial and error, as most of us do, how he could best hit the ball. He had got the *feel* of his shots thoroughly into his system and could pull them out whenever he wanted. While he was playing he inhibited any extraneous matters in the most effective way possible—*he refused to let them into that part of himself that was concerned with his golf.* So he could play his best in circumstances that would have turned gray the hair of any less perfectly adjusted player.

Please note that the Hage did *not* concentrate in the accepted sense. He did not shut extraneous matters out of his mind; he merely shut them out of his golf. While he was playing he would talk intelligently about any subject that cropped up, stocks and shares, eating and drinking, politics or puritanism. *Nothing*, neither wind nor weather, bad greens, tight corners, or unduly chatty opponents, ever made the Hage *tense*. Consequently golf never exhausted him; he was as fresh at the end of a Championship as he was at its beginning.

Incidentally this mental limberness was not left behind on the last green. I remember talking to him at Sandwich on the day he won the British Open. He had finished and we sat and chatted for a long time while waiting to see if George Duncan would deprive him of the title which otherwise he had won. Well George very nearly did it, but Walter Hagen never batted an eyelid. He was as chatty, as cheerful, and as untense as ever—at the end of a week's competitive golf with the whole issue of a three thousand mile trip in the balance.

I suppose everyone would agree that "self-control" as effective as that possessed by men like Hagen and Harry Vardon is a priceless quality. But how [to] achieve it? It can only be done by building one's golf into a closed, self-controlling circle, and then keeping extraneous matters outside that circle.

The reason why the neophyte and the player needing re-education find control so elusive is simply that *their* golf has not yet been built into such a closed circle. And if they only knew it they make things far worse by trying to *learn* golf and *play* golf at the same time. When that happens, pity the poor teacher!

The pupil, let us say, is making good progress. He is beginning to coordinate his game and build up his controls, when he suddenly takes himself off for an afternoon in an entirely different atmosphere—that of competitive golf, in which *style* means nothing and immediate results everything. Of course his budding style and incipient control go overboard and *end-gaining* dominates. Everything is subordinate to getting the ball into the hole, so Golf Bogey No. 1 wins again. It is only an intentionally established set of controls that can resist the temptation to *force and guide* the ball when much is at stake.

These controls are the thing! Their creation and development must be the constant aim of both pupil and teacher. Everything helping their development must be encouraged, everything hindering it avoided. Their building up is largely unconscious and unnoticed, indeed even a successful pupil will often feel that little progress is being made—until perhaps quite suddenly he will be surprised to find himself playing effective, confident golf.

I remember with special pleasure how that happened to a young pupil of mine, Mlle Aline de Gunsbourg. She had been in my hands since her childhood and her first experience of a major tournament was when she went over to England for the Ladies' Open. *She actually led the field in the qualifying rounds* and was only put out on the last green in the semi-final by Pam Barton, the eventual winner.

On her return she said to me, "I did not know I could play like that! No one was more surprised than I was. I just played—and everything went right."

I was delighted, but not so surprised. I knew she had the golf in her and that sooner or later the controls we were building would enable her to play it. But I was delighted, because you would not normally expect a young pupil to play a bit above her best on such a nerve-testing occasion.

So when a golfer says to me, "I must learn to concentrate-concentrate-concentrate!" I counter with: "No, you must build controls-controls-controls!"

Beyond Percy—Feel Simple Golf

Malcolm Gladwell, in his 2009 book, *What the Dog Saw*, describes the difference between panicking and choking in sports. Both involve failing when the penalty for failure is high. Someone panics when they don't have the knowledge, skills, or abilities to succeed at something; become afraid of failing; and naturally fail in their attempt. Someone chokes when they do have what it takes to succeed but their inability to handle the fear of failure leads them to underperforming and failing.

Percy's examples of crossing a narrow footbridge and teeing off to a narrow fairway are related. When the penalty for failure is high, pressure to perform increases, the brain kicks in to try to intentionally control actions, and something that is normally easy to do becomes difficult. Panicking and choking become real possibilities.

What can be done to prevent choking when faced with an important golf shot? One answer relates to Percy's story of the American crossing busy streets in England. To cross the street safely, the man followed the sequence: (1) raise right forearm, (2) clench right fist, (3) look to the right, (4) cross the street when safe.

Keeping the brain quiet leading up to and then swinging the golf club is important. A quiet brain allows automaticity to make the swing. This increases the chance of a good result and reduces the chance of choking. Following a sequence leading up to the swing keeps the brain from thinking about the consequences of a bad shot or getting overly excited about the possibilities of a good shot. A sequence is something familiar and comfortable that keeps the brain appropriately involved without causing it to become too active.

The sequence in a golf swing is a series of actions taken in order to build bracing into the starting position. A golfer's sequence might be to (1) apply upward bracing, (2) apply inward bracing, (3) apply behind bracing, (4) apply profile bracing, (5) pivot for power and direction. (Details of bracing are covered in Chapter VII.)

Once the swing begins, the brain is kept quiet through impact with the ball by thinking of a single positive swing thought, such as "full stretch" or "turn then twist." The sequence and swing thought keep the brain appropriately involved without allowing it to become too active. Fear of failure or having too much positive or negative emotion are kept out of the swing, which allows automaticity to be in charge.

In addition to the importance of breathing, we add to the value of playing with the attitude of having "fun" and "enjoying" the game. These simple mental acts help reduce the perceived penalty for failure, which keeps the emotional amygdala from becoming active and dismissing automaticity.

All this is part of the psychology of the swing.

more ON LEARNING GOLF

Part Two

On Learning and Teaching

"You must learn to feel the sensations through your intellect and then forget them intellectually and leave them to your muscular memory or control system."

Chapter Summary

PERCY TALKS TO both the student and the golf instructor about learning and teaching the golf swing. Percy's learned approach was to build upon the good qualities already in place, be positive, link together through sequence the various sensations/controls/feels of the swing, be patient, and practice.

Today's Takeaway

Part One talks about how Percy came to his theory of golf and why he believed in and instructed it. The chapters of Part Two build upon various technical and practical points of the swing. Interwoven into the chapters is relevant storytelling emphasizing important lessons. To begin Part Two, Percy covers a few things about learning the game and about teaching it that deserve our attention.

Learning golf is about developing *automaticity*, not memorizing facts or technical parts of the golf swing. Automaticity is the modern way of describing Percy's understanding of "reflex" golf and using "muscle memory." Automaticity is developed by the following:

1. Learning and doing the fundamentals of the golf swing (i.e., pivot, body balance, swing width, starting position) correctly;
2. Learning the various feels (sensations in the body) that automatically result from doing each of the fundamentals correctly;
3. Linking together the various fundamentals through repetition until the golf swing is experienced and automatically repeated as a single movement;
4. Linking together the various feels through repetition until the golf swing is experienced as a single feel; and
5. Allowing the pre-programmed learning developed through repetition (i.e., automaticity) to repeat the desired golf swing as a single movement and single feel.

There is a lot of psychology, the mental side of the golf swing, in this. This highlights Percy's insistence that the golf swing is a blending of the physical and mental.

The process of *learning* golf must be positive. This is an important part of the psychology of the swing, one of the five swing fundamentals. Percy instructs the golfer and instructor to spot the good in a golf swing and build upon that by adding more good qualities. Positive learns, negative burns.

Percy repeatedly emphasizes the importance of "building up"— building up swing fundamentals, building up feels, and building up confidence. Varying by golfer, this progressive process of building up may take place quickly or may take years. But with patience and practice, it does happen.

Percy's Teachings in His Words (p. 49-55)

Now I claim that the right way of learning golf has almost nothing in common with the "learning" we did at school; it is an entirely different process. Memorizing the capitals of Europe or a Latin declension, or "learning" chemistry or mathematics, are purely mental feats and depend exclusively upon *mental memory*, whereas I contend that to learn to play good and consistent golf you need *muscular memory*.

What you need to learn (or memorize) are not the technical or mathematical details of a good shot *but the feel of it*. If you and every component muscle in you can remember the feel of a good shot, *you can make it*—and you have become what I term a reflex golfer. That is to say, the good shot has become your "reflex," or *automatic response* to the sight of the ball. But please remember that this golf memory is a *memory of a cycle of sensations* which follow and blend into one another quite smoothly. Each sensation must be connected up with those which precede and follow it; it cannot be considered independently. The truth is that it cannot even be *felt* independently. You cannot, to take a crude example, *feel* the top of your swing as such; you can only feel a sensation between the sensations of the back swing and those of the down swing.

For that reason you must never in golf say, "I've got it!" when you think you have found the secret of some shot that has been evading you—unless what you have "got" fits into your cycle of sensations or, as we shall now call them, *controls*. Because, unless it does so fit in, it cannot become a reliable part of your game. And why do I call sensations controls? Simply because I want you to control your golf by these sensations instead of by *thought*.

There is another reason why your memory of a golf shot must be a memory of a cycle of sensations, not of a number of separate sensations. It takes an exceedingly skillful juggler to juggle with six glass balls at once, but if the six balls were threaded onto a string most of us could manage them—and the memorizing of sensations as a cycle (instead of as independent items) *does thread them up* for us very much in this way.

To turn for a moment from learning to teaching. Most of the teaching of golf is completely negative—and a purely negative thing can have no positive value. Why do I say that golf teaching is negative? Well we can all find faults in each other's game, millions of them, and we all start off to teach golf by pointing out these faults and "curing" them. I did this for twenty-five years, but I have now discovered that the right way to get a pupil to hit the ball satisfactorily is *to watch for any good natural qualities* that may be there and to build up the swing around them.

We all hit a good ball sometimes. Maybe with the beginner this is an accident, but the good teacher will use such an accidental shot, photographing it in his mind and starting away to build up controls around the qualities which made it possible.

In this way the beginner can retain his natural capacity to hit the ball and will gain confidence in his ability to do it—and so go on enjoying his game and improving it. But if the teacher merely points out to him a dozen or more faults in his swing he will become perplexed, confused, and fed up. For that reason I never tell a pupil his faults (which is negative teaching). I notice the faults, of course, *and suggest the necessary corrections* (which is positive). So I never tell a pupil that he overswings and breaks his left arm, I explain width to him. That is to say I give him a positive conception and by working on it he actually cures his faults without even being aware that he had them.

Now there is another point about teaching which I would like to emphasize. You will find that in this work I have not tried to set down a set of controls in one way and leave it at that. I have tried to set the same things down and explain them in many different ways. So when you find me repeating myself do not think it is carelessness! All good teachers must repeat, but never in exactly the same words or with just the same connections. I want to give you a clear idea of the controls which will enable you to produce an effective swing, and I do not mind if I have to say the same thing in a dozen different ways so long as one of the twelve gets home with you. I hope you will not mind either, because you should be able to pick something new out of the other eleven also.

I learned golf by the long way—trial and error—and I want to lead you away from that to a method which is methodical and is effective whatever your age or your handicap may be. If you accept my method of learning you do not need a lot of practice on the course to improve; you can assimilate the principles in your armchair and put in useful practice on the hearth rug—where you need no club because you can *feel* your muscular movements without it. You must learn to feel the sensations through your intellect and then forget them intellectually and leave them to your muscular memory or control system.

. . . .

So do not despair if you are trying to learn golf, or better golf, and getting no results. It may be that you have been trying to learn too many things (like juggling with too many balls) and when you have tried to add just one more, your whole game has broken down on you. We will simplify the things you have to learn by stringing them together into cycles of sensation because they are then easier to remember and easier to *add to*.

If you work in this way your golf will be *progressive*. You will still (being human) get bad patches, but each bad patch will tend to be less bad and each good patch will tend to be better, because you are *building up* your game.

The foundation upon which it must be built up is the *feel of the swing*; so in the first practical chapter I give you an idea of the whole swing—just as I do in the first lesson when personal teaching is possible.

The subsequent chapters are what a musician might call "Variations on the Theme!" Hence the apparent repetition. Because I believe that all golf shots should be made with the same controls, you will not find anything fundamentally different in the chapter on Putting than that which you will find in the chapter on the Full Swing. Yet you might quite possibly get a control for your driving out of the Putting chapter; it depends on your make-up and on what you read into what I have written.

Some years ago I told a pupil, in the course of a lesson, "I drive as I putt." Three years later he said to me, "You once told me you drove as you putted—what you meant was that you putted as you drove." I let him have his own way! The great thing was that we had got the two associated in his mind and controls and so proved my system to be teachable and workable in others. I have had plenty of confirmation of this since.

In finishing this chapter I will return again to the need to make your learning *positive*. Don't go out to find out what is wrong with your swing, go out to improve it.

Beyond Percy—Feel Simple Golf

Part of the psychology of the golf swing is to practice experiencing the feels of good swing fundamentals without a club in hand. Modern sport psychology research has shown that visualizing doing athletic movements correctly strengthens automaticity and results in improved performance. Adding body movements while mentally visualizing correct movements (e.g., actually shifting weight in your feet while visualizing pivoting) strengthens automaticity even more. You don't have to be on the golf course to improve.

Quite remarkably, mental visualization with body movements improves athletic performance almost as much as physical practice. Think of how a gymnast prepares for her performance by closing her eyes and moving her body as she visualizes her upcoming floor routine. She is activating her automaticity that has been developed through repeated practice. Her visualization may also have helped quiet her brain, which would add more benefits. Of course, mental visualization with body movement plus actual practice results in the greatest learning and improvement.

Paul saw the benefit of visualization to his golf swing while writing our instructional books. Without hitting a single ball, but by repeatedly visualizing the swing fundamentals over many hours while writing sections of the books, his golf swing improved.

CHAPTER VII

The Controlled Golf Swing

"The most difficult thing about learning golf is to learn to distract your mind from everything except the feeling of what you are about to perform."

Chapter Summary

PERCY NOTES HOW much of the essence of the golf swing he condensed into a reasonable number of pages. This chapter is packed with content and takes time to work through. Percy introduces the concept of a controlled golf swing in which a good golf shot results from repeating the feel of the swing that produces the desired result. The three primary feels of a good swing are (1) pivot, (2) shoulders moving in response to the pivot, and (3) arms moving in response to the shoulders. Percy's mental image of "turning in a barrel" leads to a good idea of a balanced swing powered by the pivoting of the lower body.

Today's Takeaway

There is something valuable in this chapter for every level of golfer. All golfers will finish this chapter with some level of appreciation and understanding. The less experienced golfer will easily find several important swing fundamentals on which to build a good swing. Yet much of the content will not be fully understood and will slip by the wayside—appropriately so. The more experienced golfer will need to read this chapter multiple times to fully grasp the number of interconnected concepts of a good swing and to keep the head from exploding from the depth and breadth of the concepts covered.

Percy presents the swing in *grosso modo*, which means in a general sense, but not complete in detail. The major takeaways from this chapter are the *connected* and *controlled* golf swings. Both help keep the swing simple.

Connected Swing

A **connected swing** is one in which the lower body pivot leads the swing and the connected upper body automatically follows (i.e., reacts). An analogy for it would be a set of interconnected gears. The intentional turning of one gear automatically turns all the other gears.

Connection is achieved through **bracing**. Bracing ensures the body moves as a single unit on the backswing pivot. This creates simplicity that makes the swing more repeatable, which leads to increased consistency. The shoulders are braced, so when the hips pivot the shoulders automatically move. The arms are braced, so when the shoulders are moved by the pivot, the arms automatically move.

Controlled Swing

Each of these connected movements has a feel (i.e., control). For example, the feel of the profile brace is tautness up the left side of your body. As these feels are linked together one after another through repetition, the swing is experienced as a single feel. The connected series of feels make the connected swing become a ***controlled*** swing. This keeps the active brain from getting involved in swinging the club and allows automaticity to take over. This makes the swing simpler.

Feels of a Controlled Swing

Up through this chapter, Percy lists several feels of a good (i.e., connected and controlled) swing. These feels are either primary or supplementary (secondary).

- Primary feels:
    - Pivot (hips feel up, rotating right then left inside a tight barrel).
    - Shoulders moving in response to the pivot (standing fairly erect with shoulders feeling up).
    - Arms moving in response to the shoulders.

When these three primary feels are experienced and connected, the swing is controlled by feel. Don't lose sight of these three feels, and return to them when your swing needs refreshing.

Percy's Teachings in His Words (p. 56-67)

As you have already heard, my first endeavor is to teach the pupil the whole golf swing—or better, the golf swing as a whole. I do not believe in trying to impart the swing in stages or by sections; from the first lesson I teach the swing complete.

What the pupil gets from this first lesson is a *grosso modo* idea of how the swing works; what I get from it is mainly an indication of how the *grosso modo* strikes the pupil as an individual. For do not forget that whatever I say and however I illustrate my points, *every pupil will visualize the swing differently.*

. . . .

Now for our *grosso modo* exposition of how the swing works.

The beginning of the movement is in the feet; the movement passes progressively up through the body, through the arms, and out at the club head. What we try to do is to make the club head come down in the same path time and time again—in such a way that the face of the club comes squarely into the back of the ball every time. We have one fixed point (the feet) and one moving point (the club head) which we desire to move along the same line time after time.

Again, we have not only to bring the club head down through the same line time after time; we must bring it down so that the club face is square with the ball at the instant of impact—and because the path of the club head is a curve, this means that impact must be *timed* correctly to an infinitesimal fraction of a second in the sweep of the swing. Also the club head must be *accelerating* at the moment of impact.

So we have not only to set up the mechanism to make a good swing, which we can all soon do if we only swing at the daisies, but we have to *time* this swing to the fraction of a second. Now I think that most of us overrate the value of good mechanics in golf and underrate the value of accurate timing. I was once watching, with a pupil of mine who had a most perfect swing, a fellow whose action was not pretty—to put it kindly. But he kept hitting nice long shots down the middle. "Not much to look at," I remarked to my pupil. "I would not care a damn what I looked like if I could repeat like that chap!" he replied.

The awkward one *could* repeat his best shots time after time. His mechanics were ungainly but his timing was near perfect.

Well, you may say, if that is so, why should you go to so much trouble to give us a good mechanical swing? The answer is that good timing plus a good swing is better than good timing plus an awkward swing.

. . . .

Too much thought about the mechanics is a bad thing for anyone's game. Now the reason why golf is so difficult is that you have to learn it and play it *through your senses*. You must be mindful but not thoughtful as you swing. You must not think or reflect; you must *feel* what you have to do. Part of the difficulty arises because, apart from simple things like riding a bicycle, we have never learned to do things in this way.

The most difficult thing about learning golf is to learn to distract your mind from everything except the feeling of what you are about to perform.

Now no teacher can *tell* you in exact words how it feels when you make a certain movement correctly. You will have to use your imagination to interpret what he says, and if he is wise he will encourage you to use it.

Let me give you an example. I want to teach you to pivot from the hips. Now I can show you how it is done and issue the usual mass of detailed instruction, but that does not call up your imagination and it gives you no conception of how it *feels* to pivot correctly.

So, instead of explaining all the mechanical and anatomical details of the pivot to you, I show you how to pivot and then tell you to do it yourself *imagining that you are standing in a barrel hip high and big enough to be just free of each hip but a close enough fit to allow no movement except the pivot.* At once you get the *feeling* of the pivot. Incidentally nine out of ten golfers would improve their games if they would use this image to the fullest degree in practice.

So far so good; we can learn to feel the body turn to the right and round to the left, beautifully fixed in space by the hips. Now carry the image a stage further: first, as you pivot *sink down from the knees*—you will feel that if you sink down, even ever so little, you will become stuck in the barrel. *This will not do*, so you must feel that you keep your hips *up* on a level with the top of the barrel. Do this and you will develop the feel of keeping your hips up as you pivot—a thing which unfortunately for our golf very few of us do.

Now do not think that we use *imagination* in teaching golf in order to evolve new theories. Oh no—there are too many theories already! What we use imagination for is to translate theory into *feeling*, and to keep our minds awake and our circle of golfing sensations expanding. Every new golfing sensation (if it is to be deliberately induced and not left to happen by accident) may need an introduction through the imagination in this way—but once the image has done its work of introduction it can be put on one side and the *feel* that it has made known can be relied on. But put your images on one side—do not abandon them, because if you *do* lose the feel, the image through which you learned it will bring it back.

Now the golf swing is a connected series of sensations or feels and when you get all these *feels* right and rightly connected you will swing perfectly. I have just given you the *feel* of the pivot—the movement on which the modern swing is based.

Now to that one basic feel, the pivot, we will add other feels, and every new feel gives you a new *control* until your whole game is controlled and you can play it as you will. But do not think you cannot play until you have this whole series of controls established. Lots of players go through their golfing lives and get a lot of fun out of the game without building up any controls at all! But the more controls you can build up and *link together*, the better for your game, the finer the conception of the swing you will evolve.

Let us get back to the visualizing of our swing. We have laid our foundation by getting the *feel* of the pivot from the hips. This movement goes up through the body to the next control point—the shoulders. And here I believe that wrong imagination does a great deal of damage to many people's swings.

We think that in the fine swing we see the left shoulder come down as we come back and the right shoulder come down as we come forward; so we feel that this shoulder movement is *right* and tend to encourage it—to the detriment of our swings because it is *wrong*. And I say it is wrong, cheerfully certain that it *is* wrong in spite of its almost universal acceptance. How much the shoulders actually dip depends upon how erect we stand when addressing the ball. We should stand as erect as possible and I contend that we should *not* feel our shoulders go down but should feel that we are keeping them fully up.

As we address the ball we look at it a little sideways—we *peep* at it. The head is fixed (because you "keep your eye on the ball"), and the movement of the shoulders is not an independent movement of the shoulders at all, but is due to the shoulders *being moved around from the pivot*. We can only keep the shoulder movement in a fixed groove and make it *repeatable* time after time, by keeping the shoulders at the limit of *upness* in whatever position the turn from the hips may have placed them. Any *excess* of upness (that is, actual shoulder lift) will result in the ball being lost sight of. In short, the fixed head determines the limit of lift and dip of the shoulders.

You will see that this is why you must feel you keep the shoulders up to the same degree with, say, a driver and a full swing and a mashie niblick (a more upright club) and a half swing. The closer you stand to your ball the more upright the swing and the more directly downward your sight of the ball ... also, the less extensive the swing you can make without losing sight of the ball.

Now try this conception of the shoulder action without a club, and *link it to your feel of the pivot from the hips*. Feel how the two become connected. This is the first connection in our building up of a controlled swing—and a very important one. You cannot take too much trouble in understanding it and building it up.

From the shoulders our power travels down through the arms, and as to arm action also I believe the common conception to be erroneous. Most people think they lift their arms to get them to the top of the back swing. With a modern controlled swing they do *not* lift them ... the arms work absolutely subjectively to the shoulders, that is why they *are* controlled.

But, you may say, if I do not lift my arms how do I get them up to the top of my swing? To find the answer, think this out. As you stand to the ball with the wrists slightly up, there is a straight line practically from the club head up the shaft and along your arm to the left shoulder, and as your hands are already waist high it needs only the inclining of the shoulders as we turn (on the pivot) to bring them *shoulder high*, without having altered their relative positions at all. They have not been *lifted*; they have gone up in response to the shoulder movement. This accounts for the curtailment *and* the control of the modem swing.

Now to my mind the foregoing are the three basic *feels* of the golf swing—the pivot, the shoulders moving in response to the pivot, and the arms moving in response to the shoulders. These are the basic movements of a connected and therefore *controlled* swing, and they must all be built into the framework of your *feel* of the swing.

Of course there are many additional nuances and supplementary *feels* which you will build up and recognize as your game develops, but though you will *add* to these three fundamentals you will never alter them. Therein lies much of their value. You will get used to taking a sly look at them occasionally as you go round the course, and so long as you keep these three primary *feels* right, nothing much will go wrong with your game.

And if your game does go wrong, if the shots which you thought you had mastered desert you, all you need to do is to go back to the *feel* of these three basic points. You just take a peep back at them, and then with one or two shots your mechanism will feel familiar again and all the other supplementary feels which you have built up by practice will be enticed back.

Now we might break off this chapter at this point. I realize that I have already given you plenty to think of and to work at. But there is a development in your game or in your way of playing it that I want to prepare you for; so, for that reason and for the sake of analyzing the matter out to its logical conclusion I add the following.

After a while by dint of pivoting correctly, not dipping our shoulders (i.e. *not* lifting with the arms), we begin to play some good shots, nice and straight and reasonably long. We have arrived at this stage by building on the basic trinity—pivot, shoulders up, and width—and by occasionally taking a sly peep at how they are going. *So far we have never consciously produced a good shot*; we have merely made certain mechanical movements which we have been taught will result in good shots.

But now we begin to realize how we should feel in order to produce a good shot. We are on the other side of the fence. We know

now what it feels like to produce a good shot, and now, instead of preparing for a shot by sly looks at our pivot etc., we instinctively get into the position which we feel will produce a good shot. And as we go on, the *feeling* of this preparatory state comes more and more into the foreground.

Also because we are working from a secure basis we can now begin to notice the nuances and subtleties. We find that we produce purer shots from one sensation than from another only slightly different. We are enticed to arrange our back swing according to the type of shot we wish to produce: an extra pivot if we wish to pull or a restricted pivot if we wish to slice. But please notice that this will not be a conscious, mechanical control—you will not say to yourself, "I wish to slice slightly so I will restrict my swing to an arc of so many degrees," you will simply alter your swing unconsciously in response to your *feeling* of what will produce the shot you want.

In other words, the control of your shots has now been placed outside your *conscious mind and will*. You have built up a feel that a certain swing will produce a slice—so you can produce a slice by getting that feel into your swing. This is only the beginning of control by feel to the very good golfer. He begins to hit a variety of shots, with little difference in flight or character and yet each subtly different and with its individual feel. He files away in the "feel cabinet" in his unconscious memory all these subtleties. Consequently he never has to "think out" a shot on the course—he sees the lie and the flight required, and these produce, by an automatic response, the right feel from his cabinet and so the right shot from his club.

I hope that this chapter is easier to read than it was to write. I like it as well as any in the book, because it does condense what I take to be the essence of the golf swing into a reasonable space, readable in a reasonable time, so that the beginning should not be forgotten before the end is reached. But it is a vast field to cover and much compression had to be exercised—so it might be as well if you turned back now and read it again!

Beyond Percy—Feel Simple Golf

Without close reading, you may have missed Percy's important concept of the basic "trinity of the swing." These three fundamentals of (1) pivot, (2) shoulders up, and (3) width are given more detail in *Feel. Simple. Golf.* and are three of the five fundamentals. "Shoulders up" is more broadly a feel of "body balance." Width is "swing width," which is the distance from the club head to the center of your chest. Feel Simple Golf adds "starting position" and "psychology of the swing" as the fourth and fifth fundamentals—both solidly based on Percy's teachings.

CHAPTER VIII

Preparatory to the Swing

"Whether or not he has learned deliberately to play by feel, the good player feels, through his carriage and balance as he addresses the ball, the coming movement that will bring his club face squarely against the ball."

Chapter Summary

THIS IS ANOTHER heavy-duty chapter that gives a lot of instruction on swing fundamentals. Percy talks about how you can anticipate the outcome of your shot in how you set up your swing with bracing. Upward, inward, and behind bracing that connects your body and builds balance into your swing are covered. This preparation of the swing fundamentals sets up your shot for success before you ever swing your club.

Today's Takeaway

This chapter on preparation for the swing is a critical one that contains great instruction on the fundamentals of the setup. Helping keep the swing simple, and therefore repeatable and consistent, nearly all of the intentional actions taken in the golf swing are done before moving your club. Once the pivot is started, automaticity takes over. This is quite the chapter!

Set/Starting Position

Just before the pivot is started, you have placed yourself into the **set position**. The set/starting position involves bracing to connect your body and help establish body balance and maintain it throughout the swing. The set position and the hitting position at impact are nearly identical.

Bracing for Body Balance

The centrifugal force created by your body's pivoting rotation can easily throw your body out of balance. Bracing stabilizes your body to withstand this force so a full pivot can be made. A good pivot is important because it is the source of power and direction.

Upward bracing in the golf swing keeps your body from rising up or dipping down. Behind bracing keeps your body from swaying toward or away from the target. Inward bracing keeps your body from leaning toward or away from the ball. Profiling that connects the upper and lower bodies is another brace built into the set/starting position. These braces are in your sequence when setting up your set/starting position. Keeping these braces in place as much as possible throughout your swing helps keep your body in balance, which allows a full pivot resulting in maximum power and correct direction.

Profile Bracing

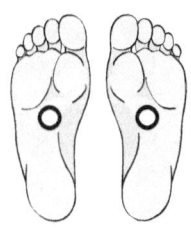
Body balance is the proper distribution of weight on your feet. Body balance is built into the starting position and is maintained throughout the swing with bracing. Weight in the set/starting position is equally distributed (fifty/fifty) between your left and right feet and equally distributed (fifty/fifty) between the ball and heel of each foot. This weight distribution results in feeling firmly planted on the ground.

Percy's Teachings in His Words (p. 68-78)

The experienced eye can make a very accurate guess at the handicap of a player after seeing him make a few practice swings, and as soon as his address is completed we can be *sure* of his quality.

Now at first glance it might seem that it would be simple enough for anyone to learn to stand correctly before the ball—to cultivate an impressive address. Yet there *is* this difference which enables the cognizant to recognize even the subtle variation between the good and the very good golfer before the ball has been struck.

It is an interesting point and one of some practical importance, because it is *directly related to the true aim and purpose of the preparatory movements*. We can recognize a golfer's quality in these movements because they express both *what* he intends to do and *how* he intends to do it. The difference between the good and the ordinary golfer is that the good one *feels his shot through his address.*

Whether or not he has learned deliberately to play by feel, the good player feels, through his carriage and balance as he addresses the ball, the coming movement that will bring his club face squarely against the ball. Briefly to analyze the feeling of carriage and balance—he feels he is set inwards and behind the back of the ball and his legs, hips and shoulders are all *braced, inside and behind the ball.*

Now this is a point where I must ask you to stop and consider and analyze carefully exactly the meaning I want to convey by the word *braced* because this is most important to a realization of the *correct feel of the body.*

My dictionary defines a brace as "anything that draws together and holds tightly," and I think that is clear and that it expresses the feeling we have when we are *braced*. But you may try it and promptly come back with the question, "But how can I feel *braced* and yet not become *stiff*?" A very pertinent question, and I will try and give you the answer.

When we take lessons in deportment we are told to walk *with our hips pulled in*, in other words to brace our hips. Yet we know that this does not make our carriage stiff; it makes it not stiff but firm and decisive.

So also, when I tell you as you address the ball to keep your elbows close together, you will immediately feel a sensation of drawing in your elbows the one towards the other. As a consequence your arms will not feel like two separate and independent arms but like a linked united *pair* of arms; yet *they will not feel stiff*. The "holding together" of your shoulder blades holds the top of your structure together and links up with the power from your hips. You will find your biceps being pulled into your thorax, your shoulders and arms being drawn together, and, if then the stomach is drawn inward, one definite (inward) *direction* of brace is set up.

The second direction in which we brace our bodies at the approach is *upwards*, yes upwards, towards the sky! The natural tendency as we stand to our ball is to droop from our hips and curve our backs. But if we are good golfers we resist this tendency by an *upward brace*—slightly bent over but pulled up to our full height and neither drooped nor curved.

Set like this we will feel our left side as straight as a poker, though not as stiff as one, and our *left foot pushing down into the ground*. Of course as the weight is equally divided between the feet, this *pushing down* is a feeling in the right foot also. The result is a highly desirable one; as a reaction to our upward brace, we feel ourselves *standing firm* as we address the ball—a thing we are frequently told to do but rarely told *how* to do!

So with our hips, shoulders, and arms braced and the body stretched upwards and braced, we no longer feel a loose, flabby, drooping figure but an upright and yet compact one. But we have one more direction of brace to add—this comes from the hips and I can best describe it as a twist forward which completes the bracing up of the whole body at the address.

As we stand to the ball our feet must not be too wide apart; the right foot should be at right angles to the line of flight, the left one pointed slightly out; a line across the toes of both feet should (like the line between the shoulders) be parallel to the line of flight. From this position, we twist our hips round (horizontally) to the left, not as far as they will go but as far as they can go in comfort, i.e., without pulling our hips out of shape. How far this is depends on how supple we are. Probably the degree of movement will be only slight, but the effect of this forward leftward twist is to tauten up the whole body without stiffening it.

Because we are anchored, first by our feet to the ground and secondly by our square-set shoulders held up against the forward pull of the hips, the right knee does not resist so we find our left side straight and our right side *bowed* inwards. And these, left side straight and right side bowed in, are very definite *feels* which come from (and can be used to check) correct bracing.

These three directions of brace should now make us feel a complete unit, which we can think of as "the set." I think they are what makes the good golfer feel *compact*.

. . . .

This feeling that the club head keeps down *is* equally necessary in the follow through, after we have sent the ball on its way. We must feel that we have dispatched the ball out and along but not up.

A pupil of mine once asked me, "But when my hands are *up* must they feel down?" My reply was, "Yes" because the *down* feeling is not a feeling of position but of *direction of pull.* We call it that because it is most noticeable in two *downward* phases, (1) as we address the ball, and (2) at the moment of impact with it.

We are frequently and wrongly told to keep our left arm straight, when we should be told to aim for the feeling of it being *down.* If we look for that, our arm will be practically straight even at the top of our swing, because we are stretching it to obtain the *down* feeling. This is the reliable way of reaching this end, because it is conditioned and controlled by *feel* not thought. Incidentally this explains why you can be a top class golfer even if your left arm is not straight at the top of your swing—not the straightness but the *downness* is the vital factor.

Now I hope you see the reason for adopting the set before the ball which I have been describing. It is so that you will feel that you will bring the club face square into the back of the ball, not from above but from behind it. When I say that I putt as I drive, I simply mean that when I putt I feel that I roll the ball along from behind—and I feel the drive is only an enlargement of this sensation, not something different from it.

"One sensation for all shots." I keep harping on this because it is not the knowledge of what we have to do which leaves us on the course—it is the *feel* of what we want to do that is apt to evaporate unless we have built up a secure feel-memory of how the swing operates. The only way in which we can *repeat* correct shots time after time (and this is the greatest of golfing assets) is to be able to repeat the correct feel of how they are produced. This feel must begin right as well as continue and finish right, and that is why I have gone into such detail in the apparently simple matter of standing in front of the ball.

. . . .

It is always a pleasure to teach intelligent analytically-minded players who think about their game, even if they are physically not capable of playing high-class golf. I remember a lady whose game had been largely messed up because to "cure" a somewhat persistent slice someone had told her to draw her right foot back a bit and hold her right hip back. Well, I squared up her stance and showed her how to brace and she began sweeping the ball away so perfectly that she could hardly believe her eyes! The next day she came back and told me she had thought over what I had told her and had found a curious resemblance between my "hip brace" and something that Miss Irene Castle the dancer had said to her some years before.

"Do you know," she said, "that while studying the dancing of Egyptians from old illustrations, Miss Castle found that they did not dance with their feet and hips and shoulders square, but with the hips profiled to the other two lines, and Miss Castle put down much of her success as a dancer to the fact that she adopted this idea?"

Now that was exceedingly interesting to me, even if it *did* upset some of the reasons I had worked out for the hips being "profiled" at golf. Like most of those who had been lucky enough to see Miss Castle dance, I had wondered how she did it—and here was part of the answer. I am more than ever convinced that the correct bracing of the body in this way is as essential to good golf as it is helpful to good dancing and that it is something that we should all seek for whatever our caliber.

I remember playing with Lord Derby and, because of his rotund figure, reminding him of the old Scotch golf adage I had heard from Sandy Herd when I was a boy. "Pull in your tummy, my Lord," I said. He looked at me and smiled. "Do you think I am Miss Wethered?" he said! At that time Miss Wethered was a slim girl, at the peak of her perfection as a golfer.

As with many other ideas which have come recently to the front, now that we know more about the brace, we find traces of it going way back into history! One of the finest pictures I have ever seen of a golfer standing to the ball was one of Mac Smith reproduced in the *American Golfer* some years ago, to my mind a perfect illustration of the correct set. I have it in my scrapbook and often take a peep at it, for we cannot refresh our memories too often. Study the photograph of Aubrey addressing the ball [...] Note especially the close relationship between this *set* and the actual hitting position; there is almost no difference between them, and that is why the good golfer can *feel his drive in his address*.

THE ADDRESS

POINTS TO STUDY

The stance is firm, compact, and braced, qualities essential to a fast swinger.

Note the triangle formed by the two arms and the shoulders.

Although the right wrist is held arched (that is, up), the right elbow is held in and down.

Note the inclination of the shoulders, due to the left side being straight and the right side curved.

The right elbow is inside the right hip.

The left arm and club are in line.

The shoulders and feet are square to the line of flight, the hips are profiled—that is, are at a slight angle to it.

The view of the ball from this position is a peeping at the back of the ball out of the left eye.

THE ADDRESS

AUBREY

When you are learning golf it is most helpful to watch good golfers and to see how they apply the doctrines which your teacher has impressed upon you. Some years ago I took a pupil of mine to study the players at Sandwich. "They look so *firm*," was his comment. They looked firm because they started braced and retained the braced feeling right through the swing.

There is one other aspect of the brace that we must consider, that concerned with the position of the head. If the head and chin are turned slightly to the right (so that the ball is seen "out of the corner of the left eye," as one of my pupils put it), it will help the feel of the correct brace—mainly because it helps us to fix our shoulders, or rather helps our shoulders to resist the movement of the hips which is trying to pull the right shoulder forward (as it does pull forward the right knee, which does not resist).

I do not mind whether you say that this position of the head fixed the shoulders or merely that it helps to fix them, but I know that it is infinitely easier to brace correctly with the head slightly side-on in this way than when looking straight down. Also, as it brings the head and chin slightly *behind* the ball, it gives the right feeling that we are looking at the back of the ball.

For those who like delving into past theories and histories of the game, the following is illuminating. It is a translation from a book called *Le Jeu de Mail* which I picked up in Paris for 10 francs. It was written nearly two hundred years ago. The extract is from the chapter on "Attitude of the Body."

"The body should not be too straight nor too curved, but slightly bent" (note the nuance "curved" and "bent." Even a couple of centuries ago they had to be careful in picking their words!) "in order that in hitting, it shall be held up by the strength of the hips (*reins*) while turning slowly backwards from the waist without losing the ball from view."

It is this half turn of the body that we call playing with the waist (or better, pivoting) which gives a wide circle to the club head.

The old book continues: "We should not lift the club too quickly but in order to (*uniquement*) and without allowing oneself to be carried away" (sway, we should say now), "wait a little (*se tenir un instant*) at the top of the swing (*la plus haute portee*) in order to hit through the plane" (amusing this, *sur le champ*) "with vigour, adding however, the force of the wrist (*la force du poignet*) without changing the position of the body, legs, or arms, in order to conserve the same union of adjustments which we have taken up at the address."

Beyond Percy—Feel Simple Golf

Because Feel Simple Golf is built upon Percy's teachings, much of what we have learned, developed, and teach is covered in our books. Here is a brief summary of two of Percy's concepts that are given more detail in *Feel. Simple. Golf.*: sequence and starting movement.

Sequence

The ***sequence*** is a very important part of getting into a good starting position to make your desired shot. The well-practiced sequence keeps your brain appropriately involved while building bracing into your swing. To run your sequence, take the following steps in the order listed, in the same amount of time, swing after swing.

1. Get into a balanced position.
2. Implement bracing:
   a. Stand tall (i.e., chin up, slight bend at your waist, flex in your knees).
   b. Pull your shoulder blades together (or push out your chest).
   c. Pull your elbows inward toward each other.
   d. Place your wrists in an up position.
   e. Activate your abdominal muscles.
   f. Turn your head to the right.
3. Make a preparatory waggle.
4. Profile your hips.

Once you have run your sequence, you are in your set position and are prepared to start your backswing pivot with the starting movement.

Starting Movement

Nearly all the intentional actions in your swing are made in setting up your swing and making your ***starting movement***. Recall our earlier analogy of the toppling dominoes. The starting movement is like tipping over the first domino in a chain.

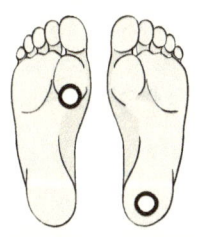

Once in the set position, the starting movement is made by bending your left knee forward toward the ball. This shifts weight onto the ball of your left foot. Pull your right knee back. This shifts weight onto the heel of your right foot. This movement of weight begins the pivoting of your hips. With bracing in place, the pivot automatically moves your connected shoulders, arms, and hands. Once the starting movement has been made, and the bracing is maintained throughout the swing, automaticity completes the connected swing. This keeps your swing movement simple.

CHAPTER IX

Interlude for Instruction: What We Mean When We Say

"The difficulty in teaching golf is that what we *have to teach* is a correct *feel*, and neither demonstration nor words can do that directly. Sometimes it is almost a chance word or movement that gives the pupil the right impression—and then he picks up the *feel* in a flash."

Chapter Summary

IN THIS BREAK from heavy content, Percy enjoys a conversation with an older student about misconceptions of the golf swing. The conversation weaves through concepts Percy thought were important to understanding the golf swing, including translating concepts into feels, actions versus reactions, opposing forces, lag, body balance (movement of weight), swing width, and backspin.

Today's Takeaway

Chapters VII and VIII are full of *intentional actions* you take in the golf swing. Most of these intentional actions are done in setting up the swing in the starting position before you move the club on the backswing pivot. Rereading these two meaty chapters on the swing as a whole will likely lead to more valuable understanding.

A major takeaway from Chapter IX is to *do nothing intentional* during the swing. This chapter is about *reactions, reactions, reactions,* which automatically occur in a good swing. There are some valuable lessons underlying Percy's storytelling.

Opposing Forces

Percy preferred the word "oppose" rather than "resist" and recognized the important role of ***opposing forces*** in the swing. Bracing enables the body to oppose the destructive centrifugal forces that can throw the body out of balance during the swing.

Pivoting and Lag

Percy gives more teaching on lag. With bracing in place, the pivoting of the hips automatically moves the connected shoulders, arms, and hands on the backswing. The body moves as a single unit for the first three feet on the backswing.

Percy didn't want the body "coming down altogether" on the forward swing pivot. Rather, the connected body starts breaking apart after the first three feet of the backswing into a one-after-the-other movement on the forward swing pivot. This lag is a source of significant power in the swing. The result is like the cracking tip of a leather whip.

Early in John's instruction of Paul, John was working with Paul's arm and hand-powered swing. One day, while hitting balls next to John, Paul saw John's pivoting action and decided to copy what he saw. For perhaps the first time, he experienced the sensation of lag in a golf swing. It was a new and great feeling. John commented, "Not bad." It was eye-opening and a turning point for Paul in his learning. His visual of John's pivot translated into a swing feel. Another eye-opening turning point for Paul was when he learned to power and direct his putt through pivoting.

Swing Width

Percy talks about *swing width*, one of the five Feel Simple Golf fundamentals, when he talks about the straightness of the left arm. The swing width feel of a full stretch results in the left arm being fully extended throughout the swing as a reaction. Along with the brace of keeping the wrists in an up position, the club is carried around and then up on the backswing pivot. The result is that the left wrist, left arm, and club shaft form a nearly straight line that continues up to shoulder height. Take note of the swing width in Percy's and John's backswing pivots.

The extended left arm gives the club path a wide sweeping arc. This adds power to the swing, just like a longer leather whip produces a more powerful crack at its tip than a shorter one. Also, the club head approaches and impacts the ball from behind, not above. This gives the desired along-and-through feel and provides the launch angle for the greatest ball distance.

Backspin—Another Reaction

Similar to the bending of the wrists, Percy notes that backspin on the ball is not something you make happen through intentional action. Backspin is an automatic reaction resulting from the angle of loft on the clubface. A wedge has a greater loft angle than a five iron and will result in more backspin. Club head speed will also impact the amount of backspin placed on the ball.

Feels

The three primary feels of the swing (see Chapter VII) are linked to the reactions in the swing presented in this chapter. To review, the three primary feels that are the foundation of a good swing are as follows:

1. Pivoting from the hips.
2. Shoulders moving in response to the pivot.
3. Arms moving in response to the shoulders.

When the swing fundamentals are done correctly and these primary feels are experienced, the following supplementary feels will also be experienced automatically:

- Backswing pivot feels:
    ○ Body moves as a single unit.
    ○ Taut and controlled (resulting from opposing forces (bracing)).
    ○ Full stretch (feel of width).
    ○ Club head down (i.e., club is carried (not lifted) around, along, and then up by the pivot).
    ○ Right hip pulls the left hip around.
    ○ Slow turn.
- Forward swing pivot feels:
    ○ Lag as the swing breaks into a one-after-the-other movement.
    ○ Full stretch.
    ○ Club head delayed and then snaps through impact.
    ○ Left hip pulls the right hip around.
    ○ Club head down (i.e., club approaches ball from behind, not above).
    ○ Fast twist.

Percy's Teachings in His Words (p. 79-88)

When my boys at St. Cloud found a particularly annoying pupil, they usually managed on one pretext or another to pass him on to the Boss! So when one day I was told that Old Zambuck insisted upon having a personal lesson from myself, I suspected trouble ahead! However it turned out to be an entertaining and thought-provoking experience.

Of course he had not been christened Old Zambuck—except by my boys! He was a retired Advocate; in his time he had been a good sportsman and a successful second-class tennis player. Now he was mad about golf and spent a lot of time at it, though up to the day of which I write he had never been a direct pupil of mine.

On our way to the sheds he informed me that he would have come to me before but for the fact that he understood that I had certain fixed ideas and considered myself "something of an impressionist."

I gasped at that! Impressionism in golf was a new one on me. I certainly have studied deeply many impressionist pictures, without understanding a thing about them, and if I have the same effect on my pupils as the pictures have on me—well, may heaven help my pupils!

"Now who told you I considered myself an impressionist?" I asked.

"Oh, Mr. So-and-So. You told him you tried to give a mind impression of how a shot was played, that the pupil had to translate into *feel*."

"Well I suppose that if trying to make you see in your mind how a movement works or what it feels like is impressionism—then I'm guilty! But I had never thought of it that way."

"I'm glad to hear it. I thought it was an attitude you assumed to impress people—knowing what snobs they are about such things."

"Oh you did!—Well, get that right out of your (silly old) head," said I somewhat piqued.

"Now don't get angry," he said. "Flaring up over nothing is another of your reputations!"

I said that he seemed to have gone around the village raking out my skeletons—and suggested that as it was a golf lesson, we might stick to the subject.

"Right," he answered. "Then how would you describe a teacher who told his pupils not to trouble about looking at the ball?"

I knew at once what he was driving at. "Well," I said, "if it were not I who had said that, I should say the teacher was a damned fool."

"But you *did* say it, to Mr. So-and-So!" he claimed in triumph.

"Of course I did, but as an individual prescription for an individual and very unusual case. He had got his eyes so glued to the ball, he was staring at it so rigidly, that he simply could not relax. In order to relax him I told him not to look at the ball."

"Did it work?"

"It did—very well, because the expression I used gave him the right impression of how he should view the ball."

"Ah, I see. You think that different pupils need different phrases to give them the same impression—and you use 'look at the ball,' 'peep at the ball,' or 'stare at the ball' accordingly?"

"Certainly. The difficulty in teaching golf is that what we *have to teach* is a correct *feel*, and neither demonstration nor words can do that directly. Sometimes it is almost a chance word or movement that gives the pupil the right impression—and then he picks up the *feel* in a flash."

"You must need a pretty good vocabulary for that," he suggested.

"Good in the sense of accurate, yes. But not necessarily extensive. You need a variety of words conveying more or less the same idea. And there are difficulties with lessons which, like this one, I give in French. For thirty years I have tried, and failed, to find the French equivalent for the English word 'swing'—and there isn't one!"

"By Jove, that is curious, but you are right."

"I know I am! But what can I do without the word 'swing'? The opposite of swing (in golf) is scoop. But no one will get the right idea of a sweeping swing by being told not to scoop!"

"Now I am enjoying this," said my pupil, warming to it. "So let us clear up some other 'teachers' phrases' that I may not have the right idea of. For instance, what about 'resist'?"

"As a matter of fact," said I, "I use the word 'resist' as little as possible. I prefer 'oppose.'"

"You do? And why?"

"Because 'resist' gives the impression that you *stop* the left side—for instance—in order to resist the blow. 'Oppose' suggests *opposition during movement* which is the correct conception."

"So! You mean that we must not feel the left side stop as we set our resistance on our way through the ball?"

"Certainly, most certainly, we must not. If you feel that it fixes your resistance on a certain spot, but if you feel you *oppose* the weight of the club head you can *oppose* it all the way up, down, and through—which is what you should do."

"But do you mean I must oppose the club head on the up swing?"

"Yes, if you will think of 'opposing' as 'force in the opposite direction'—which is the way to think of it. It is that and that alone which keeps the controlled swing *taut* and controlled."

"Good, so far! Now to the next. I have some difficulty in comprehending the word 'wait,' when you tell us to wait for the club head."

"Well 'wait' gives a fairly good impression if you take it simply in relation to the left heel. When you are told to 'wait for the club head' you are meant to delay your sweep through until your left heel has come well back to the ground. So the phrase is not well chosen. And also I do prefer the word 'delay' because 'wait' somewhat suggests stopping the whole swing—which is entirely the wrong idea. Stopping the whole swing is just as bad as not waiting at all—because in each case you will 'come down altogether.'"

"Which is wrong?"

"Certainly. The idea is to *start up all movements together but to come down one after the other*. The club head must follow the body down. If you 'wait' *for the club head to complete the up swing*, it will catch the body up and you will come down altogether."

"Let me ponder over that a bit. Now that is quite true and interesting to me because I used to wait all over, as you say, and however long I waited it never got me over the mistake it was supposed to correct, 'coming down *altogether*'—and in consequence *outside*. You have made me see why. If I delay the club head—not my whole swing—I shall feel the club head coming in *after*."

"I am very pleased with your deduction, which shows that you have absolutely grasped the idea. But just another word about resist and oppose. Arising out of a pretty *feu de mots* with which some pupils tried to trip me one evening—I evolved the following:

When I resist I will become tight,
When I oppose I will become taut.

—and from that anyone who has any sense of finesse with words can see how we poor golf Pros can go all sideways in our teaching! We must be neither tight nor slack at golf—we must be taut."

"Good! That is clear. Now there is another question I want to ask you. What is this 'lateral movement'?"

"So far as I know, it is a movement set up by the hips which allows the right hip to go to the right as we swing up and the left to the left as we go through. According to theory the closer the movement is kept to the line of flight, the less pernicious it is likely to be."

"The less pernicious? You do not like lateral movement?"

"I am totally opposed to it. How it arises you will see from the chapter on Golf Bogey No. 1 in my book."

"But I have not got your book."

"Well, hurry up and get it!"

"I will—but one more point first. Must I keep my wrists down as I address the ball?"

"You must not. If you do, the toe of your club will be off the ground. Also it is better to keep your wrists *up* with more or less a straight line through your arms, wrists, and shafts, so that you can keep the *club head down* on the way back—which is different!"

"Must I always feel that I keep the club head down?"

"You bet you must! Use whichever phrase you like—'keep the club head down' or 'don't lift the club head.' They are positive and negative of the same idea."

"Now before we leave the question of wrists. Do I have to 'cock my wrists' on the back swing?"

"No, you do not! The wrists cock themselves. If you hold your wrists free to respond to the movement of the swing and to the momentum of the club head set up by that movement, the weight of the club head itself will be sufficient to cock the wrists for you."

"Then my wrists should be cocked! So why did you say they should not?"

"I did not say they should not be cocked, I said you do not cock them, which is quite different. You do wrongly when you grab hold of the club and actively *lift* the club head back over your shoulder. We do not lift the club head up—we swing it back and it goes up. Only when you can carry your club head back from the ball, will you be able to break your wrists on the way down."

"On the way down! Surely you mean at the top of the swing," he protested.

"Well," I said, "'At the top' will do for anyone but the topnotcher; so as you don't aspire that high you can keep it! But do remember anyway *not* to lift the club head up with your hands, *or* to cock your wrists *actively*."

"Then again—must I keep my left arm straight as I go up?"

"Certainly. But there again if you feel *wide* as you go up, as you should, your arm *will* be straight. Make the straightness an effect rather than a cause."

"Is the idea of keeping it straight to be able to pull down with the left arm from the top?"

"Oh dear no, no! Your left arm is straight to give you a wide swing so that your club head will come in from behind the ball, not from above it. But you do not pull down with your arms, you pull down from the legs and left side. If you start the swing down by grounding your left heel the rest of the body, shoulders, and arms, being reactive, will respond to this pull from the leg, and your arms and hands will be started down slowly and quietly—to gather speed as they get down behind the back of the ball."

. . . .

"So do not bother about back-spin—leave that to your club, and the experts! Rely on accurate hitting, and then the fact that you have a lofted club will give you what you want."

"Why will it?"

"Because you have taken the ball below its center to give it height, you have automatically given it a certain amount of back-spin as well. You then have a combination of height and back-spin to stop the ball. The ball drops almost vertically out of the sky and would not run much even if it had no back-spin."

"You mean I ought to aim not at pure back-spin but at a kind of 'drop-shot' to stop the ball?"

"Exactly. It is the difference between throwing a ball overhand onto the green and tossing it on with an underhand lob. It is really a lob shot you want to develop. And let me tell you that the short shot played with a delicate lob is the most effective scoring shot in golf."

"Well I thank you, Professor—for a most illuminating half-hour. Good-day to you!"

And so we parted, each of us having learned something.

Beyond Percy—Feel Simple Golf

Swing analysts and instructors frequently show a stop-action shot of a professional golfer in the process of swinging a club. Lines and angles may be drawn on the photo, showing the proper position of the body in a good swing movement. Common examples are the position of the right elbow, club at the top of the backswing, or the bending/unbending of the wrists during the swing. An important question is whether those positions resulted from intentional actions taken by the golfer at those points in the swing or whether the positions were automatic reactions resulting from intentional actions taken earlier in the swing.

The golf swing becomes simpler when you take a small number of intentional actions before you begin swinging the club, which automatically set off a series of natural and good reactions as the club swings. Like Rick Bradshaw suggests in the foreword of *Feel. Simple. Golf.,* it is better "to discover one or two thoughts that make thirty things happen versus thinking about thirty thoughts to make one thing happen."

Following Percy's lead, Feel Simple Golf focuses on taking a few intentional actions to set up and start the swing and having good mechanics during the swing (e.g., positioning of the elbow and bending/unbending of the wrists) happen as natural reactions.

CHAPTER X

Fundamentals: Centered on Wrist Action

"There is no action in golf less understood than the use of the wrists, for curiously enough we do not have to work them, but we have to let them work themselves."

Chapter Summary

THIS CHAPTER FOCUSES on the proper movement of your wrists. Proper movement automatically occurs (without any intentional action) when the swing fundamentals are done correctly. Movement of the wrists is a reaction. The message is simple: do nothing to make your wrists move, or stop them from moving, throughout the swing. Although simple, for many of us, doing nothing is difficult.

Today's Takeaway

Chapter X is a good example of Percy's "variation on a theme." As Percy writes earlier, he describes the same swing concept multiple times in different ways throughout the book so at least one of the ways conveys his intended meaning to each of us. Chapter X repeats and supports what Percy covers in Chapter IX—the reactions occurring automatically in a good swing.

Wrist Action

The active wrist action that happens in the swing is an automatic reaction to the momentum in the club head. Momentum is a function of the weight and speed of the club head.

The wrists can move (1) up, (2) down, (3) forward, and (4) backward. To demonstrate, reach out your arm as if to shake hands with someone. Moving your wrist up makes your fingers point downward. Moving your wrist down makes your fingers point upward. Moving your wrist forward turns your palm toward you. Moving your wrist backward turns the back of your hand toward you. Moving your wrists forward and backward is like the opening and closing of a hinged gate.

The one and only time you should take an intentional action with your wrists is in the starting position, when you place them in an up position. Percy said that you should do as little as possible with your wrists during the swing. In other words, take no intentional actions with your wrists as the club is swinging. The wrists are passive during the swing and move as a natural reaction to the momentum of the pivot. However, your wrists *feel* highly active during a good swing. They must for power to be transmitted from the pivot to the club head!

Waggle

Percy writes earlier that you can feel in the waggle the swing you have set up in the starting position. Percy adds that the feel of the takeaway into the backswing pivot (what Percy calls the "swing in embryo") is a sign of what the remainder of the swing will produce. Experiencing the three primary feels of a good swing in the waggle and in the start of the backswing pivot leads to a good swing. Studying and practicing the very start of the swing are worth our time and effort.

Weight Movement

Percy's focus on the movement of the knees is important because the knees move body weight that is felt in the feet. Proper movement of weight provides body balance, which allows for a full pivot. Pivot provides power to the swing and direction to the ball.

Starting Movement

The starting movement is the final intentional action taken before automaticity takes over to complete the connected and controlled backswing.

Grip

"The Grip: Points to Study" remains as valid and important today as when Percy wrote his book.

Feels

Percy introduces more supplementary feels of a good swing. All these feels automatically result from doing the swing fundamentals correctly.

Percy's Teachings in His Words (p. 89-100)

There is no action in golf less understood than the use of the wrists, for curiously enough we do not have to work them, but we have to let them work themselves—like the hinges on a door.

This is important because the wrists will only be used correctly when we have the right idea of their correct mechanical action. If we get the wrong idea, the opening of the wrists in the region of the ball is bound to be mistimed. You will never get perfect timing if you try to flick the club head through the ball by wrist and hand action—perfect timing will come only when the opening of the wrists is brought about automatically by the momentum of the whole swing.

To put it in another way, the movements of the feet, legs and hips belong to the active, intentioned part of the down swing; the opening of the wrists belongs to the passive, purely reactive part of it. So keep at the forefront of your mind that the hands and wrists do not and must not "nip the club head through the ball."

The trouble in learning to let your wrists open themselves (which is what they must do) is, that at the top of the swing, the club head seems so far from the ball that you feel that, if you do not *help it down* with *wrist* and hand action, it will never get there—or will get there so late as to make a horrible slice. The result is that you *do* work your wrists, you come down too soon, and *pull* instead of slicing! Low ground shots to the left are most frequently due to this premature and faulty wrist action.

Now this feel of the club head being a long way from the ball and a long way from your left side is actually a most desirable one. Register it in your *feel* cabinet, and if you can *widen* the gap between the club head and your left side, do so; you can never get it too wide. The gap means that you are "coming down one after another."

. . . .

The hands and wrists are passive agents, they are not free agents—they do not decide in which direction they shall go; they go in the arc set out for them by the turning of the pivot. This is true of the up swing as well as the down. The pivot not only provides the power, it also controls direction—guiding the club head in its correct plane through the ball. That is why a good pivot is so important.

But we must not forget that we are going to learn golf by *feel*; so here is a little exercise that will teach you to detect and ever afterwards to recognize the difference between *feet activity* and *hand activity* at the beginning of the back swing.

Take up your normal stance before the ball. Then without movement of feet, pivot, shoulders, or arms, take the club head back a full three feet entirely by wrist and hand movement. Note the *feel*. Then re-address the ball (being careful this time to keep your left arm and the club shaft in a straight line from shoulder to club head). Now turn your body around *from the knees only* until your club head is a yard back again—making no use of any movement above the hips. Note the entirely different feel.

In the first case, your hands *lifted* the club head back; in the second, your pivot *carried* it back, and you will have felt at once that the latter is much the smoother and much the more consistent way. It is this carry back beginning at the pivot which I want you to cultivate.

Please do not think that I am making an undue fuss about a trifle in going to such lengths to introduce you to the right *feel* at the beginning of the swing. I will go so far as to say that your progress will be very largely decided by whether or not you get this back swing right—once you get the correct feel of the carry back, you will find the rest of the swing *flowing from it* naturally. So, do study this feel quite profoundly. Properly considered it is the whole golf feel, because this initial carry back is the whole swing in embryo.

But now let us carry our experiment in feel a further stage. Do it mentally this time. Go (in your mind) to the top of your swing and then get the feeling of starting the down swing by the two different methods by which you started the carry back. That is, the first time feel that you start the down swing with hand and wrist movement only, the second time feel that you start it *from the knees*.

Now if you were observant of feel in your first experiment (the carry back), this second one will give you quite a vivid idea of what the beginning of the down movement should feel like. Of course it is the movement starting from the knees that is correct; it enables you to come down without using the hands actively. You will feel your hands, arms, and wrists coming down *broken back—the* wrists beginning to drop down towards the ball. This is what we mean by "dropping the wrists from the top'" and "passive hand work."

So at each of the points we have examined there are two feels—the activity from the knees and the passivity of hands and wrists. The most notable difference is that at point 1 the wrists are straight while at point 2 they are broken. How they break on the up swing is our next study.

This introduces the question of *tension,* how tightly we hold our club and consequently our wrists—for if we grip the club with a stranglehold, our wrists will become inflexible. We want them and indeed our whole body flexible; so our grip should be light and sensitive.

As we take the club head back, from the knees, though the wrists have not taken part in the carry back, they will have been *tightened*—to hold the club shaft in a straight line with the left arm. *How much* should we tighten here? Just as little as will serve to carry away the club head where it should go; any more and you lose flexibility.

. . . .

In order to break the wrists as late as possible on the back swing, we must carry our hands back quite a long way—indeed as far as possible, before we break. "It feels like an eternity!" a pupil once remarked to me. Well it does if you have always done the opposite: that is broken your wrists as the initial movement of the carry back. *Now* you feel your wrists will never break as you go up—and as a matter of fact that is a true feeling, because they actually only break when you are beginning to feel you are on the way down [. . .][3]

Now let me describe an important little local movement hidden in this part of the swing—the *reverse.* The reverse is the part of the swing in which the club head is thrown over and pulled down. It requires a special name because it has a special *feel,* a feel curiously detached from that of the rest of the swing. We have our main feel of control and power down in our nether regions, but at the moment of reverse we are conscious of something happening up above, which is not in accordance with what we are doing down below.

What happens at the reverse is that the club head—having so far to go—takes longer to get to the end of its journey back than does the body, the turn of which is soon exhausted. So before the

---

3 See the note on the top of the swing on page 25 (change page number for published book)

club head has arrived, the body has begun to come back. As to check the return body movement, *or* to check the completion of the club head's travel, would create an undesirable pause in the flow, we let them go on, and the club finds itself *behind* the body movement both *in time* and *in position.* This is as it should be.

When we are told to allow our wrists free play at the summit of the swing, it is so that we shall not break up—by introducing muscular hand force—the flow of movement which we have intentionally set up in the reverse region.

The *feel* in this region is that the club head is still going back when our force center begins to pull forward. The wrists do not break at a given point; their break is a retarded action *set up to delay the club head* and yet to keep the movement smooth. The swing is a continuous flow of movement, and we destroy its continuous character if we divide it arbitrarily into two parts—"up swing" and "down swing." There is no upswing and no down swing; there is *the swing* complete. For the first three feet back from the ball we are "all together," but after that the club head—owing to the longer path it must take—loses ground, which it only catches up at the moment of impact with the ball. It *will* catch up then, even if you try to prevent it, and the further it has lagged behind, the faster it must travel to catch up.

. . . .

We are told and have evidence in the "flickers" that the wrists open as we come into contact with the ball, but this opening is not something that the wrists *do,* but something which they cannot help happening. And the art lies not in making the wrists open but in postponing their opening as late as possible.

As the club head arrives in the region of the ball, our body (because of its comparatively short degree of action) has already got back into its "opposing" position, with left heel back on the turf, left side straight and firm, and right hip twisted into the left one—the whole giving a sense of secure *brace* to the whole body. By this time the arms are already half-way down, but the wrists are still pulled back. But now owing to the forward pull of the hips and the gathering momentum of the club head, something must happen—and what happens is that we can no longer keep the club head from flying past the ball.

We have done everything possible to delay the club head and to inhibit wrist movement, but finally the club head gets out of control (this is literally true) and flashes through the ball as if mad with rage!

Now this is as it should be. We purposely set up a state that would leave the club head free and unchecked in this region of the swing, and we must see to it that we do not interfere in any way with its ferocious passage through the ball. There will almost inevitably be some tendency to rigidity due to local necessities in this region (as in the initial take-up), but we must not feel the slightest check or guide attempting to control the club head. *Let its furious assault die away into a perfect follow through.*

Do not hold or check or guide the club head but keep the left side firm and rigid and play on around it. That is the only way of keeping the fury of the club head on the right path. You have unleashed a storm, and all you can do is to control the center from which came its force *and from which it will die away.* Feel centered and balanced.

If after reading the foregoing you come to the conclusion that the best thing to do with your wrists is nothing at all, my exposition has been successful. Since probably no one has told you before that your wrists *are only a link,* you cannot be blamed for not having realized it!

Too many people try to do something with their hands, thinking this to be *wrist action.* But when you analyze it, there is no deliberately induced action in the golf swing which corresponds to the mythical "flick of the wrists." Anyway, the word flick is appropriate when we speak of removing ash from a cigarette—but utterly out of place in a movement which sweeps a golf ball two hundred and fifty yards down the fairway.

If you have built up a good powerful central organization around which you whirl your club, the more you leave your wrists to their own sphere of activity the better will be your stroking. And the proper sphere of activity of your wrists is to act as the link in the flail with which you sweep the ball away.

Recently I was explaining to a coming champion my deduction that hand work wrongly applied to flick the club head through the ball was the commonest misconception in golf. He thought this over, and then said that he had read (and now began to understand what Bobby Jones meant when he wrote it) that on his way through the ball Bobby Jones felt that he was "freewheeling."

The American mind is inventive of and receptive to the vivid modem expression, and Bobby Jones coined a great one in "free-wheeling" through the ball—as a corrective to the general misconception of the flick of the wrists being a sharp hand and arm attack applied directly to the ball.

THE GRIP

POINTS TO STUDY

Only two knuckles of the left hand are showing.

The right hand is held well on top of the shaft. The first finger of the right hand is held as on a "trigger" shooting down at the ball—it will be pushing against the back of the shaft. It is pinched into its position by the thumb.

The right elbow is held down, and in consequence the right wrist is arched upward.

The hands are close together, so the two wrists are close together and can operate as one large hinge.

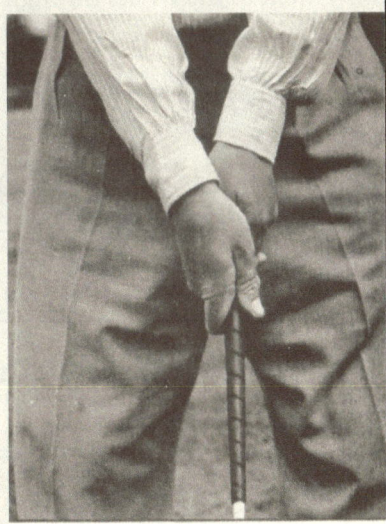

THE GRIP

PERCY

The elbows are braced. They seem to be held close to the body, but are in fact held close together by the brace.

Beyond Percy—Feel Simple Golf

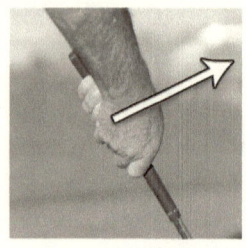

During a good swing, your wrists move up and down as well as forward and backward. In your starting position, you should intentionally place your wrists in an up position (see photo). At the "reverse" in the swing, as your pivot transitions from the backswing to the forward swing, the momentum of the pivot automatically causes your wrists to break (i.e., move to a down and back position). As your forward swing pivot pulls your shoulders and arms forward, your wrists remain in a down and back (i.e., fully cocked/hinged) position. As your hands approach impact, the momentum of the pivot automatically unhinges/releases your wrists. Your wrists explode through impact, producing tremendous club head speed. Percy describes the correct movement of the wrists through impact as "flailing."

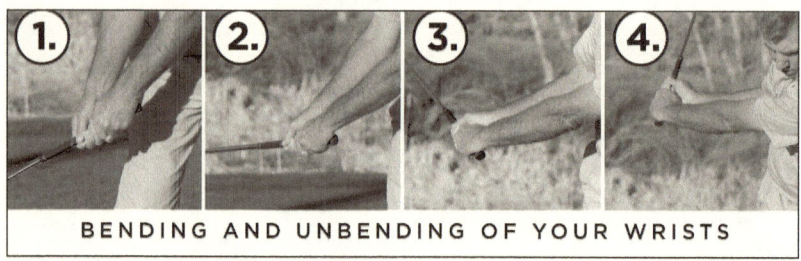

Movement of Wrists on Backswing Pivot

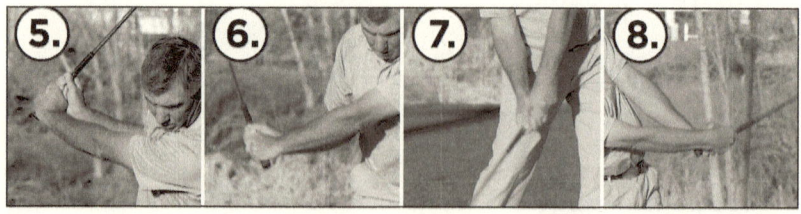

Movement of Wrists on Forward Swing Pivot

Flailing is defined as waving, swinging, or causing to wave or swing wildly. A flail is also an agricultural tool used for threshing. Holding the handle, the other whipping end strikes a pile of grain, separating the grain from the husk. The link connecting the two sticks represents the wrist in a golf swing.

The correct movement of your wrists during the swing should be passive. For this to occur, your shoulders must move in response to your pivot and your arms must move in response to your shoulders. Your wrists must remain relaxed for flailing to occur.

CHAPTER XI

To Keep-or Not to Keep-Your Eye on the Ball

"Very early in my teaching of a new pupil I tell him to keep his eye on the ball, because I know that unless he does so he will never achieve any class as a golfer. But I do not harp on the idea or rub it in—I point out that its importance actually lies less in the sight of the ball than in the reactions which it produces—for instance that it keeps our heads still."

Chapter Summary

THE GOLF BALL is incidental to the game of golf. If you set up a good starting position and rely upon automaticity, the ball is of little importance. The ball is struck as a reaction in the course of the swing and the results take care of themselves. If too much focus is placed on seeing and hitting the ball, the swing easily unravels. As with the movement of the wrists, the message about the golf ball is to take no intentional action to strike it. Just keep it in view.

Today's Takeaway

The destructive distraction of the golf ball to a good swing takes us back to the active versus quiet brain. When hitting the ball becomes a problem to be solved or the fear of a bad shot (or missing the ball completely) enters the brain, the active brain kicks in and automaticity is dismissed. The simple act of hitting the ball becomes unnecessarily hard. This is like the way in which crossing a narrow footbridge or driving into a narrow fairway can make the active brain kick in, dismiss automaticity, and make the otherwise easy action so much more difficult.

Percy said that keeping his head down was not to keep his eye on the ball, which he didn't need to do. Keeping his head down helped him *feel* his swing. Although he didn't say so, keeping his head down may have been an upward brace Percy used to make a good swing, experience the desired feels, and get the desired results.

While spectators of Percy and Aubrey commented on how long they kept their heads down during their swings, John is typically asked how he can hit the ball so far with such a short backswing. John's full swing can accurately be described as a three-quarters swing.

The adjacent photo shows that John does have a full shoulder turn. But this is an automatic reaction to his full pivoting action, not an intentional action he makes with his upper body.

Percy advises to brace yourself up when your swing is struggling. Proper bracing built into the starting position sets up a connected and controlled swing. Bracing also keeps your body in balance during the swing, which helps your body make a good swing. Using good swing fundamentals (i.e., pivot, body balance, swing width) automatically results in the three primary feels of (1) pivot, (2) shoulders moving in response to the pivot, and (3) arms moving in response to the shoulders. Going back to the basics is the best, simplest, and quickest way to fix a troubled swing.

Percy's Teachings in His Words (p. 101-112)

I suppose the most often repeated piece of advice in the whole realm of golf is "keep your eye on the ball." It is given and accepted as a profound golfing truth (which properly understood it is), but it is necessary to examine what we mean by it and how it fits into the rest of our golfing program.

Very early in my teaching of a new pupil I tell him to keep his eye on the ball, because I know that unless he does so he will never achieve any class as a golfer. But I do not harp on the idea or rub it in—I point out that its importance actually lies less in the sight of the ball than in the *reactions* which it produces—for instance that it keeps our heads still.

And I put this emphasis on the *reactions* rather than on the sight of the ball because, to my mind, it is only the bad golfer who actually sees the ball out of his eyes. The good golfer I am convinced *feels* where the ball is more than *sees* it.

Now to the ordinary golfer that may seem an absurd statement, or if he does accept it, it may be confusing. So I will try to clarify my meaning.

When Aubrey and I were playing a lot together, we were often congratulated upon the *deftness* of our short game—and the congratulations were usually followed by the comment, "How long you keep your head down after the ball has gone!" Their idea was obviously that I kept my head down because it enabled me to "keep my eye on the ball." But what I was really doing was to keep my head down in order to retain the *feel* of the swing and to keep my controls going even though the ball had been dispatched. Few of the spectators realized that I often *played these shots with my eyes shut;* yet I did so.

But when I play with my eyes shut, my *senses are wide open.* My main concern was to see that my general muscular feel and sense of balance went right through to the end. Not until the follow-through was finished did I look up to see where the ball had gone. I never miss a shot through looking up too quickly; I do sometimes miss one through fear of missing it! The primary fault is not in looking up but in *losing the feel of the swing.*

Incidentally I have taught many pupils to play pitch shots without looking at the ball.

. . . .

Do I mean by that that the beginner needs to *learn* how to see the ball? That is exactly what I do mean. He must learn *not* to see the ball to the exclusion of all his other senses. So when I tell a pupil to keep his eye on the ball I *at once* go on to the work of building up *a swing that makes looking at the ball a necessity.* Of course *every* pupil "looks up" badly at first to have the pleasure of seeing where the ball has gone, but this is a primitive stage and soon over.

In the next stage, when I am impressing him more and more with swinging correctly, I find that he often becomes so engrossed in the swing as to be unable to remember to keep his eye on the ball. But in such a case I believe the cure must come by making the "head down" a natural outcome of the swing. If I simply insist upon "head down," I run a risk of getting my pupil all stiffened up, "frozen on the ball" as we call it, and consequently only able to make hacking, chopping movements.

Now in this matter of seeing the ball, I would ask you to consider a golfer at the other end of the scale. How does a very good golfer *see* the ball? In my opinion, through his very highly developed sense of feel, he sees the ball (in some proportion) through his hands.

. . . .

Now to my mind the value of that idea to the golfer lies largely in an idea which it promotes, that perhaps the greatest value of "keeping your eye on the ball" is the assistance which it gives in building up *sight through feel.*

I can assure you that some sort of sight through feel is certainly possible. I have developed it myself, as have many other first-class golfers. I can *see* the face of the club and the angle it is at the top of my swing (when it is "out of sight" behind the back of my head), and long before I lift my head, I can *see* the ball fly away with the exact curve which I know my shot has given it.

But let us leave these metaphysical regions and come back to the ordinary golfer. Why is it that so often he can make perfect swings when the ball is *not* there, yet he becomes semi-petrified and makes the most ridiculous shots as soon as there *is* a ball, even a ball carefully perched on a perfectly prepared tee, for him to hit? And what would happen if you could put down an invisible ball for him? Is it knowing that the ball is there that upsets his swing or is it the *sight* of it?

. . . .

If you think this *too* fanciful (though the tale is true), it was recalled to my mind by a very practical job which I have recently undertaken—the re-education of a golfer who had not played *except in his imagination* for fifteen years. He was married at about that time and one of his marriage vows was not to play golf at weekends. He had little other time to play, so when now and again he was able *to* get away in the week he would lunch at the club and then play nine holes *with an imaginary ball*. Something happened to the union, and he is now playing again. And I assure you that, with two or three lessons after his fifteen-year break, he was as good as ever he had been, and now, after a dozen or so, he is quite a few strokes better than he was when he renounced playing.

But we must come back (again!) *to* the ordinary golfer who finds that the ball has a devastating effect on his swing. Why is this so?

It is so because the ordinary golfer is an unrepentant endgainer. When he sees the ball, he becomes obsessed with the idea of hitting it; the ball is made the *climax* or the *end* of his activity. That is *to* say, the highest speed attained by his club head is at the moment of impact, or, much worse still, he may try to stop the club head as soon as it has struck the ball. That is the effect of seeing the ball as something to be hit.

Now we know that for maximum effectiveness the highest speed attained by our club head (the dynamic center of our swing) must be some way past the ball—two feet past at least. So in one sense you must simply ignore the point in your swing where the ball sits on the tee. You must swing past it exactly as if it were not there.

. . . .

Let me put it this way:

a. You must not make an undue effort to keep your eye on the ball,

but

b. You must just keep your eye on the ball.

Here you see my difficulty again—the difficulty of finding a phrase that will accurately express a subtle shade of feeling. And however I express it, every reader will read and visualize it differently.

I remember one lady who came to me with her swing terribly constricted and tied up by *looking too intently at the ball*. She had no great physique, but she had patience and an analytical mind, and we soon had her sweeping the ball away in good style.

Knowing her to be an intelligent woman capable of expressing herself, and an interesting amateur painter, I asked her if she could explain the difference in her attitude to the ball since we had "united" her swing—and whether she saw it differently now. Her reply was worth pondering over.

"I cannot explain why," she said, "but now I never think of the ball. I am busy trying to feel how I should swing the club. Really I do not think I can tell you if I actually *see* the ball at all now . . . yes I do, but not in the old way. It used to look like craters in the moon, now it looks like a star in the Milky Way." Seeing my look of surprise she explained, "It used to be a huge, frightening, gray object, pitted with cavities; now it is a little star somewhere in the path of my wide sweeping swing."

Now that lady had found the joy of golf through getting an altered conception of the ball. For the joy of golf is to feel the ball snugly gathered up and thrown off the face of the club. In a sense no one can teach you that, you must find it for yourself—but some of us can certainly help you to find it, by giving you an understanding of what you are seeking.

The golf swing is governed by a chain of controls, and when the ball is introduced, it must not destroy, weaken, or dislocate any of them. Let us take four of the principal controls, purposely taken from points widely apart in the swing so as to represent the whole movement. Here they are:

1. Pivot.
2. Bring down the left heel early in the down swing.
3. Allow the wrists to break back slowly.
4. Continue the stroke on, through and around the left side.

These are just a selection of possible controls. They can be replaced by others or added to. But if a player will learn them thoroughly, by doing them slowly one after the other until they are *linked up* in his mind and muscles, he will become at least a decent golfer.

But if having got him this far, when he misses a shot I suddenly say to him, "You looked up!" the chances are that he will then look at the ball so intently, with such fixed purpose, that he will miss the next shot too! What he has to do to get things right is to try not to look up but without interfering with his basic controls. In fact, the "not looking up" must become a new link in the chain of controls. You do *not* weaken a chain by adding more links to it unless the new links are weak.

As I see it, good teaching must be based upon giving the pupil a few fundamental controls that will never need to be altered but that can be added to, packed round, and supported by other controls as the pupil's game develops. But the essentials are that the early controls shall never need to be altered and that other controls which are added later must fit in with them; *never contradict them.* I can assure you that one needs a very sound knowledge of golf (and an extensive one of human capacities and make-up) to teach that way.

Further, when something goes wrong and a pupil loses his game, it will not do to say what is wrong and so to emphasize this wrong point that it attains undue importance in the pupil's mind. If you do that he will so concentrate upon getting that one point right that he will throw everything else *wrong*.

For instance a pupil comes along for a lesson because he has gone off his game badly. I see he is ducking his right shoulder and bending his knees and showing all sorts of faults which flow from these two. Now in my experience it is no use at all pointing out these faults to him. What I normally do, if I know him well enough, is to ask him what time he went to bed the previous night—and to suggest that he brace himself up a bit or he may fall to pieces—also that it is impossible to teach golf to a fellow who is practically down on his knees.

You would be surprised at the number of specific faults which I have cured that way! In fact it hardly ever fails. When your game goes to bits, *try bracing yourself up.*

Sometimes of course one *has* to be more specific, but even then I rarely point out the obvious fault *as* being an obvious fault.

Suppose a pupil comes to me and I see that his swing is too vertical; he is picking up his club head too quickly and so breaking his wrists (and even bending his left arm) too early. Plenty of faults to point out, but I do not point them out. What I do point out is tha*t he is losing width,* and in a short time just *keeping wide* will straighten his arm and correct the other faults. To get to this stage, I say to him every now and again, "That's fine, *keep wide,* don't stiffen, don't hurry, just keep wide." Soon he will begin to feel his swing again, and in a little it will be back to normal or maybe better than normal.

You may feel disposed to remind me that this chapter is supposed to be about keeping your *eye* on the ball! So it is, but these digressions on the controls have not cropped up by accident. I have introduced them here to illustrate the point (which I keep making because it is so fundamentally important) that any *one* feature of the swing is of no use to a golfer and cannot even be understood unless it is linked up with all the other features. You can set a ball on your table and sit in a chair and learn to look at it all the evening, but that will teach you nothing at all about how to look at the ball in your swing. And as a golfer that is what you want to learn to do.

Beyond Percy—Feel Simple Golf

The potential problem of having a golf ball in front of you change and hurt your swing is a psychology of the swing issue. Running a familiar and well-practiced sequence leading up to the swing and then using positive self-talk during the swing (such as thinking of a desired feel of the swing) keeps the brain quiet. A quiet brain allows automaticity to make the swing. The club head hits the ball as an incidental event in the course of the swing. The objective of the swing is to experience the desired feels of a controlled swing. The objective is not to hit the ball a certain distance in a particular direction to a specific spot. Keep it simple—swing the club, don't try to hit the ball.

The active brain used to set up the swing quiets as the swing is made using automaticity. The pivot provides the power. Bracing is used to connect the body and provide control. Understand the role of the brain, pivot, and bracing, and your concept of the swing will change.

CHAPTER XII

Interlude for Instruction: It Is the Pupil Who Must Learn

"It is hopeless for a beginner to concentrate on some single point and work at it and struggle to get it right when what he should be doing is to get some sort of movement going, based upon the correct principles of swing—which are a good pivot and a wide-sweeping movement, with good central balance and power from the feet and legs."

Chapter Summary

THIS CHAPTER USES a fun story to review important points about the golf swing. Percy talks about a lesson he had with a stout old Englishwoman who was a poor golfer. He reviews concepts already covered in this book, including her incorrect concept of the swing, correct pivoting (not using hands and arms), the importance of not focusing on hitting the ball, and learning by listening and watching.

Today's Takeaway

Tucked away in his writing, Percy quickly summarizes three fundamentals of the golf swing: "good pivot and a wide-sweeping movement, with good central balance and power from the feet and legs." In Feel Simple Golf, they are labeled as pivot, swing width, and body balance. Percy said that trying to focus on anything else in the swing without these three fundamentals in place is futile. Again, it is like trying to hang curtains in a house under construction when the foundation has not been laid.

Where to Start

So where does one begin to learn, correct, or overhaul a swing? Since the pivot provides power and direction to the shot, start with building a very good pivot. Percy advises to "get some sort of movement going." Specifically, start with moving the knees to shift weight in the feet, which causes the hips to pivot. Once movement is happening in the lower body, apply bracing to connect the swing and maintain body balance and swing width.

Once to this point, you will be able to play an acceptable round of golf. Improvement will continue as you add more feels to your controlled swing.

Feels

Percy describes the following feels of a good swing:

- Slight bend in the knees and at the waist in the starting position.
- Pivoting like the spinning of a top.
- Club goes around and along (not up and down).
- Firm grip on the club (not loose or tight).

- Same grip tension at the top of the swing as in the starting position.
- Stretching down as you near impact with the ball.
- Club head feels slow (delayed).

Percy said that the sweeping swing, which gives maximum club head speed, feels slow, not fast. As lag starts building in the swing, the hands, with cocked wrists, are pulled down slowly by the twisting pivot. The hands continue down slowly (are delayed) until they are automatically whipped through impact with the ball.

Percy's Teachings in His Words (p. 113-123)

These "Interludes for Instruction" will show you among other things why my job is so fascinating—at least to anyone like myself who is as interested in human beings as he is in golf. That dual interest I may tell you is an effective substitute for some of the qualities which I have *not* got: patience, for instance!

Pupils are continually telling me how much they admire my patience, but my family (who know me better) will tell you that I am one of the most impatient people imaginable with an almost objectionably insistent temperament. So when a pupil tells me I am very patient, I say, "You think so! But what you take for patience is simply the result of ripe experience. I am trying to build up good golfing habits in you, and I know that habits—good or bad, in golf or outside it—need time to consolidate."

Indeed, I remember one pupil of mine who brought a Professor of Philosophy along to survey my lesson. Having watched me for some time he said to my pupil, "He is creating instincts." I said nothing to that, but thought a lot! I had visualized my work as the creating of habits, but if he was right and it went back a further stage to the creation of instincts—then I would need all the patience I could muster, if it was patience which enabled me to keep my good humor when a pupil misses the ball ten or twenty times in succession. Of course, I do not get out of patience when this happens. I simply say, "Carry on—don't worry, you will hit a good one soon." The point being that the pupil is doing as well as he can with the experience at his disposal. When he has had more experience, he will do better, but meanwhile neither my impatience nor his own will help him.

Now I want to describe a lesson which I once gave to a man and his wife. She was an Englishwoman and he a Japanese diplomat. The interesting point it illustrates is the completely different approach of two people, sympathetically akin, both wishing to learn to play a decent game of golf, yet completely opposite in inherent gifts and with absolutely different conceptions of the golf swing.

They were both playing enough *bad* golf shots to convince them that they were wrong somewhere; so they came to me for advice. Though both were temporary members of St. Cloud, I fortunately took them in my Indoor School—fortunately, because the big mirrors which I have before each driving net there happened to be the very thing necessary for one of them.

I gave each of them a couple of half-hour lessons. She was English and so should have understood me much better than he did. As a matter of fact, he hardly understood a word I said and never answered more than an unconvinced and muttered, "Yes" or "No."

Yet look at this very odd sequel. After the lessons I did not see either of them for some weeks, except to wave them good-day on the course once or twice. Then she came back to the school alone to see me.

"Do you know," she said, "my husband has made remarkable progress since those two lessons, but I have not. In fact I am worse than ever. It beats me; you did nothing for my husband but tell him to keep his balance and not dip his shoulders—and even *that* you had to do by signs, yet hey presto!—he is a reformed golfer. And I, who had the full benefit of all your eloquence, am *worse* not better. I think I shall have to give the game up."

Then we came to it. Would I please tell her frankly if she was too fat (though I don't think she used that word) to ever play good golf. She could not resist a glance at me and a queried, "You are not *thin* for a golfer are you?"

I will not say that I felt flattered by the comparison, but anyway I told her to count the question of size *out*. A very highly placed pupil of mine told me once that the lightest partner he had ever danced with was a woman who weighed over two hundred pounds. I told her this, and, from the quizzical way she looked at me, I knew I had scored a point. So I went all out for game and set!

"May I be permitted to tell you what your real trouble is, Madam?" She nodded assent. "It is nothing to do with your figure," I said. "It is that you cannot see, neither can you listen."

There was a slightly painful silence, which I waited for her to break—which she did by stammering that she did not understand.

"Don't you?" said I. "Well, I mean that, so far as learning goes, you are deaf and blind. Is *that* clear?"

"Yes," she said, "that is too brutal to be misunderstood. You might have put it in another way."

"Impossible," I said. "That is just the literal truth. You did not listen to what I told you *or* see what I demonstrated. Had you done so, you would not have got your game into its present mess.

"So far as your husband is concerned, he is deaf and dumb—so far as conversation with me is concerned—*but he is not blind*. He can see, and his eyes enabled him to pick out the essentials of my lesson."

"And what were they?"

"Well he had seen that all good golfers turn away from the ball, so he did so too. He did it wrongly because someone had told him to keep his eyes on the ball (probably *you* told him; it is an English idiom), and he dipped his shoulders in consequence. All he had to pick up from me was that to see the ball you need not dip the shoulders. He used his sense of sight and being naturally intelligent *got his pivot right*."

"But do you mean to suggest that he sees more or sees differently from the way *I* see?" she asked.

"Of course he does."

"But being able to understand what you say should more than counterbalance that?"

"Maybe!" said I. "But don't forget that you have not only two chances of being right, you have also two chances of being wrong *and you took them both!* He got an extraordinarily pure conception of the movement by sight alone—and as he has probably more brains than the two of us put together, he seems to me to have all the advantages!"

"Well," she said quietly, "I think you may be right."

"Of course I am right. *Nothing* verbal can replace an intelligent visual conception of the swing. You have never seen a swing as your husband has seen it, because it is obvious from your own swing that you think the golfer's arms produce the power, like the arms of the windmill. This is not so; the golfer's powerhouse is below the waist. If he is a good golfer, he *never* hits with his arms. He gets his power by twist or *spin.*"

I took up a wooden tee between thumb and first finger and *spun* it, like a top. "That is golf mechanics in its purest form," I said.

"But you don't expect a stout old lady like me to spin?"

"Why not! You do in the ballroom; why not on the golf course? And you need not worry about the slim flapper; she doesn't spin too well! *You* can turn on the pivot, and if you do, you will play good golf. But so long as you *slide* you are doomed."

"You suggest I slide?"

"Yes, you do," I said. "You don't turn because you are afraid of missing the ball. So you stand close to the ball and try to make up for the restriction which this puts on your power by *sliding* over the ball. It is a hopeless style.

"Your husband is a man and links cause and effect. He sees all good golfers play in a certain way; so he plays that way too. You, being a woman, do not care to consider causes, and the effect you want is to get someone to say, 'Good shot!' as your ball creeps off the tee. But you cannot earn the 'Good shot!' unless you concentrate on the *cause, on a good swing.*"

"Now," I continued, "let me see you make a few swings first without a ball and then with one."

"Oh," she replied, "I can always swing well when there is no ball."

"Why?" I asked.

"That is what *I* want to know. Why *should* a stupid little ball perched up there ruin my swing?"

I chuckled. "Because you try to hit it!" I said.

"But surely I must try to hit it."

"Surely you must not! What you must try to do is to swing your club. Which at the moment means you must concentrate on pivoting *not* on hitting the ball."

"Don't you *try* to hit the ball?" she asked womanlike.

"No. I try to swing my club head correctly (that is, from my legs), so that it swings past the ball, taking the ball in its passage."

"Then you said I was all wrong in what I did with my hands and arms. What should I do with them?"

"Just keep them out as *wide* as you can. You will feel you are stretching down when you near the ball, and that is good. What you must never feel is that you are lifting the club head, either on the way back or through. If you *lift,* you will *scoop* not *swing.*"

"But how can I get my club head up over my shoulder if I do not lift it there with my arms?"

"Study and practice the pivot *and you will see!* Actually of course, the arms *do* lift the club, but it should not be an independent arm movement; it should be reactive—simply transmitting the power from the pivot. You say you cannot keep your left arm straight, and that is another certain sign that your idea of power is up and down with the arms, whereas ours is around and along from the pivot."

She picked up a club and took a few swings, much shorter than before, the body much more stretched and with more leg work.

"Is that more the idea?" she asked.

"Much more."

"But I am not hitting the ball any better!"

"Not yet, but you will, because you are now beginning to swing correctly."

"But I feel I can never connect with the ball from away back there."

"Oh yes, you will, very shortly too, and with much more consistency than with your old scoop."

"But even if I *do*, I feel I have no *power* at all that way. I cannot use my wrists."

"You mean you cannot use your hands and arms. That is exactly what we have been aiming at! Actually *using* the wrists in golf is a most delicate business, possible only to the very good player. When you think you are using your wrists, you are simply pulling the club down with your arms as fast as it will come."

"Well if *I don't* pull it down, how am I going to get it to go swiftly through the ball?"

"Curiously enough you get maximum club head speed at the ball by exactly the opposite of your 'pulling down' plan. You get it by *delaying* the club head so that it lags behind the rest of the swing and then rushes forward. To get this effect you must let your wrists be a *free link*—any attempt to use them in your stage of experience will simply kill the speed of the club head."

"And that 'delay the club head?' Is that what you mean when you say 'swing slowly'?"

"Yes. Curiously, again, the sweeping swing which gives you maximum club head speed does not *feel* fast."

. . . .

"You mean that some day we will study the grip or the stance in detail?"

"Exactly. But not too soon. It is hopeless for a beginner to concentrate on some single point and work at it and struggle to get it right when what he should be doing is to get some sort of *movement* going, based upon the correct principles of swing—which are a good pivot and a wide-sweeping movement, with good central balance and power from the feet and legs.

"All the working members of the golf swing are related and linked up, and it is the perfect coordination of movements that makes the good player. Experience has shown me that where most people go wrong when they take up golf is in imagining that the power must be produced by the hands and arms. Yet the fact that they put nails in their shoes should tell them where the power comes from!"

My pupil took a few more swings and swept one or two balls away quite nicely.

"I admit that they begin to go a bit better and to *feel* better. But it is sheer luck if they go straight!"

"Why luck?"

"Because when I swing as you tell me, I have no idea of where the hole is *or* where I am aiming the ball. I feel too far from the ball to be able to guide it down the middle."

"Good, because that is not the way to get it down the middle anyway. Listen; when you have learned to sweep the ball away more or less truly four or five or six times in succession, you will begin to *feel* a sense of direction. You will begin to feel that when you operate in a certain manner, your ball will go in a certain direction. The ball will keep this direction as long as you keep the feel of the swing, but if you pull the swing out of shape or try to constrict it by trying to *guide* the ball, all certainty of direction *is* lost."

"Then I must definitely not try to drive the ball down the middle?"

"You definitely must not. You have tried to do that for years and have gradually become worse and worse. That is why you came to me for advice."

"Well you have given me plenty," she said somewhat ruefully.

"Yes," I replied. "It does sound very complicated all in a mass like that. It seems absurd to make such hard work of a game. But much of your trouble is in getting rid of false ideas and bad habits. Once you get on the right lines and begin to progress, like your husband, you will get a lot of fun out of working out each new problem as it arises. For each new sensation brings a new idea which must be fitted into your golfing system as a whole. That is the whole trick of progressing at golf: to add what you learn to what you already know."

Beyond Percy—Feel Simple Golf

Psychology of the Swing

Percy's decades of experience told him that the source of many golfers' troubles was getting rid of false ideas and bad habits. Both relate to the psychology of the swing. False ideas come from one's paradigm of the golf swing. Bad habits relate to automaticity with bad swing mechanics. Both are challenges to overcome.

A paradigm is a mental model of how we think something works. An old paradigm that once existed was that the earth is flat. Changing that paradigm was difficult and took a long time. In his own way and in his own time, Percy called for a paradigm shift in the golf swing. *Feel. Simple. Golf.* compares the typical golf swing paradigm with the paradigm based on Percy's teachings.

Typical Golf Swing Paradigm	Feel Simple Golf Swing Paradigm
1. Learn and use different swing movements for the full swing, short game, and putting.	1. Use one swing movement for 95 percent of all golf shots, including the full swing, short game, and putting.
2. Putt the ball using a pendulum-like swing movement of the shoulders, arms, and hands while maintaining a motionless lower body.	2. Putt using the rotation of the lower body with everything above the waist moving as a reaction.
3. Intentionally and actively move the upper body (i.e., shoulders, arms, elbows, and hands) to swing the club—keep the lower body as motionless as possible.	3. Swing from the ground upwards with an active lower body; start by intentionally moving the knees and feet and then the hips—let the upper body react.

4. Use intentional actions during the swing to control mechanics.	4. Make most of the intentional actions before and up to the start of the swing.
5. Learn and play golf using many (hundreds of) stand-alone swing tips.	5. Learn and play golf using five integrated fundamentals.
6. Learn the golf swing through many paid lessons over an unspecified/indefinite period of time.	6. Learn the golf swing following a plan of thirteen lessons over six to seven hours (see *Experience the Feel of Simple Golf*).
7. Troubleshoot a swing using stand-alone swing tips that address symptoms (applying Band-Aids) but fail to fix root causes.	7. Troubleshoot using a seven-step self-directed process that fixes root causes based on the five swing fundamentals.

While changing the automaticity of poor swing mechanics is challenging, so too is changing one's paradigm of the golf swing. Cognitive dissonance gets in the way. If, after all the practicing we have done—dollars spent on ineffective lessons, hours invested in reading and watching golf tips not based on a system, and hours spent coaching the same—to change one's paradigm of the golf swing means admitting we have been wrong and have wasted our resources, that is hard to admit. So, for many, it is easier and less painful to hold on to the old, ineffective paradigm than to change to a different, simpler, and more effective one. To some, it is just easier to continue believing the earth is flat.

Upper Body-versus Lower Body-Powered Feels

One of John's promising students and potential Feel Simple Golf instructors was an impressive-looking, tall young man. He crushed the ball a mile using his massive upper body strength. In the process of becoming a lower body–powered golfer (i.e., changing his golf swing paradigm), he experienced the feel of lag starting at the top (the "reverse") of the swing. He told John that he no longer had the comfortable feel of controlling the club head with his hands.

This is like Percy's experience with the Englishwoman who said that by following Percy's instructions she was unable to (intentionally) guide the ball down the middle of the fairway. The lesson is the same—swing the club to repeat the desired feels of a good swing and the results will automatically be there without any intentional control to hit the ball.

The desired feels of an upper body–powered and lower body–powered golfer are very different.

Upper Body-Powered Feels	Lower Body-Powered Feels
1. Club speed is felt in the hands.	1. Club speed is felt in the pivot/turn and twist.
2. Lower body is still, and feet remain planted on the ground during the backswing; the lower body reacts to the upper body.	2. Active movement of the feet, knees, legs, and hips on the backswing and forward swing; the upper body reacts.
3. Large shoulder turn (ideally to ninety degrees) and long arm/hand swing; the lower body reacts.	3. Full hip rotation; shoulders, arms, and hands react to the pivoting of the lower body.
4. Tension (i.e., torque) between the rotated shoulders and the stationary lower body.	4. Tension (i.e., torque) between the ground and the rotated hips.
5. Wrists bend early in the backswing to lift the club.	5. Club head down. Wrists naturally bend at the end of the backswing pivot.
6. Club head light in the hands at the end of the backswing.	6. Feel of hands continuing upward and wrists bending as the pivot moves forward.

7. Arms high (with the club parallel to the ground at the end of the backswing).	7. Club feels down (both backswing and forward swing pivots).
8. Arms and hands pull the club down to start the forward swing.	8. Weight shifts in the feet to start the forward swing pivot; left hip pulls.
9. Wrists unbend and forearms rotate through impact.	9. Lag; wrists unbend naturally through impact.

Shifting the desired feels of the golf swing is a necessary part of shifting paradigms.

CHAPTER XIII

The Feeling of In-to-Out

"Much of the difficulty of golf arises because the source of power (our body) is *not* in the line of flight but is away to one side of it—so we have to produce our power and use our weight *by rotation*."

Chapter Summary

THE FEEL OF an in-to-out swing produces a long and straight shot, or a gentle right-to-left draw. With bracing in place for a connected and balanced swing, and with power from the pivoting of the hips, the in-to-out swing feel is an automatic and desirable outcome. What *is* required is a change in one's concept of the club's swing path and the actual source of power.

Today's Takeaway

Percy introduces the feel of in-to-out when he talks about Golf Bogey No. 1 in Chapter IV. The feel of in-to-out seems that we will push the ball to the right of the target. The club head actually approaches the ball down the target line through impact. Take a look at your divot in the ground to confirm this.

When you feel you are swinging the club head down the target line, your club head is likely on an out-to-in swing path. The result of this "over-the-top" swing is a dreadful slice—or a straight pull to the left of the target if the club head, by chance, happens to be square at impact. Again, look at the divot in the ground to confirm this out-to-in swing path through impact. What you feel and what actually happens are not the same (Golf Bogey No. 1). The feel of in-to-out is not natural and may feel strange at first.

An exaggerated feel of in-to-out may result from the club head actually swinging slightly to the right of the target line through impact. The result is the ball starting to the right of the target then gently bending right to left toward the target in its flight.

While Percy attributes the draw to more skilled golfers, we have found that even beginners who use proper bracing and have good body balance, a wide swing, and power from the pivot (i.e., using the three swing fundamentals correctly) will naturally draw the ball gently from right to left.

The feel of an in-to-out swing is not something you intentionally try to do. It is the automatic result of using good swing fundamentals.

Bracing

Bracing is needed to maintain a single axis in the body and not be pulled around by centrifugal force. The greater the pivot, the greater the centrifugal force, and the more important bracing becomes.

Feels

Percy describes other desirable feels linked to the feel of an in-to-out swing.

- Starting position:
    - Set inwards and behind the ball (resulting from bracing).

- Backswing pivot:
  - Club and left arm feel in a straight line when at waist high (full stretch).
- Forward swing pivot:
  - Inwards and behind the ball (right hip does not spin out toward the ball or sway toward the target).
- Wide swing (full stretch).
  - Slow (arms and hands drop slowly as they are pulled down by the lower body with a delay (lag)).
- Pulling the club head along and through the ball from behind (not up and down); driving a wedge under a door.
  - Flail (as wrists open through impact with the ball).

Percy's Teachings in His Words (p. 124-132)

It is now time for us boldly to approach a subject which we have already skirted round and touched the fringes of, the in-to-out theory about which so much has been heard in recent years. We have already considered certain aspects of it in the chapters on "Golf Bogey No. 1," and "Preparatory to the Swing." Now in this chapter I want to help you to feel how to swing from in-to-out, a thing of which many people realize the importance without being able to put it into practice.

Firstly what is this "in-to-out"? It is the feeling of swinging the club head *not* directly down the line of flight, but from *inside* this line as the ball is approached to *outside* the line in the follow through. *The feeling that this is the path taken by the club head is essential to a good swing. Therefore the fact that scientific analysis can prove that at the impact the club head does actually follow the line of flight exactly can be ignored. You play golf by feeling, not by scientific analysis.*

This feeling of in-to-out is intimately connected with that other feeling referred to in the chapter on "Preparatory to the Swing," that of being set inwards and *behind the ball*. The long straight drive that covers the pin all the way is the result of a swing which you *feel* travels from in-to-out. This is what we all refer to as an in-to-out swing; a shot in which the club head does actually take this path (as distinct from being felt to take it) is only played by the first-class golfer when he wants to put *pull* on the ball. And if you will think it out, that suggests why the in-to-out feeling is something that we teachers try to instill into every pupil. The point being that, while an exaggerated

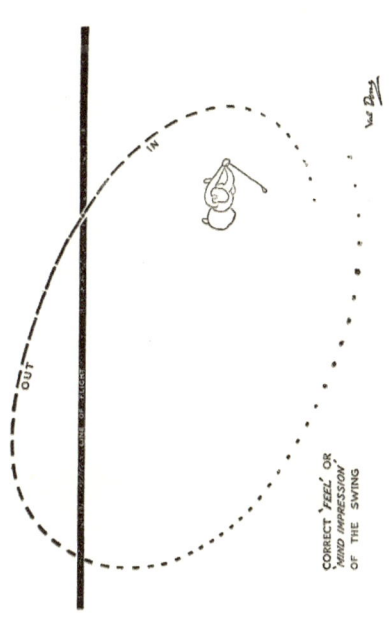

in-to-out feel gives *pull,* the correct in-to-out feel gives straightness and *no* in-to-out feel (that is, the feeling that the club head goes along the line of flight) gives *slice*.

The advantage of the modern in-to-out swing is seen in both the flight and the run of the ball. Hit with the correct in-to-out feel, the ball is given the very minimum of backspin—consequently it "floats" through the air and, when it pitches, takes its natural spin forward, instead of kicking sideways as an undercut ball tends to do, as every lawn-tennis player knows.

. . . .

From the first time we see golf played to the first time we take a club in our hands, we have instinctively formed a false conception of the movement. We visualize the club head going up and over our shoulder and down onto the ball. You need only take any neophyte to see how he immediately takes the club up and down. His conviction that this is the correct movement is strengthened by the fact that he sees the ball soaring into the air and concludes that it must have been hit with an *upward* motion. So to make matters worse, he brings his hands into play also to assist the up-down-up movement—and is fully equipped for a career of scooping.

Now here are two devastatingly false impressions, and it is astonishing how long in many golfers' lives they remain. We must not try to lift either the club head or the ball, and we shall never be good golfers until we can feel that we pull the club head along as we swing, *along* not up and down.

Let us put this in another way. If I were to ask you to:

1. Drive a wedge under a door

and

2. Drive a nail into the floor

—you would visualize two entirely different directions of hammer-head travel. Driving the wedge under the door is the direction we must feel at golf. The force must go along through the length of the wedge, along through the length of the ball.

With this in mind, it becomes clear that in swinging, the weight of the club head should be brought along from behind the ball, not from above it. This is what we call the wide swing, *wide* not high: a wide sweep that brings the club head in from behind the back of the ball.

Now another impression we get which impedes progress is that the club shaft goes up and above the right shoulder. In fact it does this not by arm or hand movement, but by the wrists being broken at the top of the swing. Consequently you must not try to get your club up by lifting it with your arms; you must feel at the top of the swing that your club and left arm are in a straight line and *are waist high*. Please ponder over this until you see its practical implications. You can try it out anywhere without a club and you will find that, if you are standing well up and your body is braced and you have the straight-left-arm-waist-high feeling referred to above, you will *not be able* to hit in a downward direction, but you *will* be able to swing the club head along through the ball—with power from feet and legs.

Now unless you have corrected your natural misconceptions of the golf movement by experience, you will have another feeling at the top of the swing. You will feel that the best you can do from such a position will be to drag the ball along the ground a matter of fifty yards or so! And because you have this powerless feeling, you try to help the club head down with arms and hands—this is "hitting from the top," one of the cardinal sins of golf.

The reason why you have this feeling of insufficiency (until experience has corrected it) is that the wide sweeping swing which comes in from behind the ball and drags it forward gives you no sensation of speed, and speed you feel you must have! The secret of this lies in the fact that speed of swing and speed of club head are entirely different, and oddly enough it is the *slow* swing which, by enabling the wrists to open at the correct instant, gives you maximum club head speed where you want it—beyond the ball.

The difficulty of accepting this is that it is opposed to the natural instincts raised by our desire to hit a long way. We feel we want club head speed so we must swing fast, not realizing that the maximum speed can only come when the momentum of the club head is free from our interference, when our opening wrists give it the speed and power of the *flail*. That is why I tell you that there is no such thing as a good natural golf swing. The natural swinger is the golf rabbit!

. . . .

Please do not think that I have forgotten that the subject of the chapter is the in-to-out feeling. That feeling is a somewhat subtle one, and it can only be induced by getting certain details of the swing right. So I must dwell upon these details. The direction of swing was the first and now the source of power is the second.

I have told you not to use your arms to hit with, that in fact you should not play golf with your hands and arms at all but with your feet and legs. Now this is an exaggeration but one that is necessary to correct the natural tendency to use our hands and arms to the detriment of foot and leg work. The arms want to work and will work, so it is necessary to emphasize the importance of foot and leg action in order to get proper balance. Also it is true that movement *should start* in the feet and legs.

Of course the arms and hands play an essential part in transmitting this power to the ball. So, if we are told that we "are hitting with the right hand" and are advised to correct this by holding less tightly with our right hand, we merely diminish our chance of hitting a long ball. The long ball feels to come out of the right hand, but the power that gives it comes from the feet, the legs, and the hips.

So it is obvious that the proper use of the legs and hips is essential if we are to pull the club head in correctly—at terrific speed into the back of the ball. Since action and reaction must be equal and opposite, we must pull *against* something, against some resistance. So at the top of the swing we must feel braced and very firmly set on the ground.

In a tug-of-war we can only use our weight and strength if we are well anchored. Also when we watch a boat race we are apt to think that it is the *arms* that are propelling the boat when actually it is the legs. But in both these cases the movement is simple, because force is applied directly along the line of flight. Much of the difficulty of golf arises because the source of power (our body) is *not* in the line of flight but is away to one side of it—so we have to produce our power and use our weight *by rotation*. We are a coiled spring, wound up by our rotation, and the heavier and more powerful the spring, the greater the force that will be implanted into the back of the ball when we "unwind" onto it. Also the greater the resistance that requires to be set up to give the springs secure anchorage. That is why it is that the farther you drive, the more important "brace" becomes.

Brace is important here for another reason also. You will remember that it is brace in general—and the several directions of brace in particular—that hold you in such a position and condition that you feel you are "inwards and behind the back of the ball." From this position, and swinging not up and down but around and along, you will find that the swing that feels to be taking the club head from in-to-out becomes not only possible but natural.

So you see that we have achieved this essential feel *not* by trying to force your club head in the direction you know you should feel it go, but by adapting a set and a conception of the correct direction of the golf movement that produces it as the natural, the almost inevitable result.

Beyond Percy—Feel Simple Golf

When you experience the feel of in-to-out, your right hip has remained in an "inside and behind" position on the forward swing pivot. In other words, your right hip did not spin out in the direction of the ball or slide to your left toward the target. This is the desired feel of your right hip being "inside and behind" on the forward swing pivot. When your right hip loses this correct position, the path of the swing becomes out-to-in. This results in pulling the ball to your left or slicing it from left to right in a big and uncontrolled curve.

A related desired feel is that your left leg pulls back on your forward swing pivot. Keeping the inward brace of pulling your elbows together keeps your right elbow close to your right hip, which also supports the feel of in-to-out.

CHAPTER XIV

The Force-Center

"And we should have felt the club head in our power center and have known that we had the secret of successful golf."

Chapter Summary

THE FEEL OF the club head in the force-center is an advanced feel of the controlled golf swing. This feel is experienced when the swing remains completely connected from start to finish. Throughout the swing, bracing connects the arms to the shoulders to the lower body, which powers the swing through pivoting.

Today's Takeaway

Percy takes us into his personal mental laboratory with microscopes and surgical instruments to dissect and examine the golf swing for a more complete understanding. You may find it difficult to follow along. Breathe easy because, similarly to the last chapter on the feel of in-to-out, this chapter is based on doing nothing—except doing the swing fundamentals correctly. Percy presents *nothing* you need to *intentionally* do. What he talks about happens as automatic reactions to doing what he has already covered.

Percy said that few of us will ever experience the feel of the club head in our force-center. To do so, you must do the swing fundamentals very well. In particular, having a connected and controlled swing (Chapter VII) from start to finish is a must. The feel of the club head in the force-center is a bonus to those skilled enough to experience it.

Feel of the Club Head in the Force-Center

Percy introduces a new and advanced feel—the feel of the club head. This feel results from having a fully connected golf swing. According to Percy, this is one of the most difficult feels to experience (and maintain) in the golf swing. Any break in the connection among the shoulders, arms, or hands that keeps the upper body from completely reacting to the pivot prevents any chance of feeling the club head. In a connected swing, what the hands experience when swinging the club head is felt in the arms, which is then felt in the shoulders, and may eventually be felt in what Percy called the *"force-center."* Percy located the force-center as being in the pit of the back.

The force-center is important because it collects the centrifugal force generated by the feet and legs and transfers it through the body to the club head. An analogy for this is a power station that collects generated electricity from a power plant and then transfers it to your house and ours.

Golf Bogey No. 1, bending the left elbow or intentionally bending/unbending the wrists to increase power, is the most likely cause of a break in a connected swing. This keeps the body from working as a single unit and feeling the club head in the swing. Percy found that the feel of the club head was easiest to experience with the shorter clubs, having heavier club heads, shorter shafts, and less club head speed.

A connected swing is easier to get with a simple swing movement that uses a small number of intentional actions. Percy describes his golf swing as a three-quarters swing. Actively using the upper body for a fuller upper body backswing would have broken his connection in the swing and kept him from the feel of the club head.

Hip and Shoulder Movement

Described in Chapter IX, as a professor, Percy taught a graduate seminar on the rotation of the hips and shoulders in a connected golf swing. The detail in his writing shows his surgical precision in dissecting the mechanics of the swing.

Upward bracing results in the hips and shoulders feeling up. This bracing keeps the hips and shoulders in the proper positions so they automatically and correctly turn in the pivot. With the left shoulder placed slightly higher from the ground than the right in the starting position, the shoulders and hips feel like they rotate in tight circles (inside a barrel) horizontally and parallel to the ground. The feel is of being up throughout the swing, not dipping. With the right elbow pulled toward the right hip, the right shoulder feels as if it goes down toward the ball through impact. The position of the hips and shoulders at impact is similar to the starting position.

What Percy describes about the movement of the hips and shoulders takes place automatically in a connected swing. No intentional action on your part is needed.

Feels

While this chapter focuses on the feel of the club head, Percy's teachings cover several other feels in a connected golf swing.

Feeling "up" in the hips, shoulders, and wrists (Chapter VIII) is balanced with the opposing force of feeling "down" with the club and arms. These opposing forces in the swing create the feel of a full stretch. A full stretch is stretching up from the feet through the body while stretching down to the ball through the arms. Some golfers with an exaggerated full stretch can be seen "hitting from their toes," with their feet barely touching the ground through impact. Upward bracing leads to these feels as well as builds width into the swing.

The feel of a club head being down is experienced in the starting position and through impact with the ball. Percy also talks about the following feels of the golf swing in this chapter:

- Feel of the club head (in the force-center).
- Braced upward with club head down.
- Full stretch (hips and shoulders up while stretching down through the arms).
- Hips pulled inward/together.
- Shoulders moving/turning parallel to ground.
- Compact and centered (connected swing).

Percy ends with the secret of successful golf: maintain a fully connected swing, let the wrists flail, focus on a good swing (not hitting the ball), feel the club head in the force-center, and play reflex golf (using automaticity).

Percy's Teachings in His Words (p. 133-145)

I think that few experienced golfers will disagree with the dictum of that great teacher Ernest Jones that our strivings to attain a good swing will have been largely in vain unless at the end we have learned "to feel our club head."

Now this is a difficult thing to feel and an exceedingly difficult thing to teach a pupil to feel, though I have often succeeded in teaching it. The real difficulty is that you cannot teach it by teaching skill in the physical movements of the swing—yet this physical skill is a basic necessity before the feel can be induced. So we have to build up the good swing and then seek for "the feel of the club head" somewhere in its cycle.

We can pick this feel out most easily with the shorter clubs. Their heads are relatively heavy and the short shaft restricts the swing.

. . . .

Now after years of study of this matter of club head feel, I came to a very curious conclusion about it, and it was this conclusion which enabled me to be quite exceptionally successful in imparting club head feel to my pupils. Here it is: we do not feel our club head with our hands; we feel it with our bodies.

What I mean is that, though the hands, being the "railhead" of our feel, do of course play an important part, yet the feel does not stay in them—the hands (and arms of course, though less consciously) *transmit this feel to the body* to the central organization of our golf mechanism. And arising from this the most common mistake we make in trying to feel the club head is to look for the feeling of it in our hands instead of at the center.

This matter of feel at the center is so important that I have coined a name for its seat, for where it is felt. I call it the "force-center." I cannot give you an exact anatomical definition of where the force-center *is,* because its position varies with different shots. As the shot (and the swing) become *longer,* so the forcecenter rises; as they become shorter, the position of the force-center drops. Yet there is always the feeling that we swing from a center, wherever that center may be. And where it is, there also must be the feel of the club head.

Having reached this conclusion as to the location of club head feel, it was easy to see why this is the most difficult of golfing feels to develop and the easiest to lose touch with. Between the club head and the forcecenter there are a number of connections in the swing (such as the wrists and the shoulders), and should any of these connections be broken, should our swing become disjointed, then the feeling of the club head cannot be transmitted back to the force-center.

This breakup of the swing most usually occurs towards the top of the swing, where we can lose connection by breaking the left arm at the elbow or by opening the hands—two very simple and common mechanical faults. When I began to realize the relationship between a connected swing and club head feel I found a curious thing, that my driving swing was cut down automatically to three-quarters. Incidentally an excellent illustration of the importance of a *right conception!*

The more you study it, the more you will see that the modern three-quarters swing is simply a *connected* swing and that the three-quarters is the limit of the swing because it is the limit to which most of us can go without breaking the connections. When first I came to this conclusion, I went to as many Championships as I could and watched the boys and tried to pick out those who followed my idea of swinging from a connected center and those who did not. One thing that I noticed at once was that the connected swingers—so-called controlled swingers—were always firmer and slower, the quicker swingers were less controlled and their swings were more liable to come unstuck. Also I noticed that as a general rule the controlled swingers did not hold their wrists down as they addressed the ball; they held them *up* in a line with the arm and club shaft.

Now that was an interesting point, and when I tried it out, I found that it had an important bearing on the whole matter. This position of the wrists gives us at once the feeling of the *club head* being *down*. Please note this is a *club head* feeling. This particular feeling, club head *down* at the address, has always been recognized as part of the correct golf feel. Our forefathers told us to keep our wrists down as we addressed the ball through a misapprehension of it; they felt *down* when they hit a good shot and thought it was their wrists that were down, whereas it was really the *club head*.

Because of that initial misconception, they had to make corrections and compensations on the way up and on the way down, but we can now eliminate these and make the swing more simple. The fewer unnecessary movements you make in a swing the better. A simple swing always has been and always will be desirable; so I aim at eliminating every unnecessary movement—and I can assure you I got rid of a big one when I concluded that the wrists should not be held down, yet the club head should feel down. Try to get this nuance, it is important.

If you try and compare these two feelings with a club, you will find you can push the club head down on the turf *with the sole flat* but not when the toe is cocked up in the air. This sole flat and down is the right feel. You see, golf force is centrifugal so the arms *must* be at full stretch when we come into the region of the ball, and we can only get this full stretch down at the foot of the swing if we feel *down* right through the swing.

I remember telling this to a pupil of mine, a good pupil in the sense that he was a good analyst, and he looked at me in astonishment. "Do you mean that I have to feel *down* when I am at the top of my swing?" he asked. "You do," I replied. He said nothing at the time, but one day later he said to me suddenly, "I can feel that down feeling when I am up now and by George! I like it! It keeps me beautifully down to the bottom of the ball automatically." The *automatically* was what I liked.

"But," you may say, "as I address the ball with my club head on the ground behind it, I must naturally feel down." Not necessarily. Feeling down is connected with the correct brace of the body. You will never feel down if you slouch over the ball; the feeling comes by opposing the club head by bracing the body. You must push down *against* something, and the down feeling is the feeling that you are braced upward against the club head as it is down behind the ball.

The first thing I do with a new pupil is to kneel on the ground and hold his club head and ask him to pull against it. I ask him to hold his position and then relax my pressure, and he at once feels what it is to feel pushing down. This is the feeling he must get as he comes into contact with the ball—which is why I repeat and keep on repeating, "Full stretch, full stretch all the time!" Even as you go through the ball you must feel down; "down while through the ball" is an exquisite golf feel.

So much for one end of the feel! What about the other end, the force-center? This is obviously a difficult feel to fix, and the best way I have found is by making the pupil stand in the imaginary barrel described in the chapter on the "Swing." You will remember that swinging in this barrel gives him the feeling of keeping his hips up; at the same time he must now *stretch down* (even when his hands are up chest high). Because the body is braced, there will no longer be any tendency for the knees to sag in towards one another; they will roll round at a constant height as he pivots and this is a very essential feel in the back swing.

Now we are building up so that you will shortly be able to feel your force-center, but first another word or two about the hips. The feel of holding them up that you get through the barrel image is a good one. So is the sort of hip brace you can get by pulling your hips in as you walk. I often tell pupils to do this. You get the feeling of holding your hips firmly together and that they no longer sag or dip first to the right and then to the left.

The good swing is based on a pivot with the minimum of to-and-fro movement. Both hips and shoulders are held up and braced, and they move in the same circular path—except that the turn of the body slightly inclines the shoulders as they go round. Now if you stand before an imaginary ball, holding an imaginary club, with your arms stretched down but held lightly (with little tension, I mean) as if you were ready to play a shot, and then turn first right and then left, rather briskly and getting the movement from the knees, calves, and feet, you will begin to feel the pull on your arms from the force-center. *The power is largely produced by the feet and legs, but it is the force-center (somewhere in the pit of the back) which collects it and is responsible for its transfer to the arms and then out to the club head.*

Now take a mashie and do very short swings to and fro with it. Soon you will begin to detect the *center* which you will feel controls both the setting up of power and the guiding of the club. Do not break the wrists or lift the club head during this experiment. The hands do nothing but keep the club straight out in front of you; let the arms feel supple and yet pushed down as the club head is down, while all the time you are moving to and fro the legs. You begin to feel connected right through, from legs to center and from center to club head. Though you make this experiment first with a mashie (that being an easy club to feel), the full drive is simply a big edition of the same movement and must be just as connected.

What I think you will find different in this braced pivot movement as compared with an uncontrolled swing is this: as your hips turn without sag, you will feel you are getting more power and getting it in a different way. You develop rotary power, largely from the legs. This is what I want you to feel, because, when you feel it, you may know that you have got your nether regions well fixed in space.

Now we have to find a similar fixing for the shoulders, to control their position and direction of movement. How should they be held at the address and what is their movement? You have to incline them forward slightly as you address the ball, but see that it is *only* slightly, only as little as your build makes necessary. And keep them both up; especially keep the left shoulder up as you go back and the right shoulder up as you come through.

. . . .

My own method of fixing the shoulders is different. It is to feel that there is a direct connection between the left heel and the right shoulder, a diagonal tie that keeps them connected and at an unvarying distance one from the other, as we go up, as we come down, and as we follow through.

This is a difficult connection to describe, but once you have grasped its full meaning you will realize its value. As we lift our left heel—going back—we will (if the tie is properly realized) feel our right shoulder move back in response. The shoulder and heel keep their distance, never getting closer or farther away; so when the left heel comes *down,* we will feel the right shoulder moving forward in a straight line against the ball—neither dipping under it nor rising over it. This is right.

The right shoulder should never feel to *dip under the ball,* though it should be felt to go down to it. As we can see when we look at the "flickers," it is true that the right shoulder *is* lower than the left as we strike the ball, but so it is at the address—and there must be no more feel of it being lower at the moment of impact than there is at the address.

. . . .

Now when you have got this diagonal tie working and can give a peep at it and at your hip brace at the same time, you will feel properly compact and *centered* as you swing. And it is only when you feel yourself to be centered that you can hope to feel the club head as you should.

For, please remember that all this discussion of brace and connections is relative to the feel of the club head. As I told you, you can only get this feel reliably at your force-center, and unless you build up a forcecenter by brace and connections, you will not feel it properly at all. For in the uncontrolled *natural* swing there is no force-center; that primarily is what is the matter with such a swing: too many separate forces are working independently in it.

So I have told you how to build up a force-center, and that when you have built it up, you should be able to feel the club head in it. You will be able to do this only if there is no break in the connections between the club head and the force-center, but one of these connections—the arms—is the most liable to disconnection of any in the whole swing.

At first glance this would seem easy enough to control, because the arms should work in exact relation to the shoulders and chest. The thorax and biceps should become one in movement. But things do not work out this way, because we do inherently—and in spite of ourselves—consider golf as being played with the arms. So we *use* our arms, ever so little it may be but enough to make us disconnected. Now this is a fine and most delicate point in which lies most of the difference between a good, a very good, and a superlative golfer. It is by the management of the arms that championships are won and lost.

. . . .

I must remind you again, because it is fundamental to this book, that *learning by a sense of feel* is something quite different to learning by the intellect. Intellectual memory may be of use in learning golf but it is never paramount. What is paramount is what I have called muscular memory, a memory for the right *feeling* of a movement which enables the muscles to repeat that movement time after time, without directions from brain or will.

What I have been trying to do in this book, and I can assure you it is no easy task, is to put on paper a method whereby you can pull the ends of your swing together and get it all properly connected.

But when you have done this, it is up to you to make yourself so familiar with the feel of your controlled swing that you can produce it automatically, practically by reflex action whenever you like.

But I warn you again that a single break in the connections will render the success of a shot a matter of chance, whereas you want it to be a matter of certainty. You know the type of player who has to depend upon his lucky day—disconnected! He can produce a good swing or he would never have a lucky day; he cannot produce it regularly because he loses connection somewhere. And the chances are that he loses it by *using his arms*. And *why* does he start using his hands? Ninety-nine times out of a hundred because he tries too hard to hit the ball!

Yes, it is usually Golf Bogey No. 1 which induces us to use our hands. That overwhelmingly common-sense impulse to *hit* the ball where we want it to go. And how can we hit *but* with our arms? So, all our carefully contrived controls go overboard, and we take vicious scoops and lashes at the ball.

What a pity! *What* a pity! For if we had inhibited our desire to hit the ball and concentrated upon producing a perfect swing—power from the pivot, shoulder controlled by heel movement, arms acting reactively to the shoulders, wrists free for the flail—we would have sent it twice as far and straighter. And we should have felt the club head in our power center and have known that we had the secret of successful golf.

Beyond Percy—Feel Simple Golf

In addition to the separate feels of a good starting position, pivot, body balance, and swing width, other feels are experienced when these fundamentals are combined into a controlled swing. This is an example of synergy in which the whole is greater than the sum of its parts. Just as the music produced by a string trio comprised of a violin, viola, and cello is richer than when each instrument is played separately, a golf swing that combines a good pivot, body balance, and swing width produces unique feels.

Feels

Following are three feels of a controlled golf swing that are experienced when your swing combines a good pivot with good body balance and swing width:

- In-to-Out Swing Path

The correct feel for the path of the club as it approaches impact is in-to-out. An in-to-out swing path feels as if your club head is swinging to the right of the target (e.g., away from your feet and body) and that the ball will also be hit right. Actually, a swing path that feels in-to-out results in your club head swinging down the target line as desired and hitting the ball toward the target. Look at your divot in the ground after hitting a ball with a path that feels like the club is swinging down the target line. Chances are the divot is pointing to the left of the target and your ball was pulled to the left of the target or sliced from left to right in flight.

There are other feels that are experienced as part of the feel of an in-to-out swing path. One such feel results from your hips rotating tightly around the axis of your spine on the forward swing pivot. This prevents your right hip from spinning outward toward the ball or swaying left toward the target. Another feel is a slight delay in the twisting forward of your right shoulder on the forward swing pivot. This keeps your right shoulder from spinning outward toward the ball or swaying left toward the target. The tight rotation of your right shoulder and hip around the axis of your spine and the delayed twisting of your right shoulder on the forward swing pivot result in the desired feel of being inside and behind the ball. This contributes to the desired feel of an in-to-out swing path.

- Slow Swing Rhythm

A controlled swing feels slow and unrushed. The turn of your backswing pivot feels slow as your lower body turns your connected shoulders, arms, and hands in one movement.

As your forward swing twisting movement begins, the feel is still unrushed. The pivoting (twisting forward) of your lower body provides only one source of power to your swing. The lag built up in your swing and swing width multiply the power. The feel of a slow rhythm makes full use of the lag by allowing your hands to lag behind your arms, which lag behind your shoulders, which lag behind your hips, which lag behind your feet. Your upper body is whipped through, naturally feeling effortless and deceptively slow but unleashing tremendous power through the ball. Using a fast rhythm by forcing your pivot risks using your upper body as a source to power the swing, which eliminates lag and restricts your pivot.

- Feeling the Club Head Movement

A highly skilled golfer can develop a feel of the club head movement within the core of his or her body. The centrifugal force of the swing produced by the backswing pivot is collected in the pit of the lower back and transferred up through the torso and down the arms to the club head through impact. The club head is felt not only through the hands holding the club but from the lower back. The transfer of centrifugal power from the lower back to the club head provides a distinct feel to the movement of the club head.

CHAPTER XV

Interlude for Instruction: Monologue

"'Now it appears that I have a very special swing; so naturally I don't want you to alter it'.... 'Oh,' I gurgled, pushing a fit back into my throat."

Chapter Summary

Mrs. de Vere de Vere was not ready for instruction. Percy, a self-proclaimed man of great impatience, and described by his pupils as gruff and overly blunt, became an unwilling, perplexed, and mesmerized audience to a rambling Mrs. de Vere de Vere during a "lesson." An old proverb says, "When the student is ready the teacher will appear." This student was not ready to learn, so Percy's greatness did not appear. Percy's reaction to this misguided golfer with a swing based on the 500 best swing tips was graciously restrained.

Today's Takeaway

Percy's simple reaction of "did he not say *'right* foot'" at the end of the monologue is a great response based on the "500 best swing tips" approach to learning golf. Mrs. de Vere de Vere appears to have been a keen supporter of that approach to the golf swing.

"Nearing the Finish"

Aubrey's follow-through in the photograph shows a full stretch in which he stretches from his feet, planted on the ground, up through his shoulders (feel of up) while also stretching down through the arms (feel of down).

Percy's Teachings in His Words

"Oh, good morning, Mr. Boomer.—You *are* Mr. Boomer, aren't you? ... I'm Mrs. de Vere de Vere; you know, Mrs. Pro Quid Quo sent me along to you, to get my swing fixed up.... Nothing much, but of course you know I'm an old golfer; so I'd better tell you all about my case. Possibly you have met my husband somewhere ... he has played golf all his life more or less ... plays very well too; no *style*, you know, but hits a very long ball and plays his irons to perfection ... and his putting, my dear fellow, you should *see* his putting; it's marvelous. You see, he was taught by that St. Andrews Pro ... famous chap...."

"Kirkcaldy?" I suggested.

"Yes, that's the fellow. People say he is funny. I can't see it.... I did have one lesson from him, but I didn't get his humor at all.... *Gruff,* I thought he was; good with the men, no doubt, but *not* with ladies...."

. . . .

"Oh!" was all I had time to ejaculate.

"Oh yes.... Now it appears that I have a very special swing; so naturally I don't want you to alter it ... of course, I never could pivot or keep the left arm straight or any of that elementary stuff you tell beginners ... but they tell me—at least, Lord Brownseed told me ... you know, that plus three gentleman who nearly beat Jobby Bones once in the championship ... well, he told me I had a most perfect and delicate grip ... 'something worth contemplating' was his phrase ... he sings you know ... between you and me, I think he is a bit poetical.... Well, as I was going to say ..."

. . . .

"But . . . " I tried to edge in.

"Oh yes, of course, my slice! . . . Well, someone gave me a very simple bit of advice—was it Ned or was it Tyril Solley? . . . you would know because you know their styles. Anyway, they said, 'turn your left hand a little more over the back of the shaft and bring your left foot back a little'—whoever it was who told *me,* and I still think it was Ned. Hey presto! I not only cured my slice but pulled my ball slap into the rough on the left. . . . I must admit that the rough on the left is no better than the rough on the right, but the moral effect was astounding. . . . Do you know, we actually won 5 and 4 that day, which only shows how simple it is when one knows."

"Knows what?" I queried, mesmerized.

"That's just it," she continued. "It's so difficult to meet simple people. Do you know what one fellow told me? . . . you don't mind, do you, but he was a Pro . . . but there, I always say that all Pros are not alike; some are better brought up than others . . . present company excepted, of course! But the Hon. Billy Bunk told me such a good story which he read in Simpson's book about the Pro who taught Balfour—the Premier, you know . . . fine man, Balfour; *he* wouldn't have let things get so complicated, my husband says. . . . Oh, where was I?"

. . . .

"Who really taught you, Madam?" I got in.

"Oh, how *silly* of me . . . . I quite forgot you would want to know that. . . . You know, last summer, I think it was, we went to Gleneagles for the week, and on the way back we stayed a day or two in London and had a lovely weekend out at Sir Bunsen Burner's place—some Park—Lent Park, is it?—such lovely daffodils—only they were over then, of course . . . and there is a dinky little course there . . . you must know it."

"Yes, I do."

. . . .

"So when you were at Lent Park, I suppose you had a lesson from Skeet?"

"Oh no... we had no time... only a few hours... so I had my lesson at a school, in London... Park Street, was it?... anyway, the Pro there is a very definite kind of chap... 'straight arm' and all that elementary stuff. I really didn't take to him... he was so cocksure of himself, which is silly when you only know 'beginners' style,' isn't it?... Anyway I only had one lesson because he nearly pulled my arm out of its socket. Do you know, it made me so stiff all down the left side that I had to walk out of the bloody place sideways."

"Oh," I gurgled, pushing a fit back into my throat.

. . . .

"But what about your swing, Madam?—Time is getting on."

"Oh yes—we really must. You see, I can't hit a ball. Put me down a peg, will you, and I will take a few swings."

She took a few swings—or, more precisely, swipes. They told me all I needed to know.

"Madam," I said, "who am I to meddle with such a swing?... As your friend said, it's something to contemplate.... Only don't say Percy Boomer told you so, please... my regular pupils might become jealous. But there *is* one thing I would like to ask you before I go on to my next pupil, and it might help you if you could answer."

"Well, what is it?"

"When Ned told you to turn your left hand more over the back of the shaft and to draw your left foot back a bit, you say it worked at first. Now are you sure, *quite* sure, that he did not say *right* foot?"

She paused, she gaped, she gasped.

"Why how *stupid* of me!... of course it was my right foot. ... What a *lucky* thing you thought of asking me such a stupid question. You don't mind, do you, but of course it *was* stupid. Of course it was my right foot, as I said..."

Beyond Percy—Feel Simple Golf

Golf is a beautifully complex game. But the golf swing is not that complex. All too often the golf swing is made unnecessarily complicated. What you need to appreciate is how the huge number of golf swing mechanics relate and how to tie them together to create a simple, repeatable, and controlled golf swing. Psychologists have found that people are able to keep seven things, plus or minus three (that is, from four to ten), in mind at any one time.

Here are the five things (a number that fits within the range) you need to do to develop a good golf swing:

1. Establish a good starting position before you move the club on the backswing.
2. Repeat a sequence of steps leading up to moving the club on the backswing. This sequence prepares you to hit the desired shot and keeps your brain from messing up your swing.
3. Establish and maintain body balance from the start to the end of your swing.
4. Pivot your lower body for power and direction.
5. Make a large sweeping swing.

That is all it takes to swing the club well. You might now be asking, "But how about the correct position of my right elbow at the top of the backswing? How about properly bending and unbending my wrists during the swing? What do I do if the plane of my swing is too upright or too flat? How do I fix my banana slice? To hit the ball farther, don't I just swing harder?"

We suggest to you that these are not the right questions to be asking. Besides, the good news is that by correctly doing these five things listed, these swing issues and everything else in the swing happen naturally. Think about this: in a golf swing that lasts from 0.5 to 1.5 seconds from the start of the backswing to impact, how possible is it that you can intentionally control the position of your elbow, wrists, swing plane, and a hundred other mechanics consistently swing after swing and have fun? Not very possible at all.

John rebuilt his golf swing on the system presented in this book and has used it successfully in the heat of competition. He has used it to teach beginner golfers with quick and satisfying results. Using this system, John has successfully fixed the swings of golf professionals as well as fellow professional golf instructors who earn a living around the golf swing.

NEARING THE FINISH

POINTS TO STUDY

The impression here is of the arms stretching upwards . . . but the essential *feel* of the *arms stretching down through the ball* is retained.

The hips have turned almost horizontally. They are braced together, the left hip has not been thrown out.

The weight of the body has not been completely transferred to the left foot, the left leg is slanting slightly back, and in consequence weight is still being taken by the big toe of the right foot.

The right leg and hip are twisted inwards: hence the fine vertical balance of the whole movement.

NEARING THE FINISH

AUBREY

The hands are almost closed, as they were at the address (very important). The wrists are close together. The shoulders are almost horizontal.

CHAPTER XVI

Rhythm

"The trouble with golf is that we are gear boxes trying to become seagulls. We have to develop rhythm on a mechanical base."

Chapter Summary

Through the first fifteen chapters, Percy has taken us through both the physical and psychological parts of the golf swing. This chapter takes us into the artistry of the golf swing. The role of timing, tempo, and rhythm is explored.

Today's Takeaway

Percy admits his difficulty in writing this chapter. We, too, were challenged more in modernizing this chapter than most other chapters. As a golf professional, John was more comfortable and able to talk about this topic than Paul. This is likely because Paul (not a golf professional, only a fair-to-good amateur) struggles more with rhythm than does John. More than once, John commented on Paul's draft of this chapter by saying, "That is basically right—given your level of skill and understanding." Touché—point made! But quite true, and not at all offensive to Paul! The topic of golf swing rhythm *is* a difficult one to get a good grip on.

Like in most chapters, Percy unapologetically touches upon a number of topics related to the main one. Percy believed you cannot think about pieces of the swing in isolation, since the swing is an indivisible unity. Before we get to rhythm in Feel Simple Golf below, here are the major takeaways from this chapter.

Accelerating Club Head

The accelerating club head reaches its maximum speed two to three feet past the line of the ball—a place Percy calls the "swing center." With the swing center in front of (past) the ball when club head speed is the fastest, "hitting the ball" is not the main focus of the swing. Impact of the accelerating club head with the ball is an incidental event in the swinging of the club as it approaches the swing center. The lesson is to let the swing happen; don't try to hit the ball.

Shortened Backswing

For the club head to accelerate through its impact with the ball, the backswing should be shortened. Let the continuous pivot shorten the backswing.

A shortened backswing does *not* mean a reduced pivot and reduced power. Percy talks in an earlier chapter about the benefits of his three-quarters swing. John's three-quarters swing includes a full pivot (Chapter XI). John's hands are only at shoulder height at the top of his swing. Yet his hips are turned fully clockwise, his feet are firmly planted on the ground, and his wrists are cocked. John's full pivot, lag in his forward swing pivot, swing width, and accelerating club head through impact provide more than enough power to his swing.

Ball on the Club Face

An accelerating club head allows the ball to remain on the club face longer through impact. This enables the ball to become more compressed against the club head, resulting in a greater rebound (i.e., trampoline effect). The speed of the ball off the club head is significantly faster than the speed of the club head. This results in greater distance.

A Golfer's Rhythm

As Percy writes, two songs can have two very different rhythms—one fast and one slow. Swinging to a song that matches your swing rhythm can improve your swing. Swinging to a song that has a rhythm faster or slower than your natural swing rhythm can throw you off, resulting in poor results.

Each golfer has his or her own unique rhythm. You must discover your natural swing rhythm; it cannot be forced or copied from another golfer. Your rhythm is your unique fingerprint of your golf swing. Rhythm reflects your inner self—your own unique soul. Your buddies will easily recognize you from a distance when they see your swing.

Feels

Percy describes several feels of a rhythmic swing:

- Flowing, continuous movement.
- Delayed dragging of the club head (lag).
- Sense of balance and an unhurried calm with time enough to feel movements blending together.
- Slow (taking a long time for the swing to develop) yet determined.

Percy's Teachings in His Words (p. 155-168)

It took me a long time to make up my mind to write this chapter, and now as I sit down to begin it I am appalled by the huge gaps in my train of thought. In fact I would like another twenty years or so to think it over in, before writing about it at all.

But that will not do, because it is no use trying to write an intelligent book on golf and leaving rhythm out, for rhythm is the very soul of golf. So I must do the best I can, and in this chapter I will endeavor to tell you what I have discovered to date about rhythm in relation to golf. And that is not going to be easy with such an abstract and subtle subject, so I ask your indulgence.

Rhythm we know in ordinary circumstances as *flowing motion,* and in golf this resolves itself into *timed movements*. Let us start with an exceedingly practical example of what this means. The most accepted theory is that as the club head approaches the ball your wrists will flick or become taut. When? you ask. That has really never been defined, and the best definition I know of it is, "co-ordination of mind and muscle which enables the player to do exactly the right thing at the proper moment" ... so you must find your own rhythm.

So we can start from the familiar word "timing," which is an advantage. But though every golfer knows the word, fewer appreciate the significance of the sense which it represents. Because until timing does become a *sense* with us, a sense of something *rhythmic,* our attempts at co-relating movements can only be on a very crude mechanical basis. It is stretching the phrase to talk of the "rhythm" by which a self-change gear box shifts gears, but a soaring seagull is charged with rhythm at its highest. The trouble with golf is that we are gear boxes trying to become seagulls. We have to develop rhythm on a mechanical base.

We want rhythm, flowing movement, in our swing. But as we have already discovered we have to dissect our swing before we can play it—just as a musician has to dissect a composition before he can even play the notes. And please note that he may learn to play the notes and *nothing more;* that is he may never get as far as the rhythm and tone in which all the delicate beauty and meaning of music are hidden. So also with our swings: we may have memorized the mechanics faultlessly and be able to perform them time after time, but, unless they can be blended by rhythm into a perfectly timed flowing whole, it will be a poor sort of soulless mechanical golf which we play. For, to repeat, *rhythm is the soul of golf.*

. . . .

The good golfer can make the ball do two things which the bad or merely indifferent golfer cannot make it do.

1. The good golfer can make the ball remain in the air a long time in the drive, or run a long way in the putt.
2. The good golfer can make the ball fly, or run, dead straight.

Now these two attributes of a good shot are due to a profound knowledge of the golf mechanics *plus* good timing. Since I have been at Sunningdale I have played often with a delightful old Blackheath golfer, Mr. A.T. Turquand Young—father of the great English Rugby forward. Though he is nearer eighty than seventy he is sweeping the ball off the tee perfectly, and, in addition to being academically faultless, his tee shots are almost as long as my own. His swing is an object lesson in effortless rhythm.

So one day I asked him to be so kind as to jot down how he came to swing so slowly and smoothly, how he came to get so far with so little effort. And did he play directly with his hands and arms? He gave me the following with permission to include it in this book.

"At the age of sixteen I found out in two things that slow movement beat 'force' every time. One was in throwing the hammer, the other was in throwing a cricket ball. As a result of this experience, I began to play golf with as slow a swing as possible, getting the power from below the waist with the result that without any effort I became a *very* long driver even in the gutty period.

"After a lapse of some years owing to illness I came back to the game just as good as when I left off, after an hour or so swinging with my clubs. The slow swing looks lazy, but the power is there and it certainly does *not* come from the arms and hands. Providing your back swing goes up all in one piece and your timing is correct, one can send the ball a very long way without effort. Of that there is no mistake, I know it from experience."

There you have it! Mr. Turquand Young found that "slow movement beat force every time." What a find—and what a grand age to make it at, sixteen!

Now as that story suggests, perfect mechanics alone are not sufficient in golf. Let us try and examine the effect of accurate *timing* and see *why* it makes such a difference—the difference which we can all recognize between the *almost* perfectly timed shot and the *perfectly* timed one.

It hinges upon the fact that golf is a *dead ball* game. We have to set the ball in motion from a state of rest and this largely accounts for the extraordinary complexity and subtlety of the game. Good shots are easier to play in live ball games than they are in golf because the velocity at which the ball comes to us sets up a *rebound*, which together with the speed of the head of the implement we wield increases the speed of our return blow. The relationship of ball velocity, club velocity, and *rebound* are simplified.

Now we can trace the two elements of rebound and club head speed in the drive, the longest of golf shots. But now because the ball is "dead" their relationship is no longer simple. It is necessary to get the correct *proportion* of each of these elements into the stroke or the resultant shot will not be perfect. A slight overemphasis on either one or other of them completely changes the flight of the shot and such slight overemphasis in either direction is not a matter of golf mechanics but is due to a delicate inflection of *timing*.

Let us see how this arises. It is generally assumed that the faster we swing the club head through the ball, the longer the ball will be. This is true if, but *only* if, the maximum club head speed is attained just *after* we come into contact with the ball. Hence the fact that we often get exceptionally long shots when we are trying to hit easy ones. With the slower swing, the club head has still been *accelerating* when it made contact with the ball and so has been able to "stay longer with the ball" *and so make use of the rebound.*

We have timed a shot well only when we feel we have remained a long time in contact with the ball, "gathering it up and slinging it off the face of the club head" as I have called it. If we are to do this, the club head must have sufficient power to take up the shock of impact *and still keep accelerating.* If at the moment of impact we stop the forward pull of the left side (which is what we will do if we aim at the ball), this power is not available and the club head cannot, as it should, continue accelerating in contact with the ball until the ball rebounds from it.

We have timed a shot well only when we feel we have remained a long time in contact with the ball. If we stop the forward pull of the left side at the moment of impact with the ball, we do not set up the resistance necessary to take up the shock of impact and *at the same time* to keep the club head accelerating until the ball rebounds from it. In fact if we let up on the forward pull when we strike the ball, we "stop the club head at the ball," an absolutely cardinal fault in swinging. That is why I always tell my pupils (and repeat it time after time in this book) *never try to hit the ball;* cultivate a sweep through the ball, and let the ball be nothing more than an incident in the swing.

. . . .

From which arises a curious and valuable illustration of teaching methods. As you know, I do not like simply to say to a pupil, "You came down outside," or "You are overswinging." These faults are mainly not mechanical at all; they arise from a *false conception,* and if I correct the false conception, the fault cures itself. In this case I found that the people who were overswinging were doing so because they were concentrating on the ball. When I had explained that the climax of acceleration must be a yard or so past the ball, their back swings began to shorten automatically—because they felt the need for a reserve of effort to enable them to go on past the ball.

. . . .

Timing, then, is: (1) The gathering up of speed through the ball from correct mechanical movement, and (2) a correct conception of the location of the swing center. These two can only be blended into a whole which can be faithfully repeated time after time by our sense of rhythm.

If, as we stand on the tee, I tell you to hum over the first two bars of the *Blue Danube* and then the first two bars of the *Sailor's Hornpipe,* you will get the sense of two quite different rhythms. You will not find it difficult to recognize which is the rhythm of the slow, flowing swing—which it is that Mme Lacoste used when each spring we went out together to play a few shots to tune her swing up. She it was who told me that if she found herself swinging too quickly, this rhythm would put her right again immediately. Incidentally until your own rhythm is well established, it is liable to be affected by that of those you play with. One of the reasons why Mme Lacoste finds a few holes with me a good tuning-up process is that my own swinging rhythm is very similar to her own.

. . . .

For though the *feel* of golf may be largely right-handed, the power of golf is centrifugal.

Next we will never get effective rhythm into our swings unless we have a proper connection of that word "wait" or, as I have told you I now prefer, "delay."

. . . .

So I analyzed it out to this conclusion: We begin the up swing all in a piece and naturally our leg and foot and hip movements are completed long before our wrists are fully broken back at the top, long before the club head begins its return journey. Since we must keep our feet, legs, and hips moving smoothly, they get far ahead of the club head. We actually *encourage* this gap by not clinging tight onto the club with our hands, but leaving our wrists flexible. What we are waiting for is the *return power,* the forward pull of the body that pulls the right hand and throws the club shaft back onto the trigger finger.

We must *not* intentionally pull with the right hand, we must wait for the body to pull it. We take up the feel of this pull mainly with our trigger finger; in a strong player the resistance may be so terrific as to burst the finger open.

So we delay while all the time we are going forward. We are *waiting in movement.*

You will now see why I explained my grip to you in some detail. But the regulated succession of movements is the same in every good swing, the point of contact (in my case the trigger finger) being the varying factor. The detail of the grip is important only in that it must have a point of contact and resistance. This can be and often is in the left hand, but I personally much prefer my own grip which I have developed out of vast experience from the so-called Vardon grip. Perhaps I should add that although I have what might be termed a family affection for this grip—for was not the genial Harry a pupil of my father?—the reason why I adopted it is simply that it is the best suited to giving you the sense of connection between *power* and *feel.*

You will realize that in developing my ideas on rhythm in golf I have come up against many interesting points which are not immediately obvious. I remember telling a pupil of mine the *Blue Danube* story. "Oh," she said, "do you really believe the ear has an influence upon golf rhythm?" Well did I? I suppose I did, as I told the story in all sincerity, but I had not thought the point out. The actual sound of a "swishing" swing cutting the daisies is different and suggests a different rhythm from the "sweeping" sound of a good shot.

The swishing sensation of the daisy cutter is too directly a simple one-two sensation; the sensation of the sweeping shot includes *drag* (from the "wait" or "delay"). When the Americans say they put draw on the ball (in English, impart a slight *pull*) they swing the ball slightly from right to left at the end of its flight. That is the result of the feeling that we are drawing the ball in. This is the basis of the in-to-out theory; we feel that, as we come in behind the ball, the club head goes *out* with a corresponding reaction by the ball in flight.

As I have suggested, I do not think either "pull" or "draw" suggests the right sensation. *Drag* suggests it much more nearly. A horse *pulls* a cart, a car *draws* a trailer (directly linked in each case) but we *drag* a fishing net, or a kite. In short, if we want to draw the ball, we must *drag* the club head. We drag the club head *in order to* draw the ball.

But you may say, "What has drag to do with rhythm?" It has all to do with it, with our feeling of flowing continuous movement.

Golf rhythm is a delayed dragging feel of the club head, developed from the power of the legs, kept under control by the braced turning of the hips, and finally loosened into a free, untrammeled movement of the arms outward and around the left side.

If to this we add a sense of balance, a sense of unhurried calm, a feeling that there is lots of time to feel each movement blending into the others, we shall begin to feel the true golf rhythm. We must swing slowly yet determinedly. When children are lost in the dark, they hurry; when *we* are lost in our swing, *we* hurry! This rhythmic swing seems slow, seems to take a long time to develop. We must cultivate this feeling and see slowly and feel slow. We lose rhythm as soon as we hurry, and we hurry as soon as we are afraid.

THE GOLF SWING IN EMBRYO

POINTS TO STUDY

For *all* golfers the most important picture in the book to study.

Above the line all movement is passive, below the line it is active.

Leg muscles have been used to push out the left knee and to pull back the right knee. No other muscle in the whole body has been used *actively*.

Relative to the club, the hips, shoulders, arms, and hands are in exactly the same position as at the address.

THE GOLF SWING IN EMBRYO

PERCY

Conversely, to bring everything back to the position of the address, all that needs to be done is to straighten the left leg and slightly to bend the right one.

The reason for keeping the wrists *up* at the address is now obvious. Had they been broken (held *down*) at the address they would be cocked up as the club was carried back.

Beyond Percy—Feel Simple Golf

When learning to dance, one of the first objectives is to learn the steps of the dance in the correct order. Then the focus moves to getting your feet moving to a certain beat or timing to the steps (e.g., one, two, three-and-four). Unless you are naturally talented, there is no fluidity or flair to your dance in its beginning stage. Your movement looks and feels very mechanical. Although you may get the steps and timing right, you probably aren't ready for a dance competition. Your dance needs tempo and rhythm.

Over time and once well practiced, your steps become linked together into a whole—into the single movement of the dance. You have added (connected) the movement of your hips, shoulders, arms, hands, and head to be in perfect unison with the gliding movement of your feet. Your body seemingly flows effortlessly to the music as if the two are inseparable. Your movements are filled with personality and your inner self (or soul) shows through. Movements have gone from clunky to rhythmic. You have moved from being a dance technician to a dance artist—from a crawling caterpillar to a floating butterfly.

Unless you are talented enough to perform in a precision dance troupe, such as the Radio City Rockettes in New York City, the unique personality of your movements sets you apart from all others. Friends can recognize you from across the dance floor by the continuous flow of rhythmic movements that make up your dance.

This dance analogy applies to the learning of golf. Let's consider how we grow from a technician of a mechanical golf swing to a rhythmic golf swing artist. Our trip must take us initially from a place that involves many separate things to a place of unity and singularity. First, a quick review.

A Review

Basic to the golf swing is bracing. Bracing connects the flexions and joints of our body so that it moves as a single unit (as a connected swing) on the backswing pivot. Bracing is built into the starting position through a sequence. With the bracing still in place, the swing breaks apart into a one-after-the-other forward swing pivot. Through repetition, the various parts of the swing become unified. Repetition of good fundamentals builds automaticity that allows the swing to be repeated without intentional actions.

Each swing fundamental done right produces a number of desired feels. Through repetition, these feels become linked to one another until they are experienced as the single feel of a controlled swing. The objective of the golf swing is to repeat that single feel.

The various parts of the swing have become connected and the various primary and secondary feels of the swing have become the single feel of a controlled swing. If done successfully, the desired results of the controlled swing are automatic.

Bracing, swing fundamentals, and feels become cemented together into the artistic soul of golf. Golf artistry involves tempo, timing, and rhythm.

Timing and Tempo

Timing leads to tempo, which leads to rhythm. ***Timing*** is the amount of time taken to do a specific action. For example, running a sequence to build bracing into the swing takes a specific amount of time. The more steps in the sequence, the longer the time taken. From the starting movement to the top of the swing when the lower body begins pivoting forward takes another specific amount of time. This swing of a single movement takes a specific amount of time from start to finish.

Tempo is the speed of action taken. Each golfer has his or her own swing tempo. Some golfers complete the swing from starting movement to follow-through in 0.7 seconds—a relatively fast tempo. Other golfers complete the swing in 1.2 seconds—a relatively slower tempo.

A controlled swing experienced as a single feel will have a specific timing and tempo. Timing and tempo are linked. Timing always leads to tempo. Your timing and tempo are unique to you. If your timing or tempo is off, they will not lead you to rhythm.

Rhythm

The timing and tempo of a controlled swing lead to **rhythm**. Rhythm is the flow of continuous movement in the swing. Percy calls rhythm the "very soul of golf." Rhythm is also an important objective of golf. When you find and stay in the rhythm of your swing, your brain is quiet, automaticity is engaged, and you may begin to find yourself "in the flow" or "in the zone." When in your rhythm, your swing simply happens without intentional control and without much thinking. Rhythm is the glue that holds the swing fundamentals together.

Body parts don't move to their own creative whim. Rather, rhythm is the smooth flow of a connected and controlled swing producing the feels noted throughout this book. Rhythm results in more than just appearance and a good feel; it leads to your best golf.

Golf's Three Rhythms

There are three types of rhythm in golf.

The first rhythm is the ***rhythm of your swing***. Once it is your turn to play, you can control the timing and tempo of your actions. These actions include determining your desired shot, setting up the starting position to make your desired swing by running your sequence, making the starting movement, and then relying on automaticity and a quiet brain to make the swing. Repeating this process following the same steps in the same amount of time leads to timing, which leads to rhythm. Intentionally shifting into this mental game mode when it is your turn to play allows you to keep the desired rhythm of your swing.

The second rhythm is the ***rhythm of your game***. This rhythm begins as you make your way to the golf course. If you are running late for your tee time and don't have a chance to warm up physically and mentally, the rhythm of your game has been disrupted. This rhythm also involves your flow of activity from shot to shot throughout your four- to five-hour round. You must learn to remain in the rhythm in which you play your best golf. After a shot, successful or not, go on a peaceful mental vacation.

You are lucky if the rhythm of your playing partners matches your rhythm. But if your playing partners or your surroundings disrupt your rhythm, you must learn to block out the disruptions and play within the rhythm that is most suited to your game. To do this, you may need to remain longer on your mental vacations as you ignore what is going on around you. To stay with the rhythm of your game, you might focus on your breathing, smile, clean your clubs or ball, or do anything that keeps you in a comfortable frame of mind and your brain quiet.

The third is the **rhythm of the round**. This rhythm involves your playing partners and those groups ahead and behind you as you play. The rhythm of the round can easily change if another golfer joins your group. The rhythm of the round can change if the group ahead of you slows down and you must wait impatiently before hitting your next shot. This rhythm can change if the group behind you is pushing you to play faster. The weather and conditions of the golf course can also affect the rhythm of your round.

Losing and Finding Rhythm

Swing rhythm is brittle and comes and goes—even during a single round of golf. If your timing or tempo changes, you can lose your rhythm.

In John's youth, he and an acquaintance made a round more interesting by making a wager. The winner would receive one of the other player's best clubs in exchange for a club of lesser value.

After a few holes, John told his playing partner that he had one of the fastest hands through the ball that John had ever seen. That apparently made his opponent begin thinking about what made the movement of his hands so fast. The playing partner's active problem-solving brain kicked in as he analyzed his swing. Whatever automaticity was involved up to that point was dismissed, and the competitor's quiet brain became destructively active. The quality of most of his next swings were worse. John's single comment hurt his opponent's timing and tempo, which hurt the rhythm of his swing. His playing partner's game crumbled, and John gained the spoils of victory.

John's comment was not intentionally made to throw off his competitor's rhythm to achieve victory. The incident made John realize the power of disrupting a player's rhythm by affecting his timing or tempo. Whether by jingling change in your pocket as your playing partner gets ready to swing, commenting on some part of your partner's swing, making your partner wait to hit the next shot, rushing your partner to speed up play, or a thousand other tactics, you can affect another player's rhythm—unless he or she has built up a strong mental game.

What can you do when you lose your rhythm? Return to the basics! Follow your sequence to build bracing into your starting position. Pivot from the lower body and allow the upper body to follow. Seek to experience the three primary feels of a good swing—pivot, shoulders moving in response to the pivot, and arms moving in response to the shoulders. Following this will lead you back to your desired rhythm.

You must know the rhythm of your controlled swing, rhythm of your game, and rhythm of your round. Your best golf depends upon learning how to get into and keep these three rhythms.

CHAPTER XVII

Interlude for Instruction: As a Dancer Sees It

"Golf is a *'passive* game; its dominating sensation is passivity.... Think of all the golfing maxims which have come down the years to us. 'Slow back,' 'Don't press,' 'Follow through,' 'Take it easy,' 'Let your club head do the work'—not one of them enjoining *activity*."

Chapter Summary

Percy asks a student, a well-known dance instructor, to give her impression of the golf swing. This opens up an interesting talk between two renowned teachers in their respective fields about what is active, passive, and reactive in movements. All these movements are present in the golf swing. Although not called lag in the conversation, this one-after-the-other movement of the passive part of the upper body in the forward pivot is discussed.

Today's Takeaway

This interlude digs into the concept of lag—the one-after-the-other movement in the forward swing pivot (Chapter III). Lag leads to increased club head speed. Lag is set up by the profile brace and set in action when the lower body pivot transitions from the back to forward swing. Lag then progressively transitions to the club head.

Percy's chat with his student touches on the three primary feels of a good golf swing that lead to lag: pivot, shoulders moving in response to the pivot, and arms moving in response to the shoulders.

As a teacher, Percy chooses his words carefully so the student correctly understands the concepts. Percy describes "active" and "passive" parts of the swing. Percy also uses the word "react" in describing parts of the swing. While Percy says that below the waist (i.e., feet, calves, knees, buttocks) is active, everything above the waist (i.e., shoulders, arms, wrists, hands) is passive. To Percy, being passive means that no intentional action is taken to actively resist or direct a force.

Muscles that are elastic work better. Loose shoulder muscles lead to an elastic feeling in the waist.

Since no action is taken by the passive upper body to resist the force of the active lower body pivot, the upper body is free to react. The word "react" allows the desired concept that parts of the swing happen automatically as a reaction to be clear. The one-after-the-other reactions of the passive upper body in the forward swing pivot lead to lag in the swing and acceleration of the club head through impact.

Percy's Teachings in His Words (p. 169-176)

I never consider I have succeeded with a pupil unless the pupil adds something to my own knowledge. A pupil who teaches me nothing has no originality, since what I am trying to impart is *sensation* and surely no two people should *feel* with exact similarity. So I encourage my pupils to talk and give their impressions of things, particularly of *feels*, and my experience is that if these impressions are banal neither the pupil nor I will learn anything! On the other hand, a pupil may come along with some quite absurd or fantastic conception of what I have tried to explain—and then I know there is fertility and that it is up to me to get a crop of ideas out of it.

So I felt I had a chance to do some good work when one day a well-known dance instructress came to me to be re-taught. Here was someone who, in addition to being intelligent, had spent her life in attaining reflex movements in their highest and most beautiful form and in learning to impart such movements to others.

. . . .

If a pupil shows any signs of life, after two or three lessons I ask him to give me his impressions of the golf movement. I did so with this lady and she gave a most interesting reply. She said she visualized the movement as "a vertical pillar with a number of circles around it." That showed enterprise and imagination, so I asked what the upright pillar represented. "Activity," she answered promptly. "But," she added, "the circles do not seem to represent passivity."

The main thing wrong with her swing when she came to me was the common fault of throwing her right hip to the right on the way back and then to the left on the way through. I explained this and showed her how she had tried to compensate for this movement by flattening the arcs of her hands and club so as to still come down inside.

"You tell me," she said, "that the pivot has two vital functions, to guide the club head and to generate power. Now I am very interested in the respective spheres of activity and passivity in movement. It is clear that the generating of power is *active,* but am I to assume that the guiding of the club head is *passive*?"

"You are," said I.

"So!" she said. "But may we first make sure we mean the same things by the use of the words 'active' and 'passive'?"

"An excellent precaution," said I, and being always one to learn, I added, "I suggest you lead off and tell me your impressions."

She thought a little and then said, "Well, I am passive when I abstain altogether from acting when I might act."

"You have quoted my dictionary," I remarked.

"Probably," she said. "Indeed, certainly, if we have the same dictionary, as I live in and out of mine—we teachers have to! But if

I have understood your analysis of the swing, you mean that that part of it which does not actively resist is purely passive?"

"Quite right," say I. "It should be. The shoulders, arms, wrists, and hands are all *passive* parts in the golf swing; the feet, calves, and buttocks are *active* parts."

"What about the hips? Are they active?"

"They are, but not prominently."

"In a subdued manner," she suggested.

"Yes that is right."

"Then," she said, "activity ends at the hips and passivity begins at the waist. That is good, for, since we have no bones in the waist except for the vertebrae, there is nothing to prevent it being a perfectly passive muscular spiral about which we can turn. Can I think of my waist as being made of strong elastic?"

"What makes you suggest elastic?" I asked. "Most people say steel."

"Well, steel in the body would feel like stays and restrict our twist, while elastic allows twist to take place and yet suggests great reactive strength. You tell me that the waist must be flexible not rigid, yet must impose its strength upon the passive part of the swing. I deduce from that, that the good golfer must be strong around the waist line."

"I will not dispute it," said I, "though some good golfers who are touchy about their figures may!"

"Now you tell me," she said, "that your shoulders, arms, and wrists are passive. How far do you go with this idea of passivity? Do you mean that you hit the ball passively?"

"I do," said I. And then, as I saw her eyebrows raised and a protest coming I hastened to add, "The greatest trial of *all* golfers is to retard the club head through the ball. And why is this difficult? Simply because they become active with their hands. Personally I almost never strike the ball too soon because I am, by instinct and training, a passive golfer."

. . . .

"Do you mean that seriously?" she asked.

"And it's not a freak idea, it is a profound golfing truth. Think of all the golfing maxims which have come down the years to us. 'Slow back,' 'Don't press,' 'Follow through,' 'Take it easy,' 'Let your club head do the work'—not one of them enjoining *activity*. I repeat, golf is a *passive* game."

. . . .

"But let's come back to your lesson," I suggested. "What part of the swing do you find it most difficult to keep passive?"

"I think the shoulders," she answered. "I either want to resist or to help with them, and I can't quite make out which it is. I know they feel they want to stiffen, while you tell me they should keep loose. For a long time I have been able to keep my hands passive; it was only recently that I found I was resisting with my shoulders, and, since I discovered that, I *have* been able to bring the club head down inside."

"Yes. You see, when you loosened your shoulders, you were able to use the elasticity of your waist, which you could not do with your shoulders held stiff. When our right shoulder pushes forward on the return swing, it is because our waist has stiffened up in conjunction with our shoulders. Relax our shoulders and we can immediately use our waist twist again."

"Yes I can see that. If I tighten my shoulders I immediately lose the feel of torsion at the waist."

"Again," I said, "if your shoulders and waist lose their flexible passivity, you can no longer *retard* your shoulders so that they will follow down, bringing the club head."

Her eyebrows went up again at that! "But you don't mean to say that I should or *can* retard my shoulders, do you?" she asked.

"Oh yes you can, and what is more, you *must*. The elastic waist and the consequent retarded shoulders have as much to do with the 'flailing' action as has the breaking back of the wrists. One is the counterpart of the other; it is the *whole action* that constitutes the flail."

"I see that. But you are always insisting on the upward stretch.

How can I stretch up through the body without actively lifting my shoulders?"

"You must stretch up with legs and hips, and then the shoulders will *come up* passively. Try it and you will see. When you try deliberately and directly to raise your shoulders, you commit one of golf's gravest faults. Keeping the shoulders up must be a *reactive* movement, reactive to the brace of the body. And now that we have cleared the ground a bit, let us return to your image of the upright pillar and the circles. The upright pillar stands for our 'power-stretch,' I suppose."

"Yes that is it."

"And the circles?"

"Well, they give us a sense of never moving any member of our body except *around* the pillar. But they also convey to me a sense of continuity in movement. Circles are continuous lines and represent the unbroken continuity of the whole movement. Also, what you good players do not seem to realize is that you make your movements *one after another,* never altogether. That gives me the image of a set of spirals moving progressively upward right out to the club head."

"Yes?" said I, interested.

"Yes. And I think it is this connecting together in progression that makes the golf feel so difficult to acquire. I feel it as a force which comes out of the ground, gets into my feet, climbs up my legs and hips, passes on through shoulders and arms, and so to the club head. Only, by the time I feel it has reached the club head, the club head is a couple of feet past the ball. *That* is what I mean by continuity."

"Oh is it!" I gasped and then when I got my second wind, "But that sounds to me less like *continuity* than *acceleration.*"

"Maybe," she said. "But if it is a gathering up of power, it is essentially a continuous gathering up. Each feel in the whole movement is joined in unison to the forthcoming one—*anticipating* it one might say."

"But do you suggest that the feel precedes the movement?" I asked.

"Of course I do. You know it does. You told me to prepare my feel as I walked to the tee, as I waggled. What is that but anticipation? You fellows excel because you anticipate. You know the correct feels and their correct succession, and you step up to a ball conscious and confident of what will happen. So there is nothing to hamper your swing, no hesitation and no hurry; the anticipation has established the correct continuous feels in you."

"How did you come to know that?" I asked, conscious that she was perfectly correct.

"Well," she smiled, "you may remember that I not only dance, I teach and therefore analyze dancing. Dancing is movement, and movement is life; so you must not be surprised if my analyzing has gone beyond my own sphere and trespassed into yours! And I *was* right, wasn't I?"

Beyond Percy—Feel Simple Golf

Power from centrifugal force is produced by an unrestricted pivoting of your lower body. When everything above your waist is allowed to react to the pivoting of your lower body, lag is created in your forward swing pivot. This lag creates more power.

When your hips complete the backswing pivot, they immediately transition to the forward swing pivot. The movement of your feet and the shifting of weight is continuous without stoppage. This keeps your upper body from catching up with the lower body, so your upper body does not come down all as one piece on the forward swing pivot. The forward twisting of your hips begins pulling your shoulders forward with a slight lag (i.e., delay). As your shoulders twist forward, they begin pulling your arms forward with another lag. Your arms pull your hands forward with yet more lag.

The lag builds up on the one-after-the-other forward swing pivot and is released through impact as the delayed upper body twists forward to catch up with the lower body that has already twisted forward. This is only possible if everything above the waist stays in a reactive (passive) position following the active lower body. Any tense muscle above the waist is like a piece of stiff metal inserted along the length of a leather whip, deadening the desired powerful whipping action.

CHAPTER XVIII

Power

"[The very good player] swings strongly from his legs upwards while we swing quickly from the club head downwards by means of our shoulders, arms, and hands. He tries to produce power in his swing; we try to impart speed to the club head."

Chapter Summary

This chapter covers something we all want in our golf swing—power! Percy teaches about the sources of power, the killers of power, and the feels of power. Power must be guided and controlled as well as produced.

Today's Takeaway

Percy's discussion of power covers a wide range of connected topics, including sources of power, killers of power, movement of the right hip and shoulder, shot direction, and feels of power—especially turn and then twist.

Power Sources

Throughout prior chapters, Percy identifies three sources of power in a pivot-driven swing:

1. Pivot (power from the ground upward based on movement of the feet, calves, knees, thighs, and buttocks).
2. Swing width (distance from the center of your chest to the tip of your right thumb).
3. Lag (one-after-the-other movement on the forward swing pivot).

Killers of Power

These power sources work best when your body is flexible. Shoulder muscles must be kept relaxed, allowing the abdominal muscles to help the pivot. Using upper body muscles to overcome a lack of flexibility reduces lag in the swing, reduces power, and leads to an uncontrolled and unconnected swing. Do Percy's experiment on flexibility (see page 203) to see if you need to be more flexible to increase the size of your pivot and generate more centrifugal force. This experiment also helps build the feel of the shoulders working correctly.

The good news is that you have control over (1) increasing your body's flexibility through stretching and exercise and (2) keeping your upper body reactive to the lower body pivot.

Right Hip and Shoulder

In a pivot-powered and connected swing, the movement of the right shoulder follows the movement of the right hip. As the right hip twists inward, the reactive right shoulder stays in the correct inside and behind position. This automatically results in the desired feel of lag, which produces power.

Shot Direction

Uncontrolled power is bad—as it is for most areas of life. If the swing is properly set up with bracing and the pivot is unrestricted, the pivot will return the club head squarely to the ball and the ball will be hit in the desired direction. Poor bracing, an unbalanced swing, and an active upper body with the resulting restricted pivot make the direction of the ball a matter of chance.

Good power and good direction require a full and unrestricted pivot.

Turn then Twist

The backswing pivot has the feel of a slow turn with the right hip pulling the left hip around. The forward swing pivot has the feel of a fast twist with the left hip spinning the right hip around. Both the turn and twist are driven by the active movement of the thighs, knees, calves, and feet. Percy describes in Chapter XIV that the torque (i.e., centrifugal force) created from the opposing forces of the feet firmly planted on the ground and the turning/twisting of the pivot is collected in and released from the force-center located in the pit of the back and hip area.

Feels

Percy refers to four feels of the swing related to power. Percy says that one of the feels, turn and then twist, should be our slogan. Other power-related feels can be added to this basic feel of power:

- Turn and then twist.
- Right hip twists inward on the forward swing pivot.
- Right shoulder follows right hip and twists inward and behind.
- Shoulder blades staying down and back allows back muscles to stay flexible.

Percy's Teachings in His Words (p. 177-186)

Most of us do not pay enough attention to what we are told, *how* we are told it, or by whom we are told it. In fact most of us need to learn how to learn. When I use the words "power," "strength," "energy," or even "moving force," some of my pupils take no notice whatever—they do not try to understand or analyze what I mean.

Some pupils of course do try to understand, and they soon realize the difference between the expressions which I have so carefully selected to indicate *power* and those which they had previously confused with them, such as "speed," "quickness," "velocity," and even "hurry." Which distinction is highly desirable, because, if they aim at speed, quickness, velocity, and hurry, they will kill any chance they may have of swinging with strength.

It is the *strength* of the swing of a very good player that intrigues us. He seems to swing slowly, even lazily, yet drives prodigious distances, and we marvel at it and wonder why we cannot do the same. For me there is nothing to wonder at; he swings strongly from his legs upwards while we swing quickly from the club head downwards by means of our shoulders, arms, and hands. He tries to produce power in his swing; we try to impart speed to the club head.

And please remember before we go on to consider its application that power at golf is centered around the hips. Please note *centered around;* the power is not *produced* by the hips (or very little of it is) but by the feet, calves, and thighs—but it is gathered up and given the correct centrifugal golf direction by the hip brace and pivot. And we will fail to drive the ball far and straight as soon as we fail *to take control of the club from the top of the swing with the feet, calves, and thighs.*

Now each shot in golf is a separate situation, and when we contemplate a situation—preparatory to playing the shot—we have to sense through our carefully built-up sense of feel how much power we need. How much *power,* not how much *swing.* A half-shot with a mashie does not mean a half-swing with that club but a swing with half power. We can play—or we should be able to play—a three-quarter shot with a full swing or a full shot with a three-quarter swing. I realize that this conception may be difficult to grasp, but it lies at the root of the superiority of the really great golfer.

I say the *really great* golfer because there are many well-known and successful players who can play nothing but full shots; a *controlled* shot is right outside their golfing range. Yet the great golfer plays every shot controlled, that is he plays every shot with what he feels to be the correct degree of power *not* at full pressure. This *control* is the secret of his greatness.

. . . .

In my opinion, we cannot lay too much stress upon this matter of *getting the right conceptions*. It is surprising what you can get people to do once they clearly understand what it is that has to be done. To reverse this, I contend that many of us are playing bad golf not because we are incapable of playing good golf but simply because we are thinking of golf in the wrong way.

I have known cases of such players who improved their swings and their games *without intending to,* simply because they came across and adopted a better conception of the swing. The truth is, of course, that just as if we appreciate good manners we will become good mannered in spite of ourselves; so also, if we appreciate the true ethics of the golf strokes, we will become good golfers.

Why do I use the word "ethics"? Well, because golf *is* a matter of ethics, that is (according to my dictionary) "relating to manners or morals." To prove this, cast your eye round the club room. The chances are you will find the most modest man in the club is also the best player *and* that he is out in the caddie shed. I have never known a great golfer who was not modest, and that goes for Walter Hagen, who in spite of his showmanship was a charmingly modest fellow and a great gentleman.

I hope that the reason why I have wandered off into moral implications in this particular chapter is clear. Our subject is power and power like fire is a good servant but a bad master. Uncontrolled power is the very devil—in golf or anywhere else.

In golf, power must be controlled in two ways: in the matter of *morals* and in the matter of *mechanics*. The mechanical control we may liken to the control of a motor car. The power at golf—the gasoline—is represented by the nails in our shoes, no gasoline, no power! But this power is not applied direct; it works through a clutch, and the clutch in the golfer's mechanism is the hips. That is where the power is gathered up, given its right direction and put into action or not. Then the hands we can compare with spark plugs—get them operating too soon or too late in the cycle of operations and your swing backfires. Your swing like the ignition on your car must be *timed*.

Without suggesting that this comparison should be pressed too far, it has its value. One of the points it emphasizes is that clutch slip must be guarded against—that is, there must be no slip, no sloppy movement in your hip work.

We must be fully conscious of how our hips should operate. If the right hip twists inwards as the hips return on the forward swing, we will have swung *from in-to-out*—that is, correctly. But if the right hip is allowed to slip outwards and around on the downward swing, this result cannot be achieved. This is because the club head performs the same actions as does the right hip; they are connected (as regards direction) by the right shoulder.

The effect of bringing our right hip inwards with a twisting movement is to guide the right shoulder in the way it should go. The right shoulder is totally subjective to the right hip; so, when the latter is braced and twisted *inwards*, the shoulder follows, coming inside and behind the ball—*in-to-out*.

Do not think that all this is a digression from our subject, power. For power must be guided as well as produced. We find that it is comparatively easy to drive the ball far; the difficulties begin when we want to add "and straight"; that is when we want our power applied with great accuracy. And in this matter of the accurate application of power, hip brace and movement are fundamentally vital.

Now this twisting inwards movement of the hips demands a muscular effort from the legs which is worth analyzing. As we pivot back, we *turn*, whereas on the forward swing, we *twist*. That is true even though a certain amount of muscular effort *is* needed to pivot back. Considering the swing as a whole, we have to gather up and increase our power gradually. The movement that starts up as a gentle turn develops on the down swing into a fierce twist. The turn is preparatory to the twist. So the effort of the leg muscles begins to be felt at the end of the backward pivot and is felt increasingly until the climax of the follow-through is reached.

The inward twist of the hips as we come down and through the ball demands great muscular activity in the calves and thighs, the generators of power in the golf swing, and it is the controlled direction of the hips that sees to it that this power is smoothly and gradually applied in the exactly correct direction. So we must incorporate into our swing a hip movement which we can recognize and control by a definite *feel*, so that by *feel* we may control the degree and direction of power in our swings.

So "turn and then twist" must be our slogan. These are the *basic* feels of the golf swing; other feels which we may add to them may help us in building up *repeatability* but they will only hinder if we have not built upon "turn and then twist" as our fundamental basis.

There is more power in the golf swing than that which comes from the legs; much of it comes from the flexibility of the body. "Flexibility" is different from "flail" yet it has similar reactions in our swing. A man of twenty-eight will be less flexible than he was at eighteen and more flexible than he will be at thirtyeight, but at eighteen it might be a *loose* flexibility, at twenty-eight a *free* flexibility, and at thirty-eight a *controlled* flexibility. Every shade and inflection of flexibility adds to or takes from our power.

A man who can only move his shoulders in conjunction with his hips has little chance of becoming a golfer. He is stiff and wooden. We must be able to "leave our shoulders behind." They have no direct torsional connection with the hips and must be able to rotate while the hips are held firm and unmoving by the brace. The fact that our whole body produces torque is what gives power to our swing, and, as we delay our shoulders, we add to the power. On the other hand, if we contract our shoulder muscles in an endeavor to give power to the blow (to "hit harder"), we produce the opposite effect. The shoulder and back muscles must be flexible so that the torque of the body can be picked up by the shoulders and flung into the club head.

....

This is very important; so let us look at it in another way also. One of the most difficult faults to cure in golf is that of the right shoulder coming forward and *outside* on the way down. It should come down *inside* and, when it does not, it is because it *has become part of the hips;* its connection with the hips is so lacking in flexibility that it is controlled by them and follows their movement. Actually we should use the flexibility of our back muscles to *delay* our shoulder action (in its relation to the pivot) in the same way that we allow our wrists to break back in order to set up delay in our club head.

It is not sufficient to delay the club head through the flexibility of the wrists only; shoulder flexibility must be added. When our right shoulder persists in coming forward, it is because this flexibility has been lost by the muscles of the back being *too tense*.

Now I have already told you that the club head follows the movement of the right hip; that is, the brace forward and to the left of the right hip will induce the swing that feels to go from in-to-out. How does the right shoulder operate in this?

When you study the *feel* of flexible shoulder action, you will find a number of sensations. One curious sensation is that we do not feel that the right shoulder comes *inside* from the front of our body but from behind it. We feel not that it is being *pulled* inside by the muscles of the chest, but that it is being *pushed* inside by the muscles of the back. I talked of this feeling to a well-known surgeon and he told me that it was indeed a correct interpretation of the anatomical facts. The muscles which hold us together and yet allow us flexibility are the cross muscles which join the base of the back (at the waist) to the shoulders. He also explained that unless these muscles are held, as we feel it, very loosely, the shoulders have no choice but to move reactively with the waist—which is in fact what we want them to do in nearly every human activity *except golf!*

Here is a little test of your own flexibility. Stand with your feet together facing the wall and close to it. Without moving your feet turn half right (so that you are looking square at the wall on your right). You can do this easily because you can turn *(a)* from the knees, *(b)* from the waist, and *(c)* from the neck; probably you will use each of the three. Now turn farther, looking into the corner which is three-quarters behind you. Then farther still, looking directly behind you. How far can you go? At the farthest stretch, you will feel coming into play the muscles which come into play at the top of your swing. Then, if you start again and this time turn *left,* you will feel the corresponding muscles which come into action as you finish forward.

You can get some interesting and quite useful *feels* from that little experiment. The point to watch is that, though the back muscles (those I have been describing) will be felt to *stretch* and so to come into action at the extremes of our turn in either direction, *they must not be held tight.* If they are held tight, shoulder flexibility is destroyed—just as wrist flexibility is destroyed by tightening the hand muscles and with just as fatal an effect upon the "flail." For the flail comes from the combined flexibility of all the muscles above the waist.

Now I know that I have been lecturing on the pivot and flexibility and that this is a chapter on power. But I know also that undirected power is no use in golf, and it is the function of the pivot to gather up power from its main sources (which are below the waist) and redirect it so that it emerges from the club head as centrifugal *swing.*

Beyond Percy—Feel Simple Golf

Percy stresses the importance of the right hip and shoulder staying in an inside and back position on the forward swing pivot. Position and movement of the knees play important roles in causing this to happen automatically.

The starting movement begins the backswing pivot by moving the left knee forward. This shifts weight onto the ball of the left foot. The right knee pulls back, which shifts weight onto the heel of the right foot. Keeping weight equally distributed (fifty/fifty) between the left and right feet, the right hip stays in the desired inside and back position on the backswing pivot. The right shoulder follows the right hip as the body rotates around a fixed axis.

Lowering the left heel to the ground to begin the forward swing pivot shifts weight to the left heel. The right knee is pulled forward and weight begins shifting to the ball of the right foot. Keeping weight equally distributed (fifty/fifty) between the left and right feet, the right hip continues to stay in an inside and back position on the forward swing pivot. Again, the right shoulder follows the right hip as the body rotates around a fixed axis.

This shifting of weight in the feet is like walking in place. Proper shifting of weight in the feet relates to the swing fundamental of body balance.

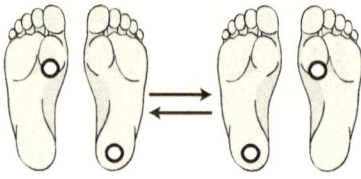

Although Chapter XXIV deals with golf analysis, problem four in *Feel. Simple. Golf.*'s troubleshooting chapter (Chapter 7) analyzes loss of distance in your swing. Lack of power could be one cause.

1. Symptom: Your swing feels forced and effortful and shot distance is very short.
2. Root Causes:
    - An incomplete or noncontinuous pivot.
    - Lack of lag on the forward swing pivot caused by using your shoulders, arms, or hands as a source of power.
    - Poor swing width.

3. Fixes:
   - Ensure good body balance in your starting position, a full hip turn, and continuous pivoting action (i.e., continuous shifting of weight within your feet).
   - Use bracing to connect your body so it starts as a single unit with everything above your waist reacting to the pivot.
   - Keep the upper body in a reactive position on the forward swing pivot so the hips pull the shoulders forward with a slight lag, followed by the shoulders pulling the arms forward with more lag, followed by the arms pulling the hands forward with even more lag.
   - Maintain swing width bracing set up in your starting position.

The three root causes relate to the sources of power in the swing. More on fixing a troubled swing is ahead in Chapter XXIV.

CHAPTER XIX

Interlude for Instruction: A Mathematician Explains

"'It is because you play golf in the simple way that you beat him! Experience has taught you the easiest way of playing. By dint of that experience and unceasing practice, you have learned to draw a straight line in the most simple way.'"

Chapter Summary

Percy seemed to always enjoy learning about the golf swing from his students during lessons. This was especially true when his students were experts in other professions. A mathematician-scientist took Percy on a journey into golf from the perspective of Einstein's theory of relativity and physics. In this interesting story, Percy's concepts, perspectives, and understanding of the golf swing are put to the test.

Today's Takeaway

This chapter is an interlude, a break, from the building up of swing fundamentals. It provides a fun glimpse into Percy's manner with his students, even frustrating ones.

In Chapter IX, Percy is described by his student as an impressionist—like a painter trying to create mental impressions of the golf swing to help his students learn key concepts. In this chapter, Percy's talk with the mathematician-scientist shows that Percy's approach to successfully playing and teaching a highly complex golf swing has been simplified.

In Chapter XII, Percy challenges his student's understanding of how she thought the swing worked. He challenges her "paradigm," or mental model, of the golf swing. Percy helps the student adopt a new paradigm that helps her better understand the golf swing. This paradigm, based on a lower body–powered golf swing, leads to a breakthrough in improving her game.

In this chapter, Percy's understanding of the golf swing and his underlying fundamentals and concepts are challenged. Viewing the golf swing from Einstein's theory of relativity and principles of psychics, the mathematician-scientist challenges Percy's paradigm of the golf swing. Although a seemingly frustrating process for Percy, he successfully handles the challenge.

Challenging how we believe the golf swing works (our paradigm of the golf swing) is a worthwhile process. If needed and useful, changing our understanding of how the golf swing works may lead to the improvement we seek. Although it may be frustrating, taking a new look and questioning our long-held beliefs and understanding of the golf swing from a fresh perspective may be helpful.

Percy's Teachings in His Words (p. 187-195)

This is another true story that will show you what an interesting variety of people I meet and how many and different ways there are of thinking about golf.

One day a player walked into my shop and inquired for me. I happened to be out, but he booked a lesson for the following day. He was an internationally famous mathematician and scientist and by no means of the abstract unpractical type.

"Do you know anything about mathematics?" he asked as we walked over to the practice ground.

If I had not known who he was, I might have dropped into the trap but, "Not a figure!" says I.

. . . .

"Do you know anything about Einstein?" he asked completely undisturbed.

"If by Einstein you mean his theory," said I getting one back on him, "of course I know nothing about it. At least, all I *do* know is that only twelve people in the world are said to understand it and you're one of them."

"Actually you probably know quite a lot about it," he said, "only you cannot express it in simple language."

"Well no more can you," said I briefly. "For if you could, many more people would understand it."

"Let us see! Firstly you must realize that golf is a four-dimensional game . . . *time* of course being the fourth."

"That is a good one," said I. "What are the other three?"

"Well, I am coming to that. Will you please play me a shot or two?"

We had a caddie out to scout the balls, and there was another watching from out to the right of us. I took a few preliminary swings and then hit a very sweet shot off the turf with my brassie, clean and long with just a little pull at the end.

"Now," he said, "what did you see?"

"Well," said I, "I did not lift my head too soon, so I did not see the ball rise. I saw it in the air and then saw it carry a bit to the left as it dropped."

"Good. Now what did the caddie see? *He* saw the ball come out of the sky too, but he saw it drop to the right. And the fellow out in the wood there saw a simple rise and fall without deviation. So you see that you three fellows would all have described the same operation quite differently; all the descriptions might have been accurate—yet they would (on the surface) have described different flights. That is relativity."

"But what has that to do with golf?"

"Nothing perhaps, except to warn you against hasty conclusions—even when you see things with your own eyes. So do not be too sure the grass is green!"

"Oh drat you and your green grass! What do I care if it is green or blue or black...."

"I knew a painter who said it *was* black," he said.

"Drat him too," said I. "You are getting me hot and bothered. What about this lesson you came out to have?"

"I am having it," he said. "In my own way. I am getting my mind right for the real work, when it comes."

. . . .

"But I am trying to understand the swing my way. The trouble with you Pros is that you only understand the swing your way; so you want us to understand it your way too. That is why you are really very little use to anyone except people of low intellectual grade. They do not understand anything anyhow so it does not matter what you tell them. Those who become good learn by imitation, those who do not work things out in their own minds—which is fatal because they have nothing to think with."

. . . .

"But what about the golf lesson you wanted?"

"I am having it and it is going very nicely. Only negatively!"

"Negatively?"

"Yes."

"But you can't learn negatively."

"Oh can't you!" he said. "Which impresses you most: $2 + 2 = 4$ or $2 + 1 = 4$?"

"Yes, I see that. I know which is right; so $2 + 1 = 4$ impresses me because of its contradiction to the truth."

"So the *negative* impresses you the more. Now!. You tell me that to make the ball roll is the greatest art of the golfer."

"Yes I do."

"You also say that to make the ball roll you must put 'top-spin' on it."

"Agreed."

"Well that, I must point out, is a negative also because no one *can* put top-spin on a golf ball."

"Oh no! You want me to believe that when I putt a ball along the ground, and it runs and runs and runs, rolling over and over and over, I have not put top-spin on it?"

"You have not put the fraction of a particle of topspin on it."

"But I can make the ball roll and you can't. Why is that then?"

"Because with your skill and experience you can make your club head 90° vertical and can pass it over the ground to connect with the ball square to its horizontal axis. Then as the bottom of the ball is stuck to the ground by the friction set up by gravity and the top is free to move, the top moves first and you set up your over and over movement. Just as if your feet suddenly stuck in the ground as you were running, you would fall flat on your face."

"But you are not going to tell me that I can't impart what I call top-spin in different degrees and so make one ball run more than another. Watch this . . . and this . . . and this . . .," I said, playing various shots.

"Yes, very skillfully done. But all you have done is to put *less* back-spin on some shots than on others. That is what I meant when I said 'top-spin' in golf is a negative. The only spin you can put on a golf ball is back-spin. To put on top-spin is a physical impossibility—as you will see if you think out where and at what angle the ball would have to be struck to impart it."

"Well, what does it matter to me what sort of spin you call it, so long as I can produce the effect I want?"

"As a player, it does not matter to you at all. The skill with which you can control spin makes you an outstanding player, no matter what you call it. But as a teacher, it does matter to you because the fact that you call things by their wrong names prevents me learning from you. Your teaching capacity is negative."

"Thank you," said I. "Fortunately there are plenty of people who do not agree with you. And anyway if that is so, why are you taking this lesson?"

"I love talking to simple people."

"Hell! Do you know that I have beaten Henry Cotton—and anyone who can do that is not so simple!"

"It is because you play golf in the simple way that you beat him! Experience has taught you the easiest way of playing. By dint of that experience and unceasing practice, you have learned to draw a straight line in the most simple way."

"A straight line?"

"What is a straight drive but a straight line?—a long one and drawn without a ruler too! Also it is in four dimensions. Yet you are simple enough to wonder why people cannot play golf—and why you cannot teach them."

"Put like that it does sound complex. But now I come to think of it, I play golf in one dimension only—straight ahead."

"And what about time?"

"I ignore it!—I play in one dimension only—straight ahead."

"Like a worm crawling straight to its hole?"

"Yes, exactly, except in my figure!"

"You mean to tell me that you only try to knock the ball along the ground?"

"Yes."

"When you play high shots over trees? When you deliberately put on *back-spin*, do you conceive all that as golf in one dimension?"

"I do."

"Well, why didn't you tell me that before? Here we have been troubling ourselves with Einstein, only to find now that you play in one dimension only."

"Well, it's a reasonable simplification, isn't it?"

"Possibly so; it is if you mean what I think you do . . . that you play golf in four dimensions with a one-dimensional outlook."

"I don't know about my dimensional outlook; what I try to feel is that I am in a position to play straight along the ground."

"Well, that certainly seems a very simple outlook and in your case it is undeniably effective. Do you think that I will ever be able to play along the ground?"

"Good Lord, no! Only twelve of us can do that *and I am one of them.*"

Beyond Percy—Feel Simple Golf

Following Percy's lead, Feel Simple Golf is driven to keep the teaching, learning, and playing of golf simple. In that vein, it is a good time to review the simple description of the Feel Simple Golf integrated system in less than one hundred words. The five fundamentals of the swing are highlighted in bold.

- **Pivot** creates power and direction.
- **Body balance** allows for a full and unrestricted pivot.
- Balance is lost when weight moves closer to or further from the (1) ball, (2) target, or (3) ground during the swing.
- Body balance is maintained using (1) upward, (2) inward, and (2) behind bracing built into the **starting position**.
- **Swing width** increases power and is built into the starting position with bracing.
- **Psychology of the swing** involves (1) an actively thinking brain to establish the starting position and initiate the starting movement and (2) a quiet brain to repeat a practiced swing movement based on feel.
- This applies from putting to driving.

After reading this far into the book, this description should be much more understandable than when you first read it. If so, well done! More ground is to be covered.

CHAPTER XX

Temperament

"The secret of success in golf lies in temperament and that is true whatever grade of golf you may aspire to play. Tournaments are not always, not even *usually*, won by the greatest stylists. They go to the men with the best balanced outlook on the game."

Chapter Summary

How we handle pressure, anger, fear, excitement, and so many other emotions we feel on the course affect how well we swing the golf club using the fundamentals of a good swing. Very much a part of the psychology of the swing, temperament directly contributes to how well we play. Temperament is based on playing with a quiet brain. Temperament in golf can be built and strengthened.

Today's Takeaway

Temperament is an important part of the mental (psychological) part of the game. Good golfing temperament means you have enough control of yourself to make your best shots regardless of your state of mind or the condition of your game. With good temperament, you have a competitive advantage over a more technically skilled golfer with a poor temperament.

Like building up controls (i.e., feels) in your swing to create a controlled swing with a single feel, you can build up mental controls in your game to create a good, stormproof temperament. Ways to build a good golf temperament include the following:

- Have a clear understanding of why you play golf (e.g., to relax, to escape life's circumstances, to win, to have fun) and a realistic view of your skill level, and play accordingly.
- Play by feel with a controlled swing and with automaticity (quiet brain).
- Use positive self-talk (Percy calls it "back-chat") to remove destructive thoughts and emotions that dismiss automaticity.

Temperament is especially important in putting because (1) confidence is a major factor in putting well and (2) the putting movement uses less force with a finer touch that is particularly sensitive to your state of mind. A sense of confidence and comfort lead to a quiet brain that allows automaticity to swing the putter, free from the intentional actions of the hands to control the putter.

Percy's Teachings in His Words (p. 196-207)

The secret of success in golf lies in temperament and that is true whatever grade of golf you may aspire to play. Tournaments are not always, not even *usually*, won by the greatest stylists. They go to the men with the best balanced outlook on the game. And how frequently we have seen the fellow with a rank, bad swing take the half-crown off a man who looked far better on the tee.

Do not mistake me. It is an excellent thing to be a stylist, if your style is supported and molded by a good golfing temperament. Harry Vardon before the Great War and Bobby Jones in the years that followed it were perfect stylists, but they were also perfectly balanced in the psychophysical sense and won more tournaments than any other golfers. On the other hand, Taylor and Braid, who were never deemed stylists at all, almost equaled these two in collecting championships because they were *temperamentally* in the championship class. But you will not find any golfer who is temperamentally weak or unreliable habitually winning big events, however brilliant a stylist he may be.

I suppose we might say that a man's style at golf is evolved from the reactions on one another of his temperament and his physical make-up. We may all learn to write from the same copy-book but we will grow up to sign our checks differently, and, though I have been teaching golf for thirty-five years now, I have yet to find two people who play alike. No matter how much you tried to teach two people to play alike, the results would be surprisingly different.

We do not all play golf for the same reason, of course, and that may affect the way we play it. Some of us play it for a living. Many play it on doctor's order and more still for exercise! There are more individual reasons too, and I have come across some odd ones in my time. A lady came to me once with her child, a girl of about fourteen. She said, "I am not going to make my daughter an intellectual; I want you to make her a golf champion." "I'll do my best," said I. "But why do you want her to be a golf champion?" "Oh," she said, "look at ... and ... and ...," and rattled off the names of champions who had made fine marriages! That was the idea, and I may tell you that in due course it proved successful.

. . . .

If a fellow is content to be able to knock the ball one hundred and fifty yards down the fairway, there is no point in explaining the flail to him—he would not be interested. Comparatively few people *are* interested in playing the game as well as they could play it. In particular, most youngsters think of nothing but hitting their tee shots "miles" and do not seem to mind missing 80 per cent of their other shots, though as we all know, it is the "other shots" which enable you to go round in a reasonable score. If you can chip and putt decently, you can always get yourself a decent score. I know lots of men who can go round St. Cloud in under 80 and never hit a clean golf shot the whole time.

．．．．

It started when a lady came to me for lessons. She did well, so well that one day she said, "Do you know, my game has improved so much that my husband is going to take a course of lessons with you. I'm so sorry." "Why be sorry?" said I. "I'm delighted." She looked at me with a slight smile. "You don't know my hubby," she said. "He is the most violent-tempered man in the world."

Well, in due course he turned up. He looked wild and he *was* wild in the sense that he let his emotions run loose! Being prepared, I naturally took up a meek and mild attitude, which egged him on to more and more furious bursts of temper every time he missed the ball—which incidentally was every time he swung at it! And every time he missed he would fling his driver on the ground and yell to me, "What did I do wrong *that* time?"

I suggested a few things which I knew would not work, and he got wilder still. Then, suddenly after a particularly furious burst of rage, I said to him quietly, "Let me see your driver." He handed it to me ungraciously. "Old friend?" I asked examining it. "Got it at Ohan," he growled. I looked him in the eye, shut my lips, took the club in both hands, and broke it in two across my knee—and threw the pieces in a corner of the shed.

He went gray and gray-white and speechless. While he was contemplating the wreckage, I bent down and put another ball on the tee. Then I straightened up and said, "Take your brassie." He went to his bag like a lamb and went on with the lesson much more quietly which was lucky for him because if he had kept on fuming I would have broken every club in his bag. He is a different man and a very different golfer today.

At a later lesson I told him the true story of a golfer who on his first appearance at St. Andrews became so enraged with his putter that he threw it out of bounds at the Elysian fields and tore up his card. Yet the next time he played there he won the Open! But he did not win the Open until he had curbed his temper.

Now these two stories are nearly everyone's. But to get as mad as the proverbial meat-axe because we miss a shot is the sign of a young golfer. The experienced golfer does not get mad when he misses a shot because he knows that if he does so the chances are that he will miss the next one too. And I doubt if it is any more difficult to build up control of your temperament in golf than it is to build up control of your swing *once you appreciate the need.*

But I think we must go back again from this point to the question of *why* you play golf. Because the state of mind and the temperamental strains of *(a)* a tired business man playing purely for relaxation and *(b)* a Pro fighting for a championship on the last green are so immensely different that their problems are different—or at least arise in very different intensities.

Many big business men and men in public life have told me how great a relaxation they found golf to be. Nothing takes your mind so completely off the daily worries as does a round of golf. Each of us, whatever his rating as a golfer may be, has to pay attention to the job in hand; so much attention that for a couple of hours we are in a new world and the problems and tensions of our normal world are forgotten.

. . . .

Again there are plenty of people, too many in fact, who play purely as a pastime. I say too many because to my mind these are the most devastating of all golf bores. A keen man is always interesting because of his keenness, but to hear a recapitulation of a round which was only played to pass the time—and is only being recapitulated to pass some more time—is the depths beyond which golf boredom cannot sink.

. . . .

Temperament is pre-eminently important in putting because good putting is so largely a matter of *confidence.* You can only *stroke* the ball when you are quietly confident; otherwise you jerk it. You can always drive or play big shots reasonably well, because that is done more with the grosser muscles, but the finer touch required for putting is a much more delicate matter and so is much more liable to be put out of gear and *jerked* by nervous tension.

Bad putters habitually *stab* the ball: that is why they are bad putters. Good putters jerk the club when they are nervous, which is basically quite a different fault.

My teaching is built up around the principle of *playing by feel*: that is, through our muscular reflexes and controls. This leaves it to our muscles to swing the club and sets us free to give a little attention to our mental state—to inhibit the urge to hurry, and to go quietly and methodically about the job. We know that when we are in a quiet state we can play the shot as well as we know how; therefore if we can *make* ourselves quiet and relaxed, we will allow our muscular control system to work.

To illustrate this point let me tell you a little story from my own experience. In 1927 I was runner-up in the Belgian Open at Knocke and won the Dutch Open at The Hague, both in the same week. They were then 36-hole tournaments, and in each I did a 69 in the second round. Now here I should tell you what you may already know, that I was never a first-class golf tournament player for two reasons: I was not physically strong enough, and temperamentally I was too highly strung.

The story is about the last hole I played at The Hague, to complete my 69 and beat Henry Cotton by one stroke. After an indifferent drive from the last tee, the home green seemed to get smaller and smaller—it was triangular in shape with the hole tucked well down in the apex, a clump of trees to the right and a bunker on the left. Henry was playing behind me, and I had a pal standing on the 17th green who signaled to me before I played my second that Henry had got his 4 and we were level over the 35 holes.

I deliberately pushed out all the surge of thoughts and emotions that came rushing into my mind and said to myself, "Now you old fool, *keep quiet* and play this shot as if you were showing a pupil at St. Cloud how it *should* be played." Well, I got myself quieted down and then played my shot—straight onto the flag but about ten yards short.

Knowing that I was a good putter, I said to myself, "Well, I shall tie anyway." But I did not a bit relish the idea of having to go out and play another 18 holes. But there it was—or rather there *I* was, on the green but ten yards from the hole. So I went through the same backchat with myself, to get quieted down. Then I putted, a firm, clean *stroking*—and when I *did* look up, it was just in time to see the ball drop into the hole, to win me the title by a single stroke.

. . . .

One day I was out on the course amusing, rather than teaching, a little girl of seven. On one occasion she showed a little impatience and I said to her very seriously, "Don't you get angry! Only badly brought-up little girls get angry, and you are a nicely brought-up little girl." I always remember the way she looked at me—sideways, like a little robin. After that she would say to me sometimes, "Am I getting angry?" And I would say, "Well, your ears *do* look a little white; let me feel your pulse," or I would put my ear to her back to hear if her heart was beating too fast. She took it all so seriously and was intensely pleased when one day I said, "Now that's better; not so angry as last time you did that!" And then one day I told her she was quite cured (which she was) and she was in ecstasies!

All very childish if you like. But those lessons in golf psychology stood her in good stead. She grew up to be a champion and her manners on the course were always a pleasure to see and a pattern to be followed.

If you wish to hide your character, do not play golf. It will be revealed on the course. I was telling this one day to a very irascible chap, and he said, "Well, what would you do about it, if you were me?" I replied quietly, "Ride a bicycle."

. . . .

When we come to bedrock, what do we mean when we say that a man has a "good golfing temperament"? We mean that he has sufficient control of himself to produce his best shots *whatever the circumstances may be*. The man who has this starts with a greater advantage than the man with the ideal golfing physique or the man with the fine natural style.

Can you acquire the golf temperament? You certainly can, as I had to do to a considerable degree. And you have got one very great help which I lacked in my novitiate—the idea of learning golf by *feel*. For one of the main advantages of this method is just that it *can* make your game storm-proof, can make you capable of producing your best shots when you need them, irrespective of your state of mind and the condition of the game.

Beyond Percy—Feel Simple Golf

Good temperament is the ability to control emotions so your performance level remains high, regardless of the situation.

If you have a good temperament, you can beat a more technically skilled golfer who may play poorly, become scared or lose his or her temper, and crumble in fear or a fit of anger. You can improve your temperament by finding ways to release anger or joy quickly and then move on to your next shot. Of course, some manageable level of anger or joy might be part of your ideal performance state that is there when you play at your best.

A short memory is a definite advantage in golf. After each shot, allow yourself a set and limited amount of time (fifteen seconds) to vent any emotions. Once that time has passed, move on and do not dwell on the past. Smile.

Quieting the Brain—During Play

Good temperament happens most easily with a quiet brain. Good preparation that quiets the brain must be followed by ways to keep your brain quiet during play. Strategies to keep your brain appropriately quiet during your round of golf include the following:

- Focus your swing on a desired feel to make the shot.
- Use positive mental framing (e.g., like Percy did when he thought to himself, *Play this shot as if you were showing a pupil at St. Cloud how it should be played*).
- Follow a sequence to set up your swing.
- Take mental vacations between shots.

During your round of golf, it is important to keep your emotions from dismissing automaticity. Once emotions kick in, large amounts of adrenaline flow through your body. Under these conditions, it is more difficult to keep a quiet brain so automaticity can be used to swing the club.

Good temperament with good intensity control quiets your brain and allows automaticity to make the next swing. The amount of intensity that leads to playing your best is part of your ideal performance state.

Ideal Performance State

You have a profile of an ***ideal performance state*** that leads to your best performance. Also, you have a performance state profile when you are likely to play poorly. You can plot your ideal performance state by writing down your thoughts and emotions when you have performed at your best and at your worst. Once you know your ideal performance state, you can find and develop strategies to get into (or closer to) your ideal performance state as you prepare to play.

Following is John's ideal performance state profile when he plays his best and his performance state profile when he plays his worst.

Ideal Performance State Profile	Poor Performance State Profile
Preparedness—High • A sense of having practiced in preparation for the round, having a confident plan of how to play each hole, having completed a proper warm-up, running my sequence to set up each shot in my starting position	**Preparedness—Low** • Being unfamiliar with the course, such as proper shot placement and slopes of the putting greens; failure to follow my sequence for getting into the correct starting position for the desired shot
Anxiety—Low • Having little concern of the unknown, feeling certain of being able to meet the upcoming challenges of the round	**Anxiety—High** • Being concerned with hitting a poor shot and injuring a spectator, playing with fear of a potentially poor result
Rhythm—High • A sense of understanding the rhythm of my playing partners and being able to maintain my own rhythm during the round	**Shot Commitment—Low** • Questioning the designed shot and losing focus of trying to repeat the feel of the desired swing
Mental Focus—Flowing • Being able to focus intensely on each shot and then allow my thoughts and feelings to drift away from golf after the shot until it is time to refocus on the next shot	**Mixed Purposes—High** • Trying to play my game as a competitor while trying to help a golf student or playing partner with their swing mechanics in my role as a golf instructor or coach
Showmanship—High • A desire to perform in front of others	

Being in your ideal performance state leads to golf that is effortless, both physically and mentally.

CHAPTER XXI

Interlude for Instruction: Largely Concerned with the Waggle

"I always start off by telling [five handicappers] that you have to be a very good golfer to be scratch. Talent and skill are not enough to get you there; your golf must be built on the right foundations."

Chapter Summary

Percy works with a good golfer, with a five handicap, whose progress was stuck. The teaching begins focused on the golfer's violent preparatory waggle powered by the hands. The teaching moves to a connected swing and finally leads to a fundamental choice. The good golfer can either continue seeking quick-fix swing tips to progress, as he has been doing unsuccessfully, or commit to a new concept of a ground-upward, pivot-driven swing to break through to the next level.

Today's Takeaway

This chapter might be more about you and your swing concerns than you think as you read. Although Percy named this chapter, "Largely

Concerned with the Waggle," the chapter gives an interesting peek into how Percy may have started his journey of helping a student change the paradigm of his golf swing.

In reading the prior twenty chapters, you have surely picked up more than a few tips you may be able to build into your current swing. Maybe these tips will help improve your swing. Even better, maybe you will be able to keep the improvements over time. If you think this is getting close to the "500 best swing tips" approach to learning and improving your swing, we are thinking alike.

Like the "five handicap fellow" who came to Percy looking to be fixed and helped forward, you may (like the majority of golfers) have similar hopes by reading this book.

Let's call Percy's potential student in the story "Tip" for ease. Percy went with Tip down a path that eventually led to seeing that what Tip needed was not a swing tip but a fundamentally new concept (or paradigm) for his golf swing.

Preparatory Waggle

Once in the starting position, a ***preparatory waggle*** is made before the backswing pivot is started. A preparatory waggle is a slow, gentle, smooth, and controlled movement of the body. A preparatory waggle helps you relax as well as regain the feel of the desired swing you want to make. With bracing in place that sets up your desired swing, the preparatory waggle allows you to feel that swing before making the starting movement and swinging the club.

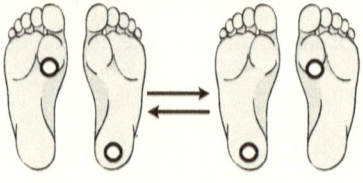

To make a preparatory waggle, move the weight in your feet as if walking in place. Weight shifts to the ball of your left foot and heel of your right foot, then back to the heel of your left foot and ball of your right foot. With bracing in place, this movement of your feet starts a small pivoting of your lower body, similar to the starting movement. Your connected shoulders, arms, and hands move as a reaction to the pivot. The waggle should be slow and gentle. This helps relieve some of the built-up tension of the swing and reminds your brain that the pivot powers the swing and that the backswing pivot should be slow.

PREPARATORY WAGGLE

Feels

Percy adds a lot of feels of the golf swing related to what is preparatory to the swing. These feels (supplementary to the three primary feels) are experienced for all shots, from driving to putting, and can be summarized as follows.

- Feels of body balance:
    - Weight equally distributed between the feet.
    - Being firmly planted with both feet pushing into the ground.

- Feel of a braced starting (set) position:
  - Overall feel: upright, firm, and compact.
  - Upward brace:
    - Tall, slightly bent over at the waist, back straight.
  - Inward brace:
    - Inside and behind the back of the ball.
    - Elbows pulled toward each other.
    - Shoulder blades pulled together.
    - Stomach pulled inward.
  - Behind brace:
    - Chin turned to the right, seeing ball out of the corner of the left eye.
  - Profile brace:
    - Hips twisted to the left, left side taut from foot to shoulder, right side bowed inward.
- Feel of club "down":
  - Carry the club back around the body and along the ground (not lifting club).
  - Left arm is stretched downward in the starting position and remains stretched.
  - Club face comes from behind the ball (not down at it), similar to an enlarged putting movement.

Problem with the Waggle

Tip came to Percy because his game was stuck. Tip was seeking a swing tip or two from Percy to help him move forward. Percy did spot a fault in Tip's swing. Specifically, Tip's hand-powered waggle was overly aggressive.

Recall that Percy emphasized the importance of the waggle and first few feet of the backswing pivot. Perform those two parts of the swing correctly and the success of the swing is nearly certain.

Problems Beyond the Waggle

Tip's upper body–powered swing lacked connection. To fix one swing problem, Tip had added something to his swing (based on a swing tip) to compensate. Swing problem after swing problem resulted in strapping on more and more compensatory movements to his swing. That relates to Percy's earlier analogy of trying to juggle six unconnected glass balls. Tip was a golf swing juggler when he came to Percy looking for help.

Two Options

Percy gave Tip two options. First, Tip could continue adding complicating compensatory movements to make his swing work. This option would surely keep Tip at a five handicap. The second option was for Tip to adopt a new concept (paradigm) of the golf swing. That new concept of the golf swing involved changing from an upper body–powered swing to a lower body pivot-powered swing. Option one involved the unwise and ultimately doomed-for-failure "500 best swing tips" approach.

Percy's Teachings in His Words (p. 208-219)

The most difficult lessons to give are those to players with handicaps around 5 and 6. They are in the "near scratch" class, and when they come to us it is either because they realize they have come to a full stop or because they have struck a thoroughly bad patch which they cannot get themselves out of.

The attitude of these players is very rarely that there is anything wrong with their game. Oh no! It is just that they miss an odd drive or two which puts them in the rough; two or three times in a round their iron shots miss the green, and then maybe a couple of putts that should go down don't, and that (they figure out in the smoke room) is why they are not scratch.

I always start off by telling these people that you have to be a very good golfer to be scratch. Talent and skill are not enough to get you there; your golf must be built on the right foundations.

The trouble with many 5 and 6 handicap men is that they have become as good as their conception of the game enables them to be. Because their swing has not been developed about the correct centrifugal principle, it is *unreliable*, and they have to depend upon a tip being given or an idea coming to them just when they need it. This is a dangerous state of affairs, and the natural result of trying to learn golf by trial and error—that is by trying one thing one day and another the next—with no basic principle to back it up. It is true that that is the way most of us Pros learned, but it takes immense perseverance and a long time!

Well, one day I had one of these 5 handicap fellows come to me for help. I made him hit a ball or two, and he asked me what I thought of his swing.

"Very good indeed," said I. "But you waggle badly. That is all there is wrong with your golf."

"Oh!" said he, a little astonished and more than a little disappointed.

You see he neither expected nor liked what I told him. Because of my reputation as a teacher, he thought that I would have a "cure" for his trouble, and I had none.

I still have no cure for it. Any pupil of mine can cure himself as well as I can cure him by referring back to first principles. If one of my pupils comes to me as to a doctor, not as to a teacher, I just run over the ground work with him, just to make sure he is setting his mechanics in motion properly, and, when we have done this, it is quite easy to put our finger on the trouble.

But to come back to the lesson. This pupil had a particularly fiery waggle, so fiery that its violence threw too much action into his hands which remained active throughout his swing and so made him a *direct hitter*.

I explained this to him and continued, "The essence of rhythmic swinging is to be smooth, for only the smooth swing *can* be rhythmic. But if you get undue club head agitation into your preparatory movement (which is what the waggle is) you will get all the feel in your hands, arms, and shoulders, *not* in your legs, hips, and back, which is where you *should* feel that you swing from."

"But I don't see why I can't feel my back and legs when I waggle my way?"

"Well, to put it as briefly as possible, when you waggle your way, the club head sets up movement to which the body must react. The club head is pulling the body; the tail is wagging the dog. It should be the other way round: you need to be subdued and waiting for the action of the body to set up club head movement."

. . . .

"Yes, that is interesting. But tell me, if I must not waggle my club with my hands—what *may* I do with them?"

"As nearly as possible—nothing," said I. "The hands are not direct agents in producing the power of a golf shot; they are a *connection* between the lower part of the body (where the power comes from) and the club head, and they must remain nothing more than a connection. If you *use* your hands, consciously or not, you break connection."

"Must a good swing be 'connected'?"

"Indeed it must. The great player is great because his swing is connected and therefore reliable. He makes an indifferent shot only when he does lose connection. The reason why he uses only a three-quarter swing is because that is as far back as he can go without the risk of breaking the connection."

. . . .

"Is a 'connected' swing the same thing as a 'compact' one?"

"Yes. How would you define a compact swing?"

"Well, a swing which seems to be working as one, without loose parts and yet free to work."

"Good. That will do for a 'connected' one too. And I assure you again that you will never develop a compact and connected swing as long as you waggle so fiercely."

....

"And you seriously think that the main thing which keeps me out of the top class is the use of my hands?"

"I do. I want you to feel your hands only as a connecting link in the whole mechanism, not as a separate working part. Try to play a short chip shot *guiding it and giving it its power entirely from the knees*. When you can do that you will know what it is to feel connected."

....

"Well your own phrase suggests the answer to that one! The basic trouble with a violent waggle is that it sets up too intense local reactions and actually *prevents us feeling the swing as a whole*. Always keep in mind that the swing is one and indivisible and must be balanced. If any part of it becomes too active (as it will if you exaggerate any phase of it), the swing is thrown out of balance and you can no longer feel it as a whole. The good golfer rarely loses the feel of the whole; when he does, he makes bad shots like the rest of us.

"Putting it another way," I continued, "any extraneous movement we perform, any *strain* we put on our swing, will push the whole out of shape. There will be a dent where there should be a smooth curve. As soon as we feel the dent we begin to make compensatory movements and before long the rhythm of our swing is completely broken up by the original dent and our subsequent efforts to correct it. The simpler the swing, the better. The ideal is to bring it down to a one point center of feel."

"Why?" he asked.

"Because the correct golf swing is the application of centrifugal force, the center whirling the periphery around. So we must have a firm center for all shots. The shorter the shot, the lower down in our body do we feel the center to be. Fundamentally the whirl around is always the same, but while in the drive we feel the whirl mainly from the hips, in chip shots we feel the whirl comes chiefly from the knees. Actually the power of a golf shot comes *out of the ground* through its resistance to the feet. The hands have nothing to do with it—What sort of a shot could you make if you were suspended with your feet off the ground?"

....

"Perhaps there are some minor mechanical faults; that we cannot know at the moment. You see, you cannot eradicate or work on a minor mechanical fault if you have a *fundamental* fault which impedes you feeling the whole swing. And who knows, when you get your preparatory movements smoother, some of those so-called faulty mechanics may smooth *themselves* out; they may be an *effect* of the strain in your swing. As you know, you do not have to throw *much* sand into a machine to put it out of order."

"So I must begin by waggling smoothly with my pivot, instead of jerkily with my hands. Is that it?"

"Exactly. That is why I use the term 'preparatory movement' instead of waggle when I can. It suggests a quiet diminutive movement of the club head—far removed from violent activity."

....

"Well the two extreme points of the golf swing are the *feet* (drawing power from the resistance of the ground) and the *club head* (free to travel through the air). Now if we are to control our swing, there must be an unbroken chain of connections between these two points. One end of the swing is fixed; the other is free but connected; but, if on the way back I (1) open the club face, (2) bend the left arm, (3) relax the right knee, and (4) open the hands—my swing will be completely disconnected. My club head will feel lost."

"Yes."

"If I start a swing in that way, I have to repeat all these breaking-up movements in the reverse way on the way down; otherwise I cannot connect with the ball. 'Some operation' as you may imagine! But if I do none of those things on the way back, if I do *not* open the club face, do *not* bend the left arm, *or* relax the right knee, *or* open the hands, I shall not have to make the corresponding corrections on the way down—and in consequence my swing will become simple and connected instead of complex and disjointed."

"Yes, I see."

"The return movement of the swing starts with the left heel returning to the ground, and this reacts on the legs, hips, pivot, and shoulders to produce the centrifugal sweep of the club head. Every part of the swing reacts naturally and immediately to the rest of it—but, if you introduce breaks and disconnections, this natural certain reaction is lost and the whole swing becomes uncertain."

. . . .

"A man's swing is largely the result of his conception of what a swing should be, and the best way of correcting a faulty swing is to *get the correct conception*. Now this lesson has altered your conception; so you can recognize faults in your swing that you could not recognize before—apart from probably introducing some new ones!"

"But I want to get better—not worse."

"True. But you came to me because you were at a dead end. You may now go much further back and become really bad, because your swing was full of compensatory movements which will not work now you have a proper conception of what a swing should be. Your choice is plain; you can either:

Go on compensating and remain 5, or

Start working on the new conception."

"Well, if I do the latter, what are the chances of real improvement?"

"It's up to you," I said. "I never knew anyone who worked on those lines without making progress. But it means work and it means that at first you must not trouble about results."

"Is it worth it?"

"It is. One day the curtain that has been obscuring your view will be pulled back, and you will play a real golf shot. Then you go on, probably losing that real shot almost as soon as you find it—but never mind. The good shots will recur and become more frequent and just as one day you found you had played a good shot, later you will *play a good hole*. Then it is only a matter of patience and work until 68 appears on your card. Is it worth it? I should say it is!"

Beyond Percy—Feel Simple Golf

Regardless of the paradigm you have of the golf swing, you want your swing to produce specific outcomes. Following is how the Feel Simple Golf fundamentals achieve these outcomes.

Integration of the Fundamentals and
Elements of the Golf Swing

In making a golf swing, you want four outcomes: distance, direction, trajectory of the shot, and to get these outcomes consistently. Distance, direction, and trajectory are determined by the five fundamentals of the swing: starting position, pivot, body balance, swing width, and psychology of the swing. Swing consistency is determined by a simple swing movement made by automaticity. Your swing's pivot is the main factor in the distance and direction of your shot.

1. Distance: The pivot generates centrifugal force in the swing that is released through the ball. An unrestricted pivot requires body balance that provides a stable base on which your pivot can take place. Body balance is established in your starting position by positioning your weight equally between your two feet and within each foot (i.e., ball and heel). Body balance is maintained throughout the swing using upward, inward, behind, and profile bracing, which are set up in your starting position. An unrestricted pivot occurs when the mechanics of the swing are completed in the correct sequence at the correct time. The power of your swing and resulting distance is increased through the lag set up in your starting position through the profiling of the hips and increased through the one-after-the-other forward swing pivot. Power is increased further through swing width established in your starting

position and maintained throughout your swing with inward, upward, and behind bracing.
2. Direction: The direction of your golf shot depends upon a good pivot that returns the club head squarely to the ball at impact as set up in your starting position. Like distance, the direction of your shot is best when a good pivot is made, which requires good body balance being established in your starting position and maintained throughout your swing, with bracing built into your starting position. Proper alignment of your shoulders and feet to the ball must be set up in the starting position. Good rhythm and timing ensure your pivot occurs with all swing mechanics completed in the correct sequence and at the correct time to return the club head squarely to the ball.
3. Trajectory: Trajectory, the curve of the ball in flight (e.g., high or low and straight, right to left, or left to right), is set up in your starting position through the grip of your hands on the club, the position of your arms, the position of the ball in relation to your feet, and the inward bracing of your arms and shoulders. Good swing width also helps provide the ideal trajectory.
4. Consistency: The consistency of your swing, being able to repeat a correct swing movement, is determined by a simple swing movement. A simple swing is created when your swing is made with good body balance so compensatory movements are not needed. Your swing is simple when few parts of your body move freely or independently throughout. A connected swing results from bracing so your lower body, shoulders, arms, and hands move as a single unit on your backswing pivot. Your swing also remains simple when a single power source (i.e., pivoting of the lower body) is used throughout your swing. Linking together the feels of a good starting position, pivot, body balance, and swing width into

a single feel that is repeated through automaticity provides more simplicity to your swing. When the swing mechanics are made in the correct sequence with good timing, tempo, and rhythm, your swing becomes more consistent.

CHAPTER XXII

Putting

"To teach yourself to putt successfully, you must study the putt in its relation to the technique of every other shot in the game, not as a thing apart. That is why I say to my pupils at the very start of their golfing days, 'I putt as I drive.'"

Chapter Summary

This chapter applies the fundamentals of the full swing to the putting movement. It shows how to "putt as you drive" and "drive as you putt." This single swing movement used from putting to driving simplifies the learning and playing of golf and helps strengthen automaticity. Like every other shot in golf, the power and direction of a putt come from the pivot.

Today's Takeaway

Percy explains the basis for his mantra, "I putt as I drive and drive as I putt." Percy's approach to the golf swing is a "system" where all the parts interact with and support each other. Being part of that system, the putting movement is basically the same as the movement for every other golf shot. The same fundamentals for the full swing are used for putting. As Percy said, golf is one whole game that cannot be pulled apart into separate pieces.

To "putt as you drive and drive as you putt" simplifies the swing movement, simplifies the playing of golf (e.g., no need to determine which swing movement to use for each shot), makes practice time more efficient (i.e., no need to invest time in a full swing movement as well as a separate putting movement), and promotes the strengthening of automaticity.

As with the full swing, no action is made to intentionally use the hands in the putting movement. Feels of the swing, including the three primary feels, are linked into a controlled putting movement.

Feels

All the sensations of the full swing are experienced in the putting movement. Additional feels for putting are as follows:

- Slight and delicate.
- Very little centrifugal force is generated.
- Rolling (not striking) the ball along from behind.
- Right hand and club head as one.
- Right hand and forearm muscles light and flexible (like holding a pen).
- Club head staying low and back as it carries through.
- Feel of correct speed leads to feel of direction.

Percy's Teachings in His Words (p. 220-232)

Take "putting is a game within a game." If you accept that and its implication—that putting needs a method of approach and technique different from that of the rest of golf—your chance of ever becoming a first-class putter drops to round about zero. Putting is *not* a game within a game: it is *the* game. It is the essence of correct golfing mechanism. If anyone who has a proper conception of the golf swing will apply this same conception to the putt, his putting will improve in consequence.

Now this chapter is on putting not on catch-phrases, but I want to deal with one more of the latter here because it may help us to get this matter of putting into perspective. "A good putter is a match for anyone." That phrase was popular and accepted as it is now when my great compatriot Harry Vardon was in his prime. Because with the limelight on him Harry had been seen to miss some absurdly short putts, some people (but not the folk he played against) put him down as "a poor putter."

The greatest putter of the time beyond doubt or question was Willy Park. So Willy was pitted against Vardon to confirm the adage that a good putter is a match for anyone. He did not confirm it; how Harry won that match is historic . . . *he pitched so close to the hole that he did not have to putt well.*

So we must rewrite the slogan and make it, "a good golfer is a match for anyone," not a good putter any more than a good driver or a good mashie player. Golf is one whole game. It is true that if you cannot putt you cannot win, for no hole is won until the ball is down—but good scores are only made possible by good play up to the green.

. . . .

To teach yourself to putt successfully, you must study the putt *in its relation to the technique of every other shot in the game,* not as a thing apart. That is why I say to my pupils at the very start of their golfing days, "I putt as I drive."

Of course, having seen with their own eyes the fierce sweeping through of a long drive and mentally compared it with the delicate accuracy with which a short putt is stroked on its way, they look incredulous when I first tell them this. Later, as their understanding of the game develops, they see the truth of it—though some of them are then inclined to argue that, "I putt as I drive," should really run "I drive as I putt!"

Now as I have told you, I wanted to find a mechanical action—a golf movement—with which *all* shots could be played, so as to develop perfect and uncomplicated reflex movements. I hope I have already made it clear why it is that if we change our fundamental golf movement for the playing of *any* shot, that shot not only fails to help build up reliable feel and reflex movements—it actually complicates and confuses the feels and reflex movements which have been built up.

Before I had reached my present conclusion on these matters, I knew that Bobby Jones had said that the putting stroke was like any other and that in actual application the Pendulum Stroke is a physical impossibility. Incidentally he had also classified keeping the head still as a fallacious golf maxim. Also one day when Walter Hagen was putting, he turned to Aubrey and said, "I can't stroke from in-to-out to-day."

Now all of this confirmed my opinion that it should be possible to putt as we drive and encouraged me in my search for the method. And you need not be surprised that it took me quite a few years to find and to master it.

REVERSED OR PUTTING GRIP

POINTS TO STUDY

The reversed overlapping grip gives more right-hand feel. (In fact, the palm of the right hand facing the hole gives the impression that the ball will be "rolled out of the hand towards the hole.")

The club is held not in the tips of the fingers of the right hand, but down at the roots of the fingers. The right thumb is on the top of the shaft.

The right elbow and forearm rest lightly in the curve made by hip and thigh.

The back of the left hand rests lightly on the left thigh. The left elbow is almost facing the hole . . . as is the back of the left hand.

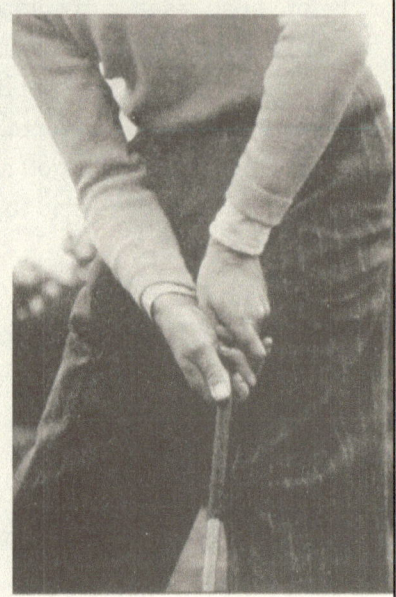

REVERSED OR PUTTING GRIP

AUBREY

Both knees are slightly bent, the weight is well back on the heels—as if sitting on a shooting stick.

The weight is more on the left foot than on the right. The ball is just inside the left heel.

Firstly, the fundamental golf movement is centrifugal, and we are used to using centrifugal forces so forcefully that to tone it down until one could stroke home a nasty four-foot putt on a fast green took some doing. But when it *was* done, I found I could sink more of these nasty short putts than I could before.

. . . .

Since in putting the movement is so slight and delicate, very little centrifugal force is generated, and it is most difficult to feel the club head; so we try to get as much feel as possible in the right hand. That is the reason for adopting the reverse overlapping grip—it gives increased right-hand feel.

. . . .

"Let the club head do the work," is just as good advice in putting as in driving. But how much work *is* there in putting—how much pressure does it need to roll a ball four or five yards? Practically none; therefore the tension in our muscular system should be practically nil. The last thing I say to myself before I take my putter back is, "Don't tighten, you old fool."

The next thing I had to work out was which was the primary of those two essentials, strength and direction. And I concluded that strength came first.

Now, before I came to this conclusion, I thought all over and around the subject and studied it in practice, especially in tournament play and in the four-ball exhibition matches which Aubrey and I used to play a great deal ten to eighteen years ago.

I remember holing three successive putts from eight to ten yards in such a match against Jurado and Perri on the Mar del Plata course. As we walked to the next tee after the third of them went down, Aubrey said to me, "How in the name of fortune do you find the line over these greens?" He might well ask [if] the greens were terrors! Well, the answer was that I did not try deliberately to find the line—I looked for the feel of the *strength* of the shot, and the direction developed out of that feel. That is why I say that strength comes before direction.

How can you learn to develop this sense of direction out of the feeling of strength? Firstly, do not putt at a hole. Just learn how far you can possibly make the ball *roll*. The farther you can make it roll with a given feel of power applied, the better you are stroking the ball. This is an essential study; it is so important that often, when I see people practicing at a hole before a tournament, I feel they would do much better to take at least a few preliminary putts without the preoccupation of the hole at all. The good putter is the one whose ball starts to *roll over as soon as it leaves contact with the club head.*

. . . .

You can do a great deal to develop *dead strength* by constant practice on your carpet. As it develops, a sense of direction will begin to appear, and it is in this sense of direction that you will begin to trust. In fact, you must *feel* direction rather than see it. Of course, what you see with your eyes does help you to find the line, but alone it is not enough.

. . . .

Incidentally, there is one reason not generally appreciated why we Pros take so long looking for the line on the greens in tournament play—it helps us to keep quiet and not to hurry. To see old Ted Ray creeping up to the ball, as he used to do after he had got his line, was a lesson in preparation for a smooth feline stroking of the ball.

. . . .

Next, do not try to take the club head back along the line of flight. Take it back low with the left hand and do not open the blade. If you will study this on a carpet with lines on it, you will find that when you do this the blade goes *inside* in spite of you. This is as it should be; in putting as in driving or playing any other shot, we should not consciously *take* the club inside on the way back; though if we are properly set well back on our heels and keep the putter blade low, that is where it will go.

To *lift* the putter blade back is putting suicide. To keep it low in the follow through is one of the signs of the great artist.

. . . .

But I warn you that all this will be of no avail if you hold yourself stiffly. To putt well we must be supple and loose. We must not be flabby; we must be conscious of our body being held up by its braces, yet not so braced as to impede movement. All our muscles must be mobilized, *but they must be mobile*. Do not sway to-and-fro, but on the other hand do not get *fixed;* there is a great deal of difference.

Remember that if we are to swing our putter head correctly *every muscle* from head to foot must co-operate. Some of their movements are invisible; some of their changes in tension infinitesimal; yet they are all essential. The putt is just as responsive a movement as is a full shot, and there must be opposition to every movement.

I have told you that I putt as I drive, so the same rules hold. If when you are driving you become a direct hitter, you will begin to pull and slice and exactly the same thing will happen (on a reduced scale of course) if you hit your putts direct.

And to close this chapter I will give you a paradox to think out. No beginner thinks putting difficult; he just goes up to the ball and taps it along to the hole, and as often as not it goes in. It is not until he misses a few as he is bound to do that he forsakes this natural and effective if inelegant style and tries to "learn how"—from then on he becomes an ordinary handicap putter. So here is the paradox: natural golfers are *bad* golfers but natural putters are *good* putters.

Beyond Percy—Feel Simple Golf

Approximately 40 percent of strokes during a round of golf are taken up by putts. The best way to improve your score is to improve your putting.

In John's decade-long journey to develop the Feel Simple Golf integrated approach to the golf swing, the unique rotational putting method presented in *Feel. Simple. Golf.* was the most challenging and interesting part of his journey.

Rotational putting is the answer to Percy's call for a single swing movement from putting to driving. This section covers what we believe to be one of the most significant contributions of John's work in advancing Boomer's teachings on the golf swing.

Unsuccessful Remedies

Golf club designers and manufacturers are involved in helping golfers try to remove the inconsistent results of putting when the arms and hands are used. Over the years, a variety of putter types have been made to do this. Examples are the long putter and the belly putter. These putters were designed to have the golfer anchor the end of the putter handle against the chest or stomach. This anchoring served as a brace, connecting the shoulders, arms, and hands and giving a simpler and more consistent pendulum swing.

In 2013, the governing bodies of golf (i.e., the R&A and the United States Golf Association) passed a rule prohibiting the anchoring of the putter or forearms to the body as part of the putting movement. Based upon these rules, Percy's setup that had the left hand rest lightly on the left thigh and right elbow and forearm in the curve made by the hip and thigh is no longer permitted.

Golfers responded to this new rule by giving more attention to how they hold the putter. A number of different putting grips developed over the years to limit the negative effects of the arms and hands, including the following:

- the cross-handed grip (i.e., switching the placement of the hands on the putter handle),
- the claw grip (i.e., not wrapping the fingers of the right hand around the putter but gripping the handle with the thumb and inside of the fingers while keeping the fingers straight), and
- bracing the long putter shaft against the left forearm.

A number of other changes to the typical putting grip can be seen. These changes all attempt to limit the inconsistent effects of using the arms and hands to power and guide the putting movement. There is no agreement on the best answer, so the search continues.

Rotational Putting
==================

Percy said he "putts as he drives," while others argued they "drive as they putt." Following is how rotational putting makes that happen.

The movement of the feet, pivoting of the lower body, and use of bracing to maintain body balance and swing width are important parts of the rotational putting movement. Longer putts involve more shifting of weight within each foot to get the right amount of centrifugal force. Body balance is established and maintained throughout the putting movement through bracing and the positioning and movement of weight in the feet. Swing width comes from bracing. A good pivot, body balance, and swing width are set up in the starting position.

This is exactly what you do for the full swing. The connected and controlled swing presented in this book is a good solution to properly using the arms and hands in the putting movement. Rotational putting involves only slight changes to the grip and alignment position in the starting position.

Benefits of Rotational Putting

Using the same swing movement from driving to putting has the following advantages:

- There is no need to develop a putting movement that is different from all other swing movements.
- Time is used more effectively, since practice putting directly benefits your other swings.
- Automaticity of the swing movement is strengthened and not confused with using different movements.

Using this rotational putting movement driven by the pivot with a connected and reactive upper body will feel strange and unnatural at first. Within minutes of practicing, the feel of greater stability and simplicity (i.e., connectedness) in the putting movement will be felt. The increased feel of power in the putting movement is very noticeable.

Introducing new students to rotational putting early in the teaching process makes a lot of sense. Experiencing the feel of the pivot is easier on the practice putting green since the reactive movement of the upper body is relatively small (e.g., arms do not raise much). Once the pivot is practiced on the putting green, using the pivot in the chipping area and on the driving range comes more quickly and more easily.

CHAPTER XXIII

Interlude for Reminiscence

"You see, the golf swing is such an unknown equation to most people that any fellow with the gift of gab and twenty years' experience of pulling and slicing can make it *sound* as though he knows what he is talking about when he expounds it."

Chapter Summary

Percy shares his amusement, and likely disgust, for golfers who know very little about the golf swing and aren't really interested in learning but take joy in sharing everything they think they know with everybody who will listen, even if those listening know much more. These are "golf maniacs."

Today's Takeaway

An old saying goes something like, "He who knows and knows that he knows is a wise man; follow him. He who knows not, and knows not that he knows not, is a fool; shun him." The golf maniac thinks he knows all about the golf swing (and is more than willing to share it *all* with you) when, in reality, he knows very little. Avoid the golf maniac, or escape, if you can. In an earlier chapter, Percy describes that the best golfer in the club house is likely the one who is most modest and humble and who spends the most amount of time in the golf shed. The golf maniac is the exact opposite.

The golf maniac is in each of us at some time or another. It is a phase we should all pass through if we have a reliable way to do it. Having the correct mental image of a sound working technique of the golf swing will keep us grounded instead of being lost in unreality. Please don't be a golf maniac.

Percy's Teachings in His Words (p. 233-239)

One of the perennial joys of golf is the way it fits in with and illuminates the character of the fellow who knows all about it: The Omniscient Golf Maniac.

There are more maniacs in golf than there are in any other sport, and they have more fun too! You see, the golf swing is such an unknown equation to most people that any fellow with the gift of gab and twenty years' experience of pulling and slicing can make it *sound* as though he knows what he is talking about when he expounds it.

There are five or six of these cranks in nearly every club, and when they get together the feathers are apt to fly! The one characteristic of every member of the clan is that he is entirely impervious to every idea and theory except his own.

I remember three of these fellows all round about the (sympathetic) 3 handicap mark having a rabid argument in our shop about that fertile subject, the shut face, and proving—to their own satisfaction any way—that one or two suggestions that Aubrey and I made were nonsense.

Well then, they took Aubrey out into a four-ball. They gave him one up and he proceeded to beat their best ball 4 and 3. They were so wrapped up in their own game and their own theories that they failed to notice that he had gone round in 64, which was eight under par.

Still, when they came back they continued to tell us how to take the club back and so on. They knew Aubrey had just beaten them, but it never occurred to them that he knew more about golf than they did.

We Pros do know quite a bit about the game. If we seem to differ a lot in our methods, it is because method is not the ultimate aim in golf, and methods (like fashions) are always changing.

One thing that the Pro nearly always has and the maniac nearly always lacks is a balanced psychophysical conception of how to go about the game so as to get par figures for 18 holes in a round for four rounds in succession, or a dozen if necessary.

These cranks spend the greater part of their lives not so much hitting the ball as figuring out *how* to hit it. They will tell you they are realists but actually they are the most visionary idealists in the world today! Their world is utterly remote from reality.

. . . .

But to return to the Golf Bore (as also we so frequently have to!). One world-famous English club numbered one of the greatest among its members. He was no great performer on the course, but in the club room he could (and did) tell exactly how every shot should be played and exactly what and why his partner and opponents had done wrong. *In theory* he was omniscient.

His fellow-members, feeling perhaps that they were too much honored in being the sole recipients of so much golfing wisdom, decided to give it wider circulation. So, to the delight and surprise of the omniscient one there appeared one day on the table in the club reading-room a beautifully bound book titled "All I know about Golf" with the omniscient one's name as author.

Delight and surprise, did I say? Well he was certainly delighted by the beautifully printed title page (how well his name looked!), by the brief but almost fulsome introduction by an amateur champion, and by the preface by a celebrated golf journalist—the surprise came in the body of the book, where All-he-knew-about-golf was set out on two-hundred-and-forty-six utterly blank pages!

Beyond Percy—Feel Simple Golf

What more can be said without making us look like golf maniacs? Well, we will try.

Learning to play golf well does not need to take years or a lifetime. After reading *Feel. Simple. Golf.,* you will have an understanding of how the golf swing works that few others have. Practice sessions will become more focused, fun, efficient, and effective. We are confident in teaching the golf swing based on this system because John first built it into his swing and uses it in competition. John truly does practice what he teaches. Second, John has seen his students build the fundamentals into their swings and regularly see quick improvement. Golf becomes fun and the motivation to practice and play increases because tangible results are there.

<u>John's Promise</u>

If you have taken golf lessons in the past, I promise you that what you will learn from *Feel. Simple. Golf.* makes more sense; is more comprehensive; is easier to understand; simplifies your swing; and makes learning, improving, and playing your golf swing more fun. (*Feel. Simple. Golf.*)

Feel Simple Golf is based on Percy Boomer's timeless teachings!

CHAPTER XXIV

Golf Analysis

"You must analyze before you can teach. It is useless just to develop a fine swing yourself and say to your pupil, 'Now copy me!' So we must analyze and base our teaching upon what our analysis reveals."

Chapter Summary

Percy gives examples of where faulty analyses of the golf swing come from superficial analyses based on limited experience. Without careful and deep analysis based on deep and wide personal experience, the real cause of a troubled swing may not be what it initially and obviously seems to be. The right correction to a troubled swing must be based on an accurate analysis.

Today's Takeaway

The golf swing is full of complexities. That must be the case, since there are 500 best swing tips. That leads one to wonder: if there are that many best swing tips, how many good swing tips might there be?

Percy gives three examples of swing problems and how each is analyzed. He gives one incorrect and one correct analysis for each problem. Percy cautions against accepting swing analyses from inexperienced individuals who fail to provide careful and deep analysis.

Without identifying the true root cause of a swing problem, identifying the correct fix is not certain. Turning to quick fixes based on swing tips from well-meaning people could lead to further swing problems.

Here is a summary of the three swing problems Percy considers. With each problem is the common (but incorrect) analysis and the correct analysis. Mixed in with the correct analyses is the important role of opposing forces in the swing.

Swing Problem 1: Hitting the top of the ball	
Common (But Incorrect) Analysis	**Correct Analysis**
Raising the head lifts the shoulders, which lifts the arms, which lifts the club head, which strikes the top of the ball.	Opposing forces. The body goes down to the ball while the arms break at the elbow. The club head is raised and hits the top of the ball. The body does not "stretch up" from the feet and legs (i.e., body sags down), restricting the opposing force of "stretching down" through the arms to the ball.
Swing Problem 2: Impacting through the ball while up on the toes	
Common (But Incorrect) Analysis	**Correct Analysis**
It "is" a problem that needs to be fixed.	No problem, the swing is good. This is a good result of using opposing forces. The shoulders are "down," and there is a sense of "stretching down" through the arms while "stretching up" through the body from the feet and legs. The opposing forces have kept the head and shoulders fixed in place. This full stretch allows the wrists to flail properly through the ball.

Swing Problem 3: Restricted follow-through	
Common (But Incorrect) Analysis	**Correct Analysis**
Faulty arm work.	The setup is off balance. The right shoulder dips below the left shoulder, causing the right hip to dip and slide toward the target; upward and behind bracing have broken and the right side has buckled, blocking the body from completing the swing in the follow-through.

Percy's swing analyses are beyond what most of us are capable of doing. Having a firm understanding of the golf swing as a system, based on the swing fundamentals of pivot, body balance, swing width, and starting position, provides a good foundation to do a careful and deep analysis of swing faults. Be aware of your knowledge of the swing and your ability to do a deep analysis before analyzing somebody's swing problem and offering corrections.

Feels

Percy identifies the following supplementary feels of a good swing:

- Stretching up through the body.
- Stretching down through the arms and ball.
- Club swinging wide through the ball and on and around the left side

Percy's Teachings in His Words (p. 240-248)

I astonish my pupils when I tell them, as I sometimes do, that for the first twenty years I was teaching golf, I taught it all wrong. They think I am simply decrying my early efforts as a teacher. Actually I tell them this to suggest what an extraordinarily difficult game golf is to analyze and to teach.

You must analyze before you can teach. It is useless just to develop a fine swing yourself and say to your pupil, "Now copy me!" So we must analyze and base our teaching upon what our analysis reveals. But here is a warning—unless your analysis is very deep and close and based upon wide experience, it may mislead you.

Now this is a matter of immediate concern and interest to every advanced golfer whether he wants to be taught or to teach himself. So in this penultimate chapter I will give you a few examples of golf paradoxes which will show you what I mean and point out the sort of traps that golf analysis holds for the unwary. I will start with a question.

Why do you sometimes top your ball?

"That is easy," I can hear you say. "I top my ball when I take my eye off it, because this raises my head which fetches my shoulders up, and *they* pull up my arms—with the natural consequence that I either hit the top of my ball or swing right over it."

Now that or something very like it would be the answer of nine-ninety-nine players out of a thousand. It would have been *my* answer for the first twenty years of my teaching life, but I now know that it is wrong. You do not top the ball because you pull up your body just before impact *but because you drop it.*

You may think that that will take some explaining. It will! Also I can tell you that it took some analyzing to discover.

The first thing to get clear in your mind is the difference between *pulling up* your body and *stretching up through your body.* This latter is essential to one of the most important feels in golf—the feel of *down through the ball.* And it is relevant to note (since it suggests where the ball is contacted) that the higher you want to pitch the ball the more essential is this *down* feeling, a feeling which is the opposite of scooping the club head up.

. . . .

"Well," says I, "here is one who says it isn't. If you take my advice, you will forget that picture and any idea it has produced in you, and go on playing as you played that shot."

"But it seems all wrong."

"It is *not* all wrong," said I. "Look! your head and shoulders are beautifully *down* and that's all you need to have down. Then see your stretch up through the body—it's marvelous; that is what gives you your wrist snap and makes you such a long hitter for such a little dainty lady."

Now, how does this up-on-the-toes position work in with that point I am always harping on—that the first movement on the return is to bring the left heel solidly and squarely back to the turf?

The return of the left heel to the ground is necessary in order to have an equal balance between the two feet. By the time this balance is achieved, we are nearing the impact—and the stretching up through the body necessary to fling the wrists open reacts as a rising-on-the-toes movement.

You can say that the up-on-the-toes is a reaction to the stretching up through the body or that the effective flinging open of the wrists is a reaction to up-on-the-toes. But whichever way you like to think of it, you will find that the prominent golfer is up-on-the-toes in the region of impact.

Now let me explain the difference between lifting up the shoulders and head and *stretching* up through the body from the feet and legs. You have only to shrug your shoulders to lift them, the stretching is rather more complex. It is an established *feel* in all good golfers that they *stretch down* through their arms as they come into contact with the ball, but you cannot stretch against nothing; so they have to stretch *up* from the feet to set up the necessary resistance in the shoulders. We have to *fix* the top of our swing by giving it something to pull against; otherwise we cannot stretch tautly down from it. We fix the top end by bracing and stretching up to hold our shoulders firmly in place.

If we relax our brace and stretch and let our body sag down ever so little, this top fixing "gives" a little and we no longer keep the feeling of stretching down through the ball. That is where the topped shots come from.

There is a clear difference between *lifting* the shoulders and *holding them up*. If we lift our shoulders, we lift our arms out of position, but if we push up from our feet, we may be using equal or greater muscular force simply to hold our shoulder in position against the terrific down-pull of the club head. Consequently, we may even *feel* that we are rising up when actually we are doing no more than resisting in an upward direction the force of the club head which is pulling down. That is why you may find, if you study a whole film with an up-on-the-toes finish, that, in spite of the up-on-the-toes movement, the head and shoulders have not been raised even a fraction of an inch.

If you wish to analyze these movements in yourself by feel, do not try it with your long clubs first. The difference between the feels of lifting the body and of holding the shoulders up through the feet is subtle, so subtle that it is easily lost in the violence of a long shot. You will recognize it much more quickly with a mashie-niblick. The feeling you want is not a gross one, but a feel that we stretch upward against the ground with our legs and feet—gradually and without haste. The push of the ground opposes the pull of the club head.

All golf is opposition. We are in a state of opposing in every phase of our swing, even in the waggle. *The very feel of the club head is only sensed when we are in a state of opposition to it.*

Close students of the game will have noticed that the body sags down as the club reaches the top, so that the player's head may be inches closer to the ball at the apex of the swing; the player is thus opposing and retaining the feel of the club head. At the bottom of the swing the forces and positions will be reversed. The body comes down when the club head is up and goes up as the club head comes down. Opposition again. These up and down movements are not something we do consciously; they are automatic adjustments of balance in opposition.

To return to the upward stretch. Some of you may have been told in a more elaborate phrase to "elongate the left side." This, I think, is a bad doctrine. It does result in some sort of stretch, but an unbalanced one—and one of its most direct results is the plunging right shoulder. We must stretch through the whole center of our equilibrium, right side as well as left, right foot as well as left, right shoulder as well as left.

The plunging right shoulder is fatal because if your right shoulder dips below its correct position relative with the left, you cannot go on through the ball—you become *blocked* just as you get past the ball. The right shoulder must be felt to come square against the back of the ball, neither under nor above it.

This dipping is a fault of the right hip as well as the right shoulder. One is the counterpart of the other. When we see a fellow with his club and hands curled around his left leg at the finish, we know that his right side has buckled on the way down, and so his follow through has been blocked.

Now let us go into this question of the right shoulder more minutely. I want you to become much more conscious of your right shoulder than of your left. When my left heel and leg are going forward I feel that my right shoulder goes back, but I have enough experience to know that what is probably happening is that my right shoulder is stationary in relation to the hips. We feel we are pushing it back when actually we are holding it back—but that is the basic difficulty of analyzing golf feels; we mistake opposition for movement.

Let me again stress here why I prefer the word "oppose" to "resist." Resist suggests something static, oppose is resistance in movement. Also, oppose suggests *direction*. If you *resist* a pull you stand stock still and resist with your weight; if you *oppose* a pull you oppose by a pull in the opposite direction, which is what we are continually doing in golf.

THE SWING

POINTS TO STUDY

Obviously a very young swing, not faultless, but fundamentally good.

1. A wide swing. Left arm straight, left wrist fully broken back. The shoulders are still turned away from the ball while the hips are turned towards it, giving body flail.
2. The left leg has straightened, but the wrists are still broken back.
3. Shoulders now square with the line of flight. Up on the toes, stretching upwards through the body so that the wrists will snap open downwards.
4. Left heel back to the ground. Head still down. Right arm straight . . . elbows still held together.

THE SWING 1, 2, 3, 4
GEORGE
(Age 17)

In the sequence, the hands, and consequently the club head, have come down yet along.

FAULTS

In position 2 and 3 the right leg is too stiff. He is looking at the ball with his right eye instead of "peeping at it with his left eye."

A boy with a catapult is a good illustration of opposition; he pulls in the direction opposite to that he wants his shot to take. He stretches his elastic; we must stretch our bodies—only upwards. And the more you can stretch *up*, the more you can feel *down*, which is what I want you to feel beyond everything.

Now I think that a lot of nearly good players would become really good ones if they learned to manage their hips correctly. I talked just now of becoming blocked just past the ball. This is not due (as it is often assumed to be) to faulty arm work, but to allowing the hips to slide out in the direction of the hole—where they effectively stop any chance of the follow through being carried on and around.

If you will brace your hips in the way I have described, you will feel them *as part of a whole* not as a break in that whole. And it is when we feel the hips and waist as a break that we go wrong. Bending at the waist must be due to suppleness of the waist *not* to disarticulation of the hips. Of course, the hips do articulate during the pivot, but they must do so controlled by the brace; they must be moved, but they must not be allowed to slop around.

The braces and stretches of the golf movement, from feet up through the body and down through arm and hands, combine into one *feel*, the feel that we swing our club wide through the ball and on and around the left side. The correct manipulation of the hips enables this feel to be maintained, but if the hips are disarticulated the whole framework of the feel is broken up.

Well, there we are! Just a few of the consideration which arise when we try to analyze that elementary and fatal fault of lifting up. So I hope you will see how essential an accurate analysis is before we can hope to effect a true correction.

Beyond Percy—Feel Simple Golf

In Rick Bradshaw's foreword to *Feel. Simple. Golf.*, he wrote, "I often say to my golf students that I want them to discover one or two thoughts that make thirty things happen versus thinking about thirty thoughts to make one thing happen." Percy stresses that it takes a highly experienced person to do the careful and deep swing analyses to identify those one or two things to fix the root cause of a troubled swing. Swing analysis is difficult because a single root cause of a swing problem (e.g., in the pivot, body balance, swing width, or starting position) might show up in the form of many symptoms.

Percy's decades of teaching experience prepared him to spot

the root cause of a swing problem very quickly. Percy could have overwhelmed the student with the details of the analyses that were performed to get the diagnosis. Or he could have simply suggested a better concept for the student's swing that would resolve the problem. How much depth Percy went into might have depended upon the knowledge level of the student and the student's desire for a deeper understanding of the golf swing.

John's Consultation with Paul

Not long ago, Paul told John of an ongoing swing problem. After weeks having not observed Paul's golf swing, John had him take a few swings. John immediately saw the source of his problem.

John took Paul on a journey of discovery. Like Percy, John has studied and experimented with the golf swing his entire life and is a golf swing scientist as well as teacher. To confirm his growth as a teacher, John experimented with Paul using two teaching approaches.

First, John focused on swing mechanics using a "500 best swing tips" approach. John had Paul take the club straight back on the backswing pivot up to waist high. John worked with him on how he was setting up his swing in the starting position. John reviewed with him the desired swing path of the club as well as faulty swing paths. These and more were all pieces related to Paul's swing problem.

Looking into Paul's eyes, John could see that his brain was overloaded with mental processing. He was becoming overwhelmed, confused, and frustrated. Paul's swing fault was not going away.

John quickly shifted to a second teaching approach—one based on the swing fundamentals and the correct concept of the swing. John helped Paul see that he was using too much of his hands in the swing, which broke connection and restricted his pivot. John suggested a better concept—a connected swing powered by the pivot, keeping the hands reactive throughout the swing. With the correct concept of the swing back in his brain, Paul said, "Oh, okay. I can do that." The next few swings showed that, indeed, his swing fault was fixed.

This journey of discovery confirmed that teaching within a system based on integrated swing fundamentals and a correct concept of the golf swing is easier, less confusing, less frustrating, and more effective than following the 500 best swing tips approach.

CHAPTER XXV

Inverse Functioning

"When you watch a good golfer driving, you may feel that he has a perfect conception of the pivot, but you would probably be much nearer the truth in thinking that he had a perfect conception of the follow through."

Chapter Summary

Percy describes his process of teaching golf and how golf is best learned by students. While teaching and learning the golf swing begin with mechanics, the desired end is to play by feel with all the mechanics happening automatically. The learning of the golf swing is a step-by-step process without shortcuts. The good golfer understands the feels that get the desired outcome and is able to repeat those feels consistently. In the "set" before the swing is made, the good golfer anticipates a good swing with the desired outcome by knowing, recalling, and repeating the feels of that swing.

Today's Takeaway

In this final chapter, Percy once again takes us into his laboratory of the golf swing and gives some important lessons. Inverse functioning provides a process for how to best teach and learn the golf swing. The "set" is part of what separates a great golfer from a mediocre one. Lastly, the importance of continuous movement of the feet is explained.

Inverse Functioning

Inverse functioning involves teaching and learning certain movements directly in order that they may later be used indirectly. Percy's process with a student was to (1) teach a swing mechanic, (2) develop a concept of the mechanic that includes what the mechanic caused to happen in the swing and how it felt, and then (3) concentrate on the feel to get the desired results. This is how Percy taught, how he knew students learned best, and how a student would be able to swing well regardless of the circumstances.

Although the pivot is involved in (as a means to) a good swing, the concept of the follow-through is the basis for a good swing (the end objective).

The "Set"

A good golfer succeeds before ever making a swing. This player knows the feel of a good shot in his or her "set" prior to the swing. The set is the feel the golfer has before the swing that makes the desired shot. In this pre-shot feeling, the golfer (1) has a concept of the desired swing, (2) knows the feel of the desired swing, and (3) knows the movements needed to achieve that concept and feel. The set helps the golfer make the proper swing movements and avoid poor ones.

Feel

While the set is more likely to be felt by the better golfer, all golfers must experience the feel of the feet moving continuously. Your knees must continue shifting weight at the "reverse" (Chapter X) when the backswing pivot transitions to the forward swing pivot. If your knees pause to allow the upper body to catch up with the lower body, the one-after-the-other forward swing pivot doesn't happen, and no lag is created in your swing.

Final Thoughts

As you grow in the game of golf, your concepts and theories will grow. Through experience, you become better able to visualize the swing and your feels. Over time, you can more effectively set up and make your desired shots. Learning golf is a step-by-step process without shortcuts. Having and following an integrated system of the golf swing makes the process simpler and quicker and leads to more consistent power and direction. Regardless of your skill level, take your time and be sure the pieces fit together for you into a unified whole, and the game will reward you.

Percy's Teachings in His Words (p. 249-258)

There is a curious evolution in the learning of golf which for want of a better phrase I have called inverse functioning. It arises because we have to teach certain movements *directly* in order that they may later be used *indirectly.*

Consider the pivot. We have to teach you how to pivot by telling you or showing you how it is done and asking you to do it that way. That is, we teach it directly as if it were an end in itself. Yet, no good experienced golfer pivots directly like that—his *pivot is the outcome of his correct conception of the follow through.*

The act of pivoting has two basic functions:

1. to guide the club head,
2. to generate power.

We know that we must feel that the club head is brought onto the ball *from in-to-out* and that the peak of the activity of the club head is reached two or three feet *beyond* the ball. So we do not hit *at* the ball *or* down the line of flight—and the experienced golfer has found that the pivot is an essential factor in producing the in-to-out sweep, through the ball that he has found to be correct because effective.

Now it is really important for you to get this difference in outlook or feeling clearly realized, because until you do, you cannot be anything but a mechanical golfer. So I will put the same thing to you in another way. When you watch a good golfer driving, you may feel that he has a perfect conception of the pivot, but you would probably be much nearer the truth in thinking that he had a perfect conception of the follow through.

If you asked that same golfer *how* he pivoted, he would quite possibly propound some involved and elaborate theory to you when actually he would have been more truthful had he said, "I don't really know how I pivot, but I do know that when I feel like I felt today I can sock that ball *miles!*" In other words, again, his beautiful action has evolved not out of the study of how to turn his body but out of a feeling of how to swing past the ball.

So, when I explain to a beginner the mechanical workings of the pivot, I know that I am beginning backwards. But, just as soon as I can, I reverse the pupil's conception. As soon as the pivot is sufficiently well established for the pupil to feel the club head move from *in-to-out,* I switch over from the pivot as a movement to be made to the pivot as a means of encouraging the club head to travel from in-to-out. And soon most of the emphasis can be put on the feeling of in-to-out, because if he retains this feel his pivot cannot have been lost.

I have just told you that the pivot has two functions, to guide the club and to generate power. Some good golf analysts combine the two and compare the body to a lever, and while this means practically nothing to the moderate golfer, it *is* suggestive to the top-notcher. For he may feel his body as a steel bar turning around between his two feet, with all the time the bones of his big toes *opposing* the movements of the club head—the extremes of the swing.

We must never lose sight of the fact that we are all in different stages of evolution as golfers and that a technique *or a conception* may be good in one stage and yet disastrous in another. For those who can reach it, the turning bar analogy may be fruitful; it certainly is true as you can feel for yourself that the leverage in golf comes up and out from the bones of the feet.

You will feel it better (even the greatest expert can feel it better) if you swing *without* a club rather than with one. There is so much more going on when you swing a club that delicate feels are more difficult to detect. There is, of course, *still more going on* when we add a ball—and yet more again when it is zero hour and our name is called out on the tee! Do not forget that I was a scratch golfer years before I hit a decent shot off the first tee at Meyrick Park.

What has this to do with our subject? A great deal. The point of this chapter is that, while you have to learn golf by direct mechanics, you must play it—as soon as you are able *not* mechanically but through your conception of how it should be played and the *feels* which you have built around this conception. The correct conception is the basis, and that is why I have told you in this book many things that are possibly too advanced for you to make practical use of.

You will probably never come up to the standard which I have set you, but if this book has given you a more correct and comprehensive conception of golf movements, you will get nearer to the highest standards than you would have had you been content with a purely mechanical concept. And, which is perhaps equally important, you are much less likely to recede under pressure.

Even if you do recede a little and if you are unable to play your shots in a tournament as well as I have taught you to play them on the practice ground, remember this: Your opponent is equally anxious to win his match; you will *both* (in consequence) fall back from your normal standard—but, other things being equal, the one of you with the more correct and comprehensive conception of the game will fall back the less.

"But," you may say, endeavoring to pull me back to a point from which I may seem to have wandered, "do you suggest that I must not *think* of pivoting?"

That is exactly what I *do* suggest, *if you are ripe for it*. Your shot and my shot both depend upon the pivot. In the early stages you have to concentrate upon pivoting in order to be able to pivot at all. But I have reached a stage where I can concentrate upon playing a good shot *via* a good follow through which is quite a different outlook.

Do I neglect my pivot in consequence of this? Oh no! I continue to pivot because I know that if I do not I cannot follow through, and I know the consequences of not following through. *Inverse functioning,* that is all! And I do not even follow through because I know I have to but because I feel that there will be no shot unless I do. In fact I have evolved through to *inverse feel.*

On this matter of inverse feel, I must digress for a few minutes. Long before he plays a shot, the first-class golfer has made up his mind how it should feel. The beginner of course has no such pre-shot feeling—which is why he so frequently makes shots which surprise him!

Now I call this pre-shot feeling and its results, *the set.* My dictionary tells me that to "set" is to "put into condition for use," and that is exactly what the set does for a golfer's mechanism. The average golfer walks up to the tee and addresses the ball—we *set ourselves* before we get to the tee and then, through the feeling which the *set* has produced, address the ball.

Do not think that this is mere playing with words. It is in hard fact one of the fundamental differences between the good golfer and the great one. It will be obvious that, if the set is the state of the feel that precedes the mechanical movements necessary to play the desired shot, then the feeling of the set and the stance which it induces will differ when we play a chip shot to when we play a full drive. For though the principle underlying every golf shot is the same, the manner of approach to the shot in hand will differ with the lie of the ball and the distance it is desired to propel it.

And note also that *the set is not static.* It is an image of the whole operation—stance and swing—and if this image is correct and is correctly followed out by the mechanism of the body, the shot *must* be one hundred per cent effective. The set is the image of the whole operation from stance to follow through.

As I have said before, the swing is a continuous unbroken movement that cannot be cut into sections for analysis. So I was delighted when one day an ardent pupil of mine remarked, "I can now play with my set in motion." I was delighted (1) because he had presented me with a clever piece of sense phraseology, (2) because he must have truly sensed the golf shot in order to be able to make such a remark, and (3) because here was proof that after many years I had been able to teach what I feel to be the correct approach to the matter.

You have only to watch a great golfer to realize how much of his secret lies in his pre-shot attitude and approach. To see him walk up to the ball and address it is all you need to tell you *this is a golfer*. His quality is demonstrated before his actual stroke, which merely confirms it. His set *is* his game.

The set has two practical purposes, to induce the right movements and to eliminate faulty ones. To take the second first, it is through his set that the good golfer feels his faults before he swings; the bad golfer only knows *his* after he has missed his shot.

. . . .

But the beginner or moderate player must not become discouraged. We attain the ultimate in golf by stages of evolution and it is undesirable to jump a stage—those who do usually come a cropper. If our evolution is gradual, it is all the better for it, for each stage is well founded before the next is added. And concepts are like food—they need to be well masticated and digested before they can be any good to you.

There is another aspect of the concepts by which we play that is worth considering. I will illustrate it by listing four things that the good golfer does that the bad golfer cannot or does not do. The good golfer:

1. Twists his hips *into* the ball.
2. Thanks to (1), twists his shoulders into the ball.
3. Thanks to (2), keeps the feel of his club traveling outwards, and

4. Takes his divot out straight.

Now this is an interesting little study. You will see that 1, 2, and 3 were all directed towards an effort to swing from *in-to-out*—yet as No. 4 proves he has played down the line of flight with his club head. In short No. 4 is a result which can only be brought about by the setting up of 1, 2, and 3, each of which appears to have a different aim.

Actually all the three factors 1, 2, and 3 are illusionary. No. 3 is the easiest to prove this of. It is *only* when we feel that we are swinging from in-to-out that we do play directly down the line of flight and take our divot out straight.

As to points 1 and 2, I suppose nothing in golf so puzzles the poor player as the way in which the good golfer keeps his right hip and shoulder *inside,* instead of letting them slop out and round. Their puzzlement is due as usual to a wrong conception. The bringing down of the right shoulder inside is *not* a thing that is done directly, a mechanical trick to be learned; it is a *result* of the proper conception of the *timing* of the golf swing.

Except for the initial start back from the ball, the golf swing is a one-after-the-other movement. The feet are one extreme of this movement, the club head is the other; the former move through a very small arc, the latter through a wide one. As a result, the feet finish their movement long before the club head does, if both are moving at the same pace as they should be in the initial stage. The bad golfer, finding that his footwork would be completed long before his arms and club head had even got to the top of their arcs, *waits with his feet* so that he can come down with his feet, shoulders, arms, and club head *all* together. This is why he comes down *outside* and is a bad golfer.

Footwork like everything else in the golf swing must be continuous. It is this continuous, unchecked feel that sets up a *flow* of power. And you can only come *inside* with your hips and shoulders if you keep your feet moving continuously *ahead* of your hips and shoulders. This enables you to twist from inside and behind, behind both in *position* and in *time.*

If you ask if the *altogether* descent, with feet and hips and shoulders coming in at the same time, inevitably brings the right hip outside and around, I answer that it does, inevitably.

Today you must come down inside and swing from in-to-out to play championship golf. Why today? Well, it was not always so. Vardon, Taylor, and Duncan seldom tried to get inside any shot. Taylor told me himself that he had never been able to play a shot with intentional pull, and Harry Vardon rarely played a wooden shot to the green dead straight; there was almost always a slight fade or slice to it. All of which was due, of course, to having learned with the old "guttie" ball; the chief difficulty with that ball being to make it rise quickly enough out of indifferent lies. Naturally the slightly *cut* shot gave additional lift.

Beyond Percy—Feel Simple Golf

Percy often said the good golfer is able to anticipate the result of a shot before swinging the club. The good golfer can feel the swing in the starting position and the preparatory waggle. The good golfer has the right concept of the swing and knows the feel of a good swing in his or her set.

As a case study on this anticipatory aspect of playing golf well, Paul accompanied John onto the golf course. Finding two spots on the course from which John had never made a prior shot to a target, John talked through his entire two pre-shot routines. Paul recorded the following.

Shot 1 Commentary

This shot is 295 yards. Standing with the ball between me and the target, I see large trees between me and the green. The driver is the right club. The area to the left of the green slopes gently from left to right. The area to the right of the green slopes away severely into thick bushes. The best shot with a driver is a large left-to-right cut (i.e., slice) around the trees and onto the green.

To get the desired trajectory, my club face needs to be open through impact. To get this, my arms must be set up in my starting position with my right elbow closer to my belly button. My feet must be in an open stance with my left foot pulled back from the target line about one to two inches and the toes of both feet turned slightly toward the target.

I begin running my sequence, still standing behind the ball and facing the target. I begin building bracing into my starting position by (1) putting my wrists in an up position, (2) pulling my elbows inward, and (3) pulling my shoulder blades together and down (causing my chest to be pushed out). Keeping the braces in place, I move into my hitting position. I establish an open stance and position my right elbow closer to my belly button. I build the remaining braces into my starting position by (4) pulling my abdomen in, (5) pulling my hips in (i.e., activating my muscles below the abdomen), (6) placing my head behind the ball (i.e., turning my head to the right), and (7) profiling. Feeling comfortable in my set position, I bend my left knee forward to begin my starting movement.

My brain remains quiet as I allow automaticity to make my swing. My only thought is to experience the feel of a cut shot.

The shot is not good. The ball goes straight and lands left of the target. The swing felt out of balance, and my arms and hands were active. I had no sense of ball control and just hoped to pull off the desired shot.

While walking to my ball, I take a few seconds to debrief my swing. The comfortable set position was not a good one because I didn't feel a cut set up. My swing started and remained out of balance. I set up too far from the ball, making me bend forward too much at my waist toward the ball. Being out of balance kept me from a full pivot. Knowing that my restricted pivot was not giving the swing enough power, I automatically engaged my arms and hands to get more power. My swing became disconnected. My bad pivot was not able to control the shot—the pivot ended up following the shot.

I know it all has to do with how much time I've invested in playing right now. I have to play and practice enough to be able to start to feel the different shots. Right now, I don't feel much at all, so it's difficult. That doesn't mean I won't play good golf. It just means my feel won't be as sharp. On to the next shot.

Shot 2 Commentary

This shot is straightaway, slightly uphill, and with no hazards. The yardage is 260 to the green.

Standing behind the ball, facing the green, the ideal shot that I see is a high driver. The setup is neutral with nothing special needed with the arms and hands in the starting position. A smooth, full pivot will do—no need for extra power to really rip the drive.

I begin running my sequence while standing behind the ball and facing the target. I begin building bracing into my starting position by (1) putting my wrists in an up position, (2) pulling my elbows inward, and (3) pulling my shoulder blades together and down (causing my chest to be pushed out). Keeping the braces in place, I move into my hitting position. I establish a square stance with my arms and hands in a neutral position. I build the remaining braces into my starting position by (4) pulling my abdomen in, (5) pulling my hips in (i.e., activating my muscles below the abdomen), (6) placing my head behind the ball (i.e., turning my head to the right), and (7) profiling. Feeling comfortable in my set position, I bend my left knee forward to begin my starting movement.

My brain remains quiet as I let automaticity make my swing. My only thought is to have a quiet or passive upper body. Being quiet would delay the club head from moving forward and delay the hit as long as possible, allowing maximum lag, which adds power.

Woo, that was really well done. I like that a lot. The shot came off almost exactly like I wanted. I could feel something there, that I had a chance. The ball lands five yards short of green on the desired line of flight.

While walking to the ball, I quickly analyze my swing. I hit the shot on the line I wanted, the shape I wanted, and the trajectory I wanted. It was exactly what I had in mind.

I felt movement through the ball. I had enough pivot to create the power I needed. I didn't have to use my arms and hands in the shot. When I pivoted correctly, I knew the shot had a chance to be pulled off the way I want.

My arms and upper body were quiet, reactive, and passive. It felt like I wasn't trying to move my arms and hands to the ball—they just came along after. That's the overall feel I was going for. That was a sweet shot! On to the next shot.

Afterword

PERCY'S BOOK WAS likely key to his induction into the first class of the World Golf Teachers Hall of Fame in 1998. Following are what we believe to be the major contributions of Percy's book

1. The golf swing is a blend of physical and mental.

Physical Parts of the Swing	Mental Parts of the Swing
• Movement of bones, muscles, joints, and soft tissue to swing club • Lower body-powered swing • Simplifying the complexity of the swing movement	• Active brain and quiet brain • Sequence • Playing by feel, not conscious, controlled actions • Automaticity

2. Percy's book presents an integrated system of the golf swing. Each part of the system affects and is affected by all the other parts. Everything needed to play good golf is in the system. For the system to be effective, all parts must be followed. You can't pick and choose which parts to use.

3. One swing movement with the same sensations is used from putting to driving and driving to putting.

In modernizing *On Learning Golf*, it is clear that almost all of Percy's teachings are key to good golf today. His teachings are timeless. This book, *More On Learning Golf*, has added to Percy's teachings by (1) expanding the fundamental of the mental part of the swing (the "psychology of the swing"), (2) adding detail on how to do the fundamentals of the swing (i.e., pivot, body balance, swing width, starting position), and (3) providing additional instruction on rotational putting.

What a pleasure it would have been to meet Percy and be his pupils! How much more exciting it would be to talk with him today, after digging into his fundamentals, concepts, and words for the past decade and writing three books based on his teachings.

Throughout his book, Percy provides glimpses into what he must have been like as a person and as a teacher. Here are how students describe Percy and how he describes himself: a plodder; a made golfer, not a natural one; an impressionist who translates golf swings into feel; someone who flares up over nothing; a professor; impatient; having an insistent temperament; a scientific teacher; an advanced slogan-monger; and a high-strung golfer.

Writing a modernized version of Percy's *On Learning Golf* will hopefully bring Percy's ideas to more golfers, including those who have never heard of him. We hope this book extends Percy's legacy as the number one swing guru of all time. Writing this book has truly been an honor, a pleasure, and a work of admiration and love for Percy Boomer. We hope we have done justice to Percy's teachings and that he would have been proud of our work.

Having finished reading this book, return to the one-hundred-word description of the Feel Simple Golf integrated system of a simple golf swing. The meaning of this summary should now be more understandable than when you read it at the start of this book.

- **Pivot** creates power and direction.
- **Body balance** allows a full and unrestricted pivot.
- Balance is lost when weight moves closer to or further from the (1) ball, (2) target, or (3) ground during the swing.
- Body balance is maintained using (1) upward, (2) inward, and (3) behind bracing built into the **starting position**.
- **Swing width** increases power and is built into the starting position with bracing.
- **Psychology of the swing** involves (1) an actively thinking brain to establish the starting position and initiate the starting movement and (2) a quiet brain to repeat a practiced swing movement based on feel.
- This applies from putting to driving.

If you have valued our additions to Percy's own words, we hope you will read our two previous books based on Percy's work: *Experience the Feel of Simple Golf* (2016) and *Feel. Simple. Golf.* (2017). Both books give more detail on what we have included in this book.

Thank you very much for reading our book and best wishes! Hit it, chase it, and have fun.

John Ward can be reached at: www.FeelSimpleGolf.com.

Acknowledgments

WE WISH TO thank Koehler Books and John Koehler, president and publisher, for choosing to be our playing partners in this project. Along the course, John Koehler admitted his golfing skills are not up to the standard of his world championship boomerang skills.

Thanks to Courtney Meunier of Koehler Books for her excellent editing of our words and for Kellie Emery's work in producing a great book cover and interior page layout. Both have made us look good!

Thanks to the many students over many years who helped John Ward develop and refine Feel Simple Golf based on Percy Boomer's swing principles. *(More to be added)*

John and Paul
May 2022

Appendix: Feels of the Golf Swing

Following are the feels of the golf swing Percy describes throughout *On Learning Golf*. Many of the feels are repeated throughout the chapters.

Primary feels:

- Pivoting from the hips
- Shoulders moving in response to the pivot
- Arms moving in response to the shoulders

Chapter	Feels
1. What Teaching Taught Me	None
2. Fundamentals: Golf and the Senses	None
3. Fundamentals: The Swing	• Swing as a single unity felt in the waggle • Weight between both feet, perfectly free and active yet firmly planted • Back and along, then along and through (pivot feel)

3.	Fundamentals—The Swing (CONT.)	• Full stretch • Lag • Nonstop movement from backswing to forward swing pivots (no "checks") • In-to-out
4.	Golf Bogey No. 1	• In-to-out • Back and along, then along and through • Hammering a wedge under a door, not driving a nail into the floor • Weight equally distributed (fifty/fifty) between the feet
5.	The Road to Golfing Health	• In-to-out • Swing as all one piece
6.	The Concentration Fallacy	None
Part Two: Learning and Teaching		None

7.	The Controlled Golf Swing	• Primary feels:
		  ○ Pivot (hips feel up, rotating right then left inside a tight barrel)
		  ○ Shoulders moving in response to the pivot (standing fairly erect with shoulders feeling up)
		  ○ Arms moving in response to the shoulders
		• Supplementary (or secondary) feels:
		  ○ Swing as a single unit felt in the waggle
		  ○ Weight between both feet, perfectly free and active yet firmly planted (body balance feel)
		  ○ Back and around, then around and through (pivot feel)
		  ○ Tautness up the left side of the body (profile brace)
		  ○ Full stretch (swing width feel)
		  ○ Lag (pivot feel)
		  ○ Nonstop movement from backswing to forward swing pivots (no "checks") (pivot feel)
		  ○ In-to-out (combined body balance, pivot, and swing width feel)
		  ○ Upness (in hips and shoulders) (body balance feel)
		  ○ Swing as all one piece

8.	Preparatory to the Swing	Feels of body balance:
		• Weight equally distributed between the feet
		• Being firmly planted with both feet pushing into the ground
		Feel of a braced starting (set) position:
		• Overall feel: upright, firm, and compact
		• Upward brace
		  ○ Tall, slightly bent over at waist, back straight
		• Inward brace
		  ○ Inside and behind the back of the ball
		  ○ Hips pulled inward
		  ○ Elbows pulled toward each other
		  ○ Shoulder blades pulled together
		  ○ Stomach pulled inward
		• Behind brace
		  ○ Chin turned to right, seeing ball out of the corner of the left eye
		• Profile brace
		  ○ Hips twisted to left; left side taut from foot to shoulder and right side bowed inward
		Feel of club "down":
		• Carry the club back around the body and along the ground (not lifting club)
		• Left arm is stretched downward in the starting position and remains stretched
		• Club face comes from behind the ball (not down at it), similar to an enlarged putting movement

9.	Interlude for Instruction: What We Mean When We Say	Primary feels: • Pivoting from the hips • Shoulders moving in response to the pivot • Arms moving in response to the shoulders Backswing pivot feels: • Body moves as a single unit • Taut and controlled (resulting from opposing forces (bracing)) • Full stretch (feel of wide) • Club head down (i.e., club is carried (not lifted) around, along, and then up by the pivot) • Right hip pulls the left hip around • Slow turn

9.	Interlude for Instruction: What We Mean When We Say (CONT.)	Forward swing pivot feels: • Lag as the swing breaks into a one-after-the-other movement • Full stretch • Club head delayed and then snaps through impact • Left hip twists the right hip around • Club head down (i.e., club approaches ball from behind, not above) • Fast twist

10.	Fundamentals—Centered on Wrist Action	• Club head being a long way from the ball and your left side (feel of swing width)
		• Flexible, light, and sensitive grip on the club handle
		• Backswing pivot
		  ◦ Knees moving weight on the feet to make the backswing pivot with the hands and wrists following as a reaction
		  ◦ Carrying the club back
		  ◦ Wrists and hands taut as the left arm and club reach parallel to the ground
		  ◦ Feeling that wrists will never break; breaking as late as possible
		  ◦ Tension of hands on club handle decreases at the top of the swing
		• Transition from backswing to forward swing pivot
		  ◦ The "reverse" (club head still going up while lower body pulls forward; wrists cock/break)
		  ◦ Nonstop movement from backswing to forward swing pivots (no "checks")
		• Forward swing pivot
		  ◦ Hands, arms, and wrists coming down one after the other; wrists flail through impact with the ball
		  ◦ Tension of hands on club handle increases toward impact
		  ◦ Left side firm and taut as club nears impact; feeling centered and balanced
		  ◦ Freewheeling—club head feels out of control as it flashes through the ball

11.	To Keep—or Not to Keep—Your Eye on the Ball	None
12.	Interlude for Instruction: It Is the Pupil Who Must Learn	• Slight bend in the knees and at the waist in the starting position • Pivoting like the spinning of a top • Club goes around and along (not up and down) • Firm grip on the club (not loose or tight) • Same tension on grip at the top of the swing as in the starting position • Stretching down as you near impact with the ball • Club head feels slow (delayed)
13.	The Feeling of In-to-Out	Starting position: • Set inwards and behind the ball (resulting from bracing) • Standing tall Backswing pivot: • Club and left arm feel in a straight line when at waist high (full stretch) • Right hip pulls (left hip follows) Top of the swing: • Coiled spring • Braced and firmly set on the ground • Powerless feel (undesirable feel resulting from a wrong conception of how power is generated; power is not from the arms and hands but from the wide sweeping arc and lag powered by the lower body) Forward swing pivot: • Inside and behind the ball (right hip does not spin out toward the ball or sway toward the target) • Left hip pulls (right hip follows) • Wide swing (full stretch) • Slow (arms and hands drop slowly as they are pulled down by the lower body with a delay (lag)) • Pulling the club head along and through the ball from behind (not up-and-down); driving a wedge under a door • Flail (as wrists open through impact with the ball)

14. The Force-Center	• Feel of the club head (in the force-center) • Braced upward with club head down throughout the swing and through impact (opposing forces) • Shoulders up • Shoulders moving/turning parallel to ground • Hips up and pulled inward (together) • Knees roll round at a constant height on the backswing pivot • Full stretch; arms fully stretched • Compact and centered • In-to-out • Inside and behind the ball on the forward swing pivot • Slow and unrushed • Turn (on the backswing pivot) then twist (on the forward swing pivot)
15. Interlude for Instruction—Monologue	None
16. Rhythm	• Ball on the club head a long time before rebounding • Flowing continuous movement; feet, legs, and hips moving continuously • Delayed dragging of the club head on the forward swing pivot (lag) • Sense of balance with an unhurried calm with time enough to feel movements blending together • Slow (taking a long time for the swing to develop) yet determined • In-to-out

17. Interlude for Instruction: As a Dancer Sees It	• Primary feels:
	  ◦ Pivot
	  ◦ Shoulders moving in response to the pivot
	  ◦ Arms moving in response to the shoulders
	• Lag
	• Shoulder muscles loose with elastic feel in the waist
	• Legs and hips stretching up
	• Feet continuously moving

18.	Power	• Lag • Turn (on the backswing pivot) and then twist (on the forward swing pivot) • Right hip twists inward (not out toward the ball) on the forward swing pivot • Right shoulder follows right hip and twists inward and behind (driven by the muscles of the back) on the forward swing pivot • Back muscles (which are kept flexible) feel naturally stretched at the full backswing pivot and on the follow-through • In-to-out
19.	Interlude for Instruction: A Mathematician Explains	None
20.	Temperament	None

21.	Interlude for Instruction: Largely Concerned with the Waggle	• Swing as a whole
		• Waggle as a quiet, diminutive movement of the club head
		Feels of body balance:
		• Weight equally distributed between the feet
		• Being firmly planted with both feet pushing into the ground
		Feel of a braced starting (set) position:
		• Overall feel: upright, firm, and compact
		• Upward brace:
		  ◦ Tall, slightly bent over at the waist, back straight
		• Inward brace:
		  ◦ Inside and behind the back of the ball
		  ◦ Elbows pulled toward each other
		  ◦ Shoulder blades pulled together
		  ◦ Stomach pulled inwards
		• Behind brace:
		  ◦ Chin turned to right, seeing ball out of the corner of the left eye
		• Profile brace:
		  ◦ Hips twisted to the left; left side taut from foot to shoulder; right side bowed inward

21. Interlude for Instruction: Largely Concerned with the Waggle (CONT.)	Feel of club "down": • Carry the club back around the body and along the ground • Left arm is stretched downward in the starting position and remains stretched • Club face comes from behind the ball (not down at it), similar to an enlarged putting movement
22. Putting	• Slight and delicate • Very little centrifugal force is generated • Rolling (not striking) the ball along from behind • Right hand and club head as one • Right hand and forearm muscles light and flexible (like holding a pen) • Club head staying low back and through • Feel of correct speed leads to feel of direction
23. Interlude for Reminiscence	None
24. Golf Analysis	• Stretching up through the body • Stretching down through the arms and ball; feeling down • Equal balance between the two feet • Club swinging wide through the ball and on and around the left side
25. Inverse Functioning	• The "set" (of the desired shot/swing) • In-to-out • Feet moving continuously

Index

A

Actions and reactions, 26, 29, 30, 33, 39, 46, 52, 53, 56, 68, 85, 89, 99-103, 109-114, 122-124, 137, 140-142, 152, 153, 182, 188, 201, 205, 214, 215, 230

Active and passive, 37, 42, 109, 112, 114, 115, 121, 140, 142, 153, 181, 187-194, 197, 228, 230, 271-273, 278, 279

Alignment, 22, 23, 60, 93, 234, 245

Aubrey Boomer, 14, 24, 95, 123, 124, 166, 241, 248

Automaticity, 36, 38, 54-56, 59, 61, 62, 68, 74, 78, 81, 89, 99, 113, 122, 123, 130, 140, 141, 155, 182, 184, 185, 214, 221, 233, 235-237, 245, 271, 272, 274

B

Backspin, 103, 109, 210

Barrel (turn/pivot/swing in), 1, 79, 81, 83, 154, 158

Basic trinity, 86

Bobby Jones, 14, 119, 214, 239

Body balance, 16, 17, 34, 37, 43, 62, 74, 88, 90, 91, 98, 100, 101, 113, 123, 132, 138, 145, 162, 163, 169, 204, 205, 212, 225, 233, 234, 245, 253, 259, 275, 276, 279, 284

Bracing, 17, 22, 47, 53, 60, 68, 80, 89-91, 93, 95, 96, 98, 99, 101, 104, 119, 123, 129, 130, 132, 144, 145, 150, 152, 154, 158, 159, 182, 183, 186, 196, 197, 200, 205, 212, 224, 233, 234, 242, 244, 245, 253, 255, 271, 272, 276, 280, 282

    Behind bracing, 17, 68, 89-91, 97, 212, 226, 234, 253, 276, 280, 284

    Inward bracing, 68, 90, 92, 151, 226, 234, 280, 284

    Profile bracing, 68, 80, 90, 93, 95, 98, 187, 226, 233, 279, 280, 284

    Upward bracing, 68, 90, 92, 123, 154, 226, 284

Brain

    Active brain, 12, 17, 30, 34, 36, 55, 60-62, 81, 122, 123, 130,

186, 274

Amygdala, 30, 56, 62, 68

Basal ganglia, 30, 56

Prefrontal cortex, 30, 55, 56, 62

Quiet brain, 12, 17, 34, 36, 55, 56, 59-61, 68, 122, 130, 184, 186, 212-214, 218, 220, 221, 274, 276

C

Centrifugal force, 6, 38, 39, 90, 101, 118, 136, 145, 150, 153, 157, 164, 178, 193, 196-198, 203, 228, 230, 232, 233, 237, 240, 241, 245, 285

Choking, 56, 67

Concentration, 61, 63

Compensatory movement, 227, 230-232, 234

Connected swing, 80, 86, 99, 101, 123, 153-157, 161, 182, 196, 223, 229, 231, 234, 246, 260

Conscious control, 30, 32, 34, 40, 42, 56-58, 274

Control by remembered feel, 33

Controlled swing, 6, 80, 81, 85, 86, 107, 123, 130, 132, 152, 153, 157, 162-164, 183, 184, 186, 214, 245

Controls (line of controls), 22, 25, 27, 30, 58, 59, 61, 62, 66, 67, 73, 75-77, 84, 124, 128, 129, 162, 214, 218

D

Dead strength, 242

Direct hitter, 228, 243

Direction, 16, 50, 51, 53, 68, 90, 91, 113, 114, 130, 132, 139, 169, 195-198, 201, 212, 233, 234, 236, 237, 241, 242, 264, 276, 285

E

End gainer, 49, 57, 62, 66, 126

Ernest Jones, 155

F

Feel, 2-4, 6, 17, 30, 32, 33, 35-38, 40-43, 48, 50, 51, 55-65, 73-97, 100-109, 112-117, 123, 124, 132, 138, 142, 145, 148, 153, 154, 173, 188, 197, 201, 225, 237, 253, 254, 263, 278-285

    Feel cabinet, 87, 114

    Playing by feel, 30, 36, 37, 54, 56, 58, 61, 62, 75, 83, 87, 89, 91, 94, 125, 161, 214, 218, 262, 264, 274

Flail, 118, 120, 121, 146, 149, 155, 162, 191, 201, 203, 215, 252, 258, 281, 282

Follow through, 22, 41, 47, 49, 93, 118, 124, 146, 160, 166, 187, 201, 242, 253, 257, 259, 262-267

Force-center, 117, 152, 153, 155, 156, 158, 197, 283

Freewheeling, 119, 281

Fundamentals (swing fundamentals), 3, 16, 17, 34, 37, 38, 43, 44, 46, 52, 54, 55, 59, 62, 74, 88, 102, 104, 123, 132, 141, 145, 162, 182-184, 204, 212, 233, 236, 253, 275

G

George Boomer, 13

Golf maniac, 247, 248, 250

Grip, 60, 113, 116, 119, 132, 179, 234, 240, 244, 245, 281, 282

H

Harry Vardon, 13, 15, 66, 214, 238, 270

Henry Cotton, 211, 218

I

Ideal performance state, 220-222

In-to-out, 35, 37, 41, 46. 47, 51, 52, 57, 58, 62, 144, 147, 151, 152, 163, 179, 200, 239, 264, 265, 269, 270, 279, 282-285

Integrated system, See "System"

Inverse functioning, 262-264, 285

L

Lag, 37, 40, 100, 101, 104, 107, 114, 117, 133, 138, 143, 146, 164, 172, 173, 179, 187, 188, 193, 196, 201, 204, 205, 233, 264, 269, 279, 281-284

M

Muscle memory, 29-31, 33-36, 40, 59, 62, 73-75, 77, 161, 218

O

One-hundred-word description, 16, 212, 276

Opposing forces, 42, 100, 101, 104, 106, 154, 197, 252, 256, 258, 280, 283

P

Panicking, 67

Paradigm, 140, 207, 224, 227

Pivot, 16, 23, 34, 37, 39-43, 48, 49, 53, 62, 74, 79-88, 90, 97-99, 101, 104, 112-114, 120, 123, 128, 130-132, 136-138, 142, 143, 145, 146, 151, 153, 159, 163, 164, 169, 172, 186-189, 193, 195-197, 200, 201, 203-205, 212, 223, 225, 227, 233, 234, 236, 245, 263, 264, 271, 273, 276, 278-284

Power, 6, 16, 17, 20, 23, 38-41, 53, 68, 85, 90, 101, 103, 112-114, 132, 136-138, 142, 149, 150, 152, 153, 159, 162, 164, 169, 172, 175, 178, 189, 193, 195-199, 201, 203, 204, 212, 229, 230, 233, 234, 236, 246, 264, 269, 276, 282, 284

Preparatory waggle, 35, 38, 42, 43, 60, 91, 98, 112, 140, 223-226, 228-231, 270, 278, 279, 284

Psychology of the swing, 17, 33, 43, 53, 55, 58, 59, 61, 68, 74, 78, 88, 130, 140, 212, 213, 233, 275, 276

Putting (rotational putting), 17, 22, 24, 28, 35, 36, 38, 55, 77, 140, 212, 214, 217, 225, 236-246, 275, 276, 285

R

Reflex golf, 31, 74, 75, 155, 239

Reverse, 44, 116, 120, 142, 263, 281

Rick Bradshaw, 5, 110, 259

Rhythm, 164, 171, 173-175, 178, 180, 183-186, 222, 228, 230, 234, 235, 283

    Rhythm of the round, 185

    Rhythm of your game, 184

    Rhythm of your swing, 184

S

Sequence, 29-31, 33, 36, 53, 60, 67, 68, 90, 98, 130, 169, 182-184, 186, 221, 222, 271, 272, 274

Simplicity, 15, 16, 36, 38, 52, 80, 99, 110, 153, 157, 212, 230, 231, 234-236, 246, 264, 274

Slice, 51, 58, 87, 114, 145, 147, 151, 163, 243, 269, 270

Starting movement, 17, 53, 60, 98, 99, 113, 183, 184, 204, 212, 224, 225, 271, 272, 276

Starting/Set position, 17, 22, 23, 34, 37, 43, 52, 53, 60, 62, 68, 90, 91, 93, 96, 98, 101, 112, 120, 122, 123, 132, 145, 154, 157, 160, 169, 182, 186, 205, 212, 224, 226, 233, 234, 245, 263, 267, 268, 270-272, 276, 280, 282, 284, 285

Swing center, 126, 172, 178

Swing width, 17, 34, 37, 39, 41, 43, 47, 62, 74, 88, 100, 102, 109, 116, 123, 129, 132, 133, 137, 138, 148, 154, 162-164, 169, 172, 196, 204, 205, 212, 233, 234, 245, 253, 258, 276, 279, 281

System (integrated system), 3, 4, 16, 19-21, 25, 27, 28, 43, 170, 212, 236, 253, 261, 264, 274, 275

T

Ted Ray, 13, 242

Temperament, 65, 133, 213-221, 275

Tempo, 171, 182-186, 235

Three-quarters swing, 123, 153, 156, 157, 172, 229

Timing, 82, 113, 171, 174-176, 178, 181, 183-185, 234, 235, 269

Troubleshooting, 21, 38, 44, 55, 123, 129, 132, 141, 186, 204, 231, 251

W

Waggle, See "Preparatory waggle"

Walter Hagen, 65, 199, 239

Miss Wethered, 95

Willy Park, 238

Wrists, 36, 41, 42, 44, 85, 96, 98, 102, 108-121, 128, 129, 133, 138, 142, 143, 146, 148, 149, 153-155, 157, 170, 172, 174, 178, 181, 188, 190, 191, 202, 203, 252, 255, 258, 271, 272, 281, 282

About The Authors

JOHN E. WARD is a professional golf instructor with more than forty years in the golf business. John's credentials include playing since the age of eight, equipment manufacturing, equipment technician, golf caddie, and more than twenty years earning a living as a golf coach to thousands of golfers from beginners to advanced, including professional golfers.

Since playing in the 2009 US Senior Open at Crooked Stick (Carmel, IN), John devoted nearly a decade to gaining a complete understanding of and building his golf swing on the methods presented in Percy Boomer's 1946 book, *On Learning Golf*. The journey was successful; his swing stood up in the heat of competition as he finished as an alternate in the qualifying for the 2013 US Senior Open.

John has taken his success as a player and adapted his knowledge and experience to create a unique approach to teaching golf based on Boomer's principles. This book is the culmination of John's decades of golfing experience, years of studying the golf swing, and more years refining his instructional approach for making learning the golf swing simple and enjoyable. The methods presented in this book have been successfully tested at the highest level of competitive golf as well as at the golf practice facility helping students learn to play, improve, and enjoy golf quickly and easily.

With a focus on simplifying the swing to a single movement that is used for most golf shots from putting to driving; providing a foundation to learn, diagnose, and fix one's own swing problems; and freeing students from an endless series of paid lessons through rapid, simple, and painless improvement, John is admittedly and proudly a bit of a rebel in the golf coaching industry. John does not adhere to the belief that the best golf student is one with lots of money to spend on never-ending lessons. John's motto in golf is to "Hit it, chase it, and have fun."

John co-authored the golf instructional books *Experience the Feel of Simple Golf: Making Percy Boomer's Putt as You Drive and Drive as You Putt Come Alive* (2016), *Feel. Simple. Golf.: A Simple Guide Inspired by Percy Boomer: Drive as You Putt and Putt as You Drive* (2017), and a companion instruction and seminar manual.

John lives in Denver, Colorado, and can be reached at www.FeelSimpleGolf.com.

DR. PAUL K. WOODS is an industrial-organizational psychologist and one of John Ward's students. Paul came to John after failing to understand the causes of and corrections for a lifelong slice. He continued as John's student even after the slice was corrected and desire to deeply understand the golf swing was satisfied.

With more than thirty years of experience in education, university administration, university teaching as a graduate school adjunct professor, human development, corporate employee training, management consulting, and improving organizations through organizational development interventions, Paul teamed up with John to put his thoughts into a written format and get it out to golfers.

Paul's professional experience in analyzing, improving, and assessing organizational performance, including a focus on continuously improving work processes, as well as being an intermediate golfer with a basic understanding of the golf swing and ability to understand and apply John's instruction to improving his own game, made the partnership with John mutually beneficial and satisfying. Paul's improved golf swing, resulting from successfully applying John's coaching, made Paul a loyal and enthusiastic supporter and follower of what is contained in this book.

Paul joined John in co-authoring the two golf instructional books. Paul lives in Littleton, Colorado.

www.ingramcontent.com/pod-product-compliance
Lightning Source LLC
Chambersburg PA
CBHW020518080526
44583CB00013B/651